Mandarin Chinese Characters
Fast Finder

Laurence Matthews

TUTTLE Publishing

Tokyo | Rutland, Vermont | Singapore

ACKNOWLEDGEMENTS

I have made use of a number of books, websites and dictionaries, primarily the *HanYing Cidian* ('*A Chinese English Dictionary*,' Commercial Press, Beijing, 1978 and subsequent editions). My thanks also to Flavia Hodges and Nancy Goh at Tuttle for their friendliness and efficiency.

Most importantly, my heartfelt thanks to my wife Alison, for her love, support and encouragement, for numerous suggestions, the many hours shared poring over dictionaries, the computer macros to generate and format the pages of the book, the quality control—a wide spectrum echoing the richness of our life together.

INTRODUCTION

Chinese characters are fascinating, but can be frustrating. In particular, looking them up in a traditional dictionary can be a nightmare, as there is no 'alphabetical order.'

With this book you can find a character in seconds from its appearance alone. From the finder chart inside the front cover, you can turn to the correct page immediately, and finding the character on that page has also been made as simple as possible. As an optional feature you can make a double thumbnail index (see page xiv) to speed things up even more.

The Fast Finder is designed primarily for serious learners of modern Chinese and serves as a quick reference for experts, but it is also suitable for beginners, or people who wish to dip into characters, browse, or simply discover what a street sign means. With this book you can:

- Find characters quickly, reliably and intuitively—from their visual appearance alone;
- Quickly check the meanings, pronunciations, stroke-counts and radicals of characters;
- Look at traditional characters to see how they have been simplified;
- Look up newly encountered characters or check on those you have temporarily forgotten;
- Find elusive characters more easily in large character dictionaries;
- Simply browse and explore, comparing similar characters.

There are some hints on finding characters on page vii, but the system is so intuitive that you can try it right now: for example, try finding 独 or 空.

I wish you success, fun and enjoyment in your study of Chinese characters!

Chinese Characters

Several tens of thousands of characters exist, but two or three thousand suffice for almost all purposes, and in many circumstances far fewer are needed. A knowledge of the 500 most common characters covers 75 per cent of Chinese writing, 1,000 gives 86 per cent, 2,000 gives 96 per cent, and 3,000 gives 99 per cent (the numbers depending very slightly on the context).

There is no 'officially approved' set of characters (as exists, for example, in Japan), and so each book or dictionary has to choose its own selection. The Fast Finder contains approximately 3,200 characters. Among these, all the 2,905 characters contained in the Chinese Proficiency Test (the *Hanyu Shuiping Kaoshi*, administered by the office of the HSK State Commission under the Chinese Ministry of Education) are included, and additional characters have been chosen to cover the characters found in well-known textbooks, with an eye also to frequency of occurrence in Chinese as measured by the databases now available on the internet.

This book uses the modern simplified characters, as used in modern China. (Traditional characters, however, are still found in the People's Republic, and are in widespread use in Chinese communities around the world. You can look up traditional characters using the appendix. For more on simplified and traditional characters, see page xiii.)

Pronunciations are given in the 'pinyin' system for modern *putonghua* (or 'Mandarin'). The pronunciation of characters is different in, say, Cantonese, but the meanings of the characters are basically universal.

Modern Chinese dictionaries are often organized alphabetically by the pronunciation of the characters. However, in many circumstances you will want to look up a character you have encountered, and yet you don't know the pronunciation for this character. For this reason dictionaries usually include an index or indexes to help locate characters by their appearance alone.

One type of index uses a system of character components called 'radicals' to classify characters. This is the system long used to organize traditional dictionaries in China, but has many pitfalls for the beginner (and even for native speakers!), even in its modern versions. Another system arranges the characters by stroke-count (the number of pen-strokes, or traditionally brush-strokes, needed to write the characters), but this is very slow to use, and counting strokes is also not without its pitfalls. A few other systems have been devised to help with this problem, notably the 'four-corner' method. This book arose out of my own frustration with these various methods when learning characters, and uses instead the human brain's pattern-recognition abilities directly.

The radical system is basically a good one, but not as logical as one might hope, and experts tend to forget how difficult it was to master the radical system initially. The Fast Finder uses 'intuitive radicals': character components which you think *ought* to be radicals *are* treated as such. However, most symbols in the finder chart are traditional radicals (or their modern equivalents), and so as you become more familiar with radicals and their quirks, you will find it easy enough to use the many books based on more traditional systems.

Information given

The purpose of this book is to *find* characters quickly, and to this end the amount of clutter on each page has been kept to a minimum. Thus the information given for each character is basic. However, it is sufficient to determine the meaning of a character, to check at a glance any characters you have confused or temporarily forgotten, or to look up the character quickly in your favorite dictionary or character guide for fuller information.

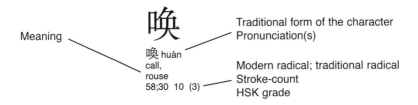

Below each character are four lines of information. The first line gives the character's traditional form (or forms), and its pronunciation(s). An absence of traditional forms (or an asterisk *) means that the character is a traditional form in its own right. For more details on traditional characters, see page xiii. Pronunciations are separated by spaces if the character has more than one. For more on pronunciations, see page x.

The next two lines give the basic meaning(s) of the character and are meant to be read together; if only one line is needed then the symbol '–' is printed on the following line. For more on meanings, see page xi.

The last line of information gives the modern and traditional radicals, separated by a semicolon (the numbers referring to Tables 4 and 5 at the back of the book); the stroke-count of the character; and finally in parentheses its grade in the HSK (Chinese Proficiency Test).

Hints on finding characters

It is a good idea to start by looking through the book to get a feel for how the characters are organized and displayed. The Fast Finder is organized with many characters to a page, so that you can see at a glance the characters which share a particular radical—and you can profitably browse this way too.

Dividing up a character

Take a look at pages 38, 39, and 40, the 'indivisible' characters. Initially you might find you have a tendency to regard any character which doesn't split left-right as indivisible; but you will see that the characters on pages 38–40 are generally quite simple ones. The vast majority of characters *do* divide into components.

To find a specific character, first look at how it 'naturally' breaks down into components. The split will usually be left-right or top-bottom, and will usually (although not always) be 'clean' with white space on the page between the two components. Having split the character, choose the simpler component as your radical, which you will use to look up the character. If the components look roughly equal in simplicity, choose either; if you already recognize one of the components as a radical, you can use that. The same character may be found in two places: for example you will find 引 under ■ on page 14, and also under □ on page 41.

In fact many characters are to be found in several different locations in the Fast Finder. A consequence of having compact information for each character is that the whole entry can be repeated in each of these locations, thus eliminating the need for cross-references, and avoiding any need to decide which radical is 'correct.'

Although most characters split left-right or top-bottom, don't forget the other patterns (pages 32–37). For these characters, use the enclosing component as the radical.

Sometimes there is a choice of 'how much' of a character to take as the radical. For example, when looking for 雇, is the radical 丶 or 户? In such cases, both radicals will be on the same page to make it easier to find the character (in odd cases where they are not, then the character will be found in both places, or there will be cross-reference of the form 启 → 32). Character with several reasonable possibilities are listed under all of these. But I rely on you not to make 'unnatural' divisions: 望 is in the ■ section under 王, not 土.

Finally, if looking for a character which also happens to serve as a radical, treat it as a character in its own right. For example, you would look up 柱 under □ on page 16, but 木 itself under ■ on page 38.

Finding the right page

Look for your radical in the finder chart inside the front cover. Remember to look in the correct section (■ or ▮, etc.) as several radicals appear in more than one section. The arrangement of the radicals in the finder chart is intuitive, with similar radicals grouped together, and the simpler ones generally coming before the complex ones. If you can't find the radical on the finder chart, look on the relevant 'others' page (these are pages such as 30, 31, 57 or 69, which contain radicals which have only one or two characters each). You will very quickly become familiar with the common radicals, which appear explicitly in the finder chart, and hence sense when to look on the 'others' pages.

As illustrated on the inside front cover, if a radical has many characters then they will be subdivided according to how the remainder of the character divides up. In the case of a few particularly common radicals which flow onto two or three pages, this idea is used in the finder chart too.

For 'indivisible' characters, the shape of the top of the character is used; you can see how this works by glancing through pages 38–40. The same idea is used for the 'others' pages and implicitly elsewhere.

Finding the character on the page

When you turn to the page, check at the top of the page that your chosen radical is there. (The thin vertical gray lines in the finder chart inside the front cover indicate whether to look on the left hand or right hand page.)

The characters for the same radical are grouped together: again, the arrangement is intuitive with the simpler ones coming before the more complex. Characters which are very similar and likely to be confused, such as 何 and 伺, or 勒 and 勤, are placed close together. As mentioned above, if a radical has many characters then they will be subdivided according to how the remainder of the character divides up.

If the character itself is printed in gray, then you were not really looking for it in the right place: never mind, at least you have found it! However, the same character will appear elsewhere in the book, printed in black. As you use the Fast Finder, taking a closer look at these gray characters will help you to appreciate more precisely how character components fit together and to distinguish between similar and easily-confused components. You are bound to find some gray characters where you would not imagine that anyone would look for them, but rest assured that there are people who would, and did!

Important distinctions

If you are new to Chinese characters, then there are several points to watch out for. Make sure you distinguish between radicals such as ⼀ and ⼇, or 力 and 刀, for example. You will learn these distinctions with time (in fact, pretty quickly).

On the other hand, unfortunately, some variants denote the same character. A few characters have minor variations from one typeface to another, or are slightly different when hand-written. Many traditional characters exist in several variant forms, and some slightly older versions of character components are still around (see the appendix). Fortunately this is not much of a problem for simplified characters.

Characters also incorporate remnants from much earlier times. For example, many traditional radicals have several forms, depending on whether they appear to the left, right, top, bottom, etc. of the characters to which they contribute. Thus:

犭 and 犬 are different forms of the 'dog' radical;

忄 and ⼼ are different forms of the 'heart' radical.

To further complicate matters, many of these forms have different stroke-counts, which can sometimes make finding even the radicals a problem! In the Fast Finder these forms are treated as though they are different radicals, in the belief that although such facts about the characters and their historical derivations can be fascinating, they should not frustrate your attempts simply to *find* a character.

Pronunciations

Pronunciations are given in pinyin, with the tones marked by accents above the vowels. All pronunciations for a character are given (even if a subsidiary pronunciation is only used for proper names), and the pronunciations are generally in order of frequency, with the most common pronunciation first. A character may have two or even three common pronunciations, but the vast majority of characters have only one, or at least one dominant one.

Characters can change tones for reasons of euphony (notably a 3rd tone changing if it precedes another), and these changes are ignored. The tones taken by 一, 七 and 不 also depend on the character which they precede; otherwise different tones tend to imply different meanings, or shades of meaning, of the character.

Meanings

The English meanings given are as short and concise as possible; their purpose is to 'suggest and remind' as one book puts it. Current rather than original historical meanings are given. From the meanings supplied, you will usually be able to deduce the meaning of the characters in a given context, but there are some points you should note.

Firstly, characters do not usually correspond neatly to single English words. Also, like an English word, a character may have several distinct meanings. (If so, it is safer not to assume that the meanings correspond in any one-to-one manner with the pronunciations. Although I have tried to list meanings in the same order as pronunciations, this is not always possible. A large character dictionary will make it clear which pronunciations can take which meanings.)

Where several meanings are given, similar meanings are separated by commas and distinct meanings by semicolons. If two meanings are separated by commas then they may qualify each other: thus 'firm, hard' indicates 'firm to the touch' rather than either 'industrial organization' or 'difficult.' Sometimes a character has a large range of meanings depending on context, and the symbol '&' alerts you to the existence of further meanings.

Conversely, several characters may share a common English meaning, so be wary of using this book to translate in the English-to-Chinese direction. Familial relationships and forms of address are particular cases of this: for example the single word 'aunt' in English corresponds to various characters in Chinese with meanings such as 'wife of father's younger brother,' and forms of address such as 'you' similarly depend on relative age, status, etc.

Characters can often serve as several parts of speech (for example acting as both a verb and a noun). Where the English word is ambiguous I have used 'a' to denote a noun and 'to' to denote a verb; for example 飞 is 'to fly' whereas 蝇 is 'a fly.' On the other hand the meaning of 舞 is given simply as 'dance' since it acts as both 'to dance' and 'a dance.'

The following notation and abbreviations are used:

EB, HS   The so-called 'Earthly Branches' and 'Heavenly Stems,' which are used in enumeration, old notation for dates and various astrological purposes (see Table 3 at the back of the book).

[ ]   Brackets [ ] are used when the character is only likely to be encountered as part of a compound word made up of two or more characters; the meaning in brackets is that of the compound. For example 啤 is given as meaning '[beer],' since you will only find it in the compound 啤酒 meaning 'beer.'

( )	Parentheses ( ) are used in explanations, such as 'right (hand)' or '(bus) stop.' The word 'literary' means that the character is confined to written Chinese and is somewhat flowery or bookish. Sometimes a word such as 'particle' is given in parentheses instead of a meaning: some terms used in this way are discussed below.
(particle)	These are words which give a gloss to the sentence as a whole, and are often difficult to pin down concisely. Fortunately, if you are learning Chinese, you will know the common ones already as they are bound to be included in any book or course you are using.
(sound)	Some characters are used mainly to convey sounds, as for example in 'spelling out' the syllables of foreign names: Samoa is 'sa-mo-ya' (萨摩亚); in many cases the syllables in the foreign language have to be shoehorned to fit. Sometimes this phonetic rendering only applies to part of a word: for example 'saxophone' is rendered 'sa-ke-pipe' or 'sa-ke-se-pipe.' (Conversely, of course, Chinese words such as 'Beijing,' familiar to many English speakers simply as sounds, all have meanings which you can discover by using the Fast Finder.)
(surname)	Many characters are used as surnames or family names, and for some characters this is their only modern usage.
(measure word)	Several dozen characters serve as counting units for nouns, analogous to the word 'head' in 'six head of cattle' or 'sheet' in 'three sheets of paper.' Measure words are usually easily recognized in Chinese as they always directly follow numbers.

Many other characters take on roles of 'surname,' 'sound' or 'measure word' in addition to their main meanings. I only list these roles in the Fast Finder if the character has no other (modern) meaning.

Finally, as far as compounds (words made up of two or more characters) are concerned, their meanings can be guessed, more often than not, from the context and the meanings of the individual characters. But of course many derived meanings are somewhat oblique, in the same way that English words such as 'laptop' and 'honeymoon' have meanings not implicit in their component parts. Compounds are listed in large dictionaries under the first character of the compound.

Simplified and Traditional Characters

During the twentieth century simplified characters were introduced in the People's Republic of China. Although the modern characters are all you need to know in many circumstances, you will still see traditional characters around, and the written literature, going back thousands of years, is written in traditional characters. Thus, although the Fast Finder is based on simplified forms, the traditional forms of the characters are given as well. The appendix, which contains all the traditional character equivalents of the characters in the main pages (but not repeating those which are unchanged on simplification), will let you look up a traditional character to find its modern simplified form. It uses the same method as the main book (except there is no thumbnail index) and has its own finder chart. For more details see the notes at the beginning of the appendix.

Chinese characters have evolved (slowly) since time immemorial, but the recent simplification was more drastic. Depending on the character, the radical may simplify (as in 詞 ➞ 词) or the remainder (燈 ➞ 灯), or both. Some characters change completely (頭 ➞ 头), and particularly tricky are cases where simplification changes the apparent radical (葉 ➞ 叶). Many characters remain unchanged (本 ➞ 本), including some surprisingly complex ones.

Several traditional characters can simplify to the same modern character, as in 發, 髮 ➞ 发. Sometimes the traditional forms in question are variants of the 'same' character: in the world of traditional characters these may have more or less equal status, or one may be an 'older' form. I have given some of the more common variants, but there is no hard and fast cut-off point for variants, and dictionaries have been accused of listing too many. In any event, there will be only one simplified form.

Quite often a simplified character is identical to its traditional form, but also acts as the simplified form of another traditional character, e.g. 里, 裏 ➞ 里. This situation is denoted by an asterisk * in the Fast Finder entry for the simplified form.

Only rarely does a traditional character simplify to different simplified forms (the choice depending on meaning and context). There are, however, a few characters which sometimes simplify and sometimes don't (depending on context or to avoid ambiguity). The traditional form thus qualifies as a 'simplified character' in that it will be seen in texts written in simplified characters. Table 1 at the end of the book lists those characters in the Fast Finder to which this applies.

Thumbnail index

A unique feature of this book is the option to make a double thumbnail index, as illustrated in the diagram below. This speeds up the use of the Fast Finder even more (and this is especially noticeable if you are using it repeatedly to look up many characters).

The thumbnail index allows immediate access to any page directly from the finder chart inside the front cover. Simply find the desired radical in the chart as normal, then put your right thumb on the tab with the chosen page number to open the book at the correct page. This tab will be on the same horizontal line as the radical you have found (thus actually bypassing the need to note the page number).

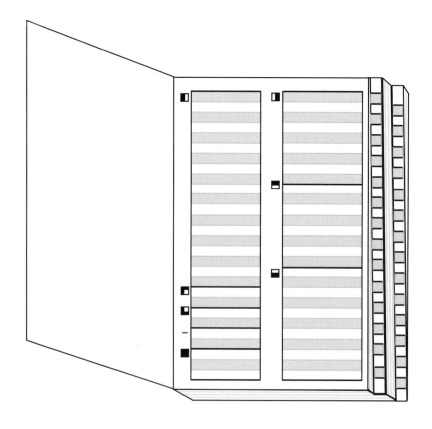

To make the thumbnail index, cut the main pages (1–79) as indicated by the heavy black lines in the block on the right hand side of each right-hand page, as indicated in the diagram below:

Pages 1–39   Page 40   Pages 41–79

For the main pages it is best to make the horizontal cut first, followed by the vertical cut or cuts. Be careful when cutting the pages; make sure that you are not unintentionally cutting two pages at once.

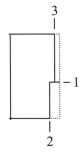

In order to have the thumbnail index visible from the finder chart, you will also have to cut these introductory pages, including the finder chart itself. Cut along the dotted line marked on the right hand edge of the right hand pages.

小 xiǎo
small; young; petty
79;42 3 (1)

办 辦 bàn
manage; set up; punish
28;160 4 (1)

火 huǒ
fire
-
83;86 4 (1)

心 xīn
heart; core; feelings
81;61 4 (1)

必 bì
necessarily; certainly
1;61 5 (1)

州 zhōu
state, prefecture
1;47 6 (4)

刃 rèn
blade; sword, knife; kill
27;18 3 (4)

刁 diāo
cunning
-
6;18 2 (4)

苏 蘇 嚇 sū
revive; ('su' sound)
50;140 7 (4)

亦 yì
also, too (literary)
162;8 6 (4)

尔 爾 ěr
you; like that, that (literary)
79;89 5 (3)

忄□→
灬□→

丫 yā
fork (in tree), bifurcation
24;2 3 (-)

业 業 yè
business; already
140;75 5 (1)

亚 亞 yà
inferior; Asia
168;7 6 (3)

严 嚴 yán
tight; strict, severe
168;30 7 (2)

半 bàn
half, semi-; partly
3;24 5 (1)

米 mǐ
rice; meter (length)
159;119 6 (1)

平 píng
flat, even, level; calm; average
2;51 5 (1)

乎 hū
(suffix; particle)
2;4 5 (2)

来 來 lái lai
come, arrive; do; bring; future; during; approx.; &
94;9 7 (1)

寸 cùn
very small; inch
54;41 3 (2)

勺 sháo
spoon, ladle
26;20 3 (2)

为 為 wéi wèi
do, act, act as; become; be equal to; for the sake of
1;86 4 (1)

归 歸 guī
return; converge; &
70;77 5 (3)

帅 帥 shuài
commander; smart, graceful
57;50 5 (4)

师 師 shī
teacher, expert; lesson; army; &
3;50 6 (1)

临 臨 lín
arrive; about to; copy; to face
3;131 9 (2)

旧 舊 jiù
old, former, outdated; worn
103;134 5 (1)

门 門 mén
gate, door; family; sect; &
46;169 3 (1)

卜 *蔔 bǔ bo
divination; foretell
16;25 2 (2)

以 yǐ
using; so as to; according to; &
23;9 4 (1)

八 bā
eight
-
24;12 2 (1)

儿 兒 ér
child, youth; son; ('r' suffix)
29;10 2 (1)

川 chuān
river; a plain
4;47 3 (4)

顺 順 shùn
obey; suitable; along; in order
170;181 9 (2)

么 麼 me
[what; such as] (suffix)
4;200 3 (1)

从 從 cóng cōn
from; to follow secondary; &
23;60 4 (1)

斗
*鬥 dòu dǒu
fight; dovetail;
dipper; &
82;68 4 (2)

头
頭 tóu tou
head; top; first,
chief; end; &
52;181 5 (1)

须
須 鬚 xū
have to, must;
beard
63;181 9 (1)

非
fēi
not, no, non-;
wrong; evil
205;175 8 (1)

永
yǒng
eternal,
forever
1;85 5 (1)

水
shuǐ
water; liquid;
river, lake
125;85 4 (1)

承
chéng
undertake;
indebted; &
5;64 8 (2)

泉
quán
spring,
fountain
150;85 9 (4)

汞
gǒng
mercury
-
48;85 7 (4)

浆
漿 jiāng jiàng
thick liquid,
syrup; starch
125;85 10 (3)

双
雙 shuāng
two, twin, dual,
bi-, double
35;172 4 (1)

劝
勸 quàn
advise; urge,
encourage
35;19 4 (2)

欢
歡 huān
pleased,
happy, joyful
35;76 6 (1)

邓
鄧 dèng
(surname)
-
34;163 4 (4)

对
對 duì
correct, yes; regarding; versus;
to face; towards; deal with; &
35;41 5 (1)

戏
戲 xì
to play; make
fun of; a show
35;62 6 (2)

艰
艱 jiān
difficult
-
35;138 8 (2)

观
觀 guān guàn
observe; view;
Taoist temple
35;147 6 (1)

鸡
雞 鶏 jī
chicken,
cock, hen
35;172 7 (1)

难
難 nán nàn
difficult; nasty;
disaster; blame
35;172 10 (1)

1	41
2	42
3	43
4	44
5	45
6	46
7	47
8	48
9	49
10	50
11	51
12	52
13	53
14	54
15	55
16	56
17	57
18	58
19	59
20	60
21	61
22	62
23	63
24	64
25	65
26	66
27	67
28	68
29	69
30	70
31	71
32	72
33	73
34	74
35	75
36	76
37	77
38	78
39	79
40	80

忆 憶 yì
recollect
-
41;61 4 (2)

怀 懷 huái
bosom; cherish;
yearn; pregnant
41;61 7 (3)

忧 憂 yōu
worry, anxious;
grief
41;61 7 (4)

快 kuài
quick; soon;
sharp; happy; &
41;61 7 (1)

性 xìng
quality, nature;
sex
41;61 8 (2)

怔 zhēng
terrified
-
41;61 8 (-)

恨 hèn
hate;
regret
41;61 9 (2)

惟 wéi
solely;
thought
41;61 11 (4)

慨 kǎi
angry; touched;
generous
41;61 12 (4)

惭 慚 cán
ashamed
-
41;61 11 (3)

懒 懶 lǎn
lazy;
sluggish
41;61 16 (2)

惦 diàn
think of;
concerned
41;61 11 (3)

慷 kāng
generous;
vehement
41;61 14 (4)

怖 bù
fear
-
41;61 8 (3)

恢 huī
vast;
resume
41;61 9 (2)

忧 憂 yōu
worry, anxious;
grief
41;61 7 (4)

悯 憫 mǐn
pity,
sympathize
41;61 10 (-)

忙
máng
busy;
hurried, hasty
41;61 6 (1)

恼
恼 nǎo
angry;
worried
41;61 9 (4)

惊
驚 jīng
startled,
alarmed
41;187 11 (2)

怕
pà
afraid; worried;
possibly
41;61 8 (1)

惶
huáng
fear
-
41;61 12 (-)

愧
kuì
ashamed
-
41;61 12 (3)

忧
憂 yōu
worry, anxious;
grief
41;61 7 (4)

怯
qiè
timid,
cowardly
41;61 8 (4)

惋
wǎn
sigh;
sympathize
41;61 11 (4)

愤
憤 fèn
resent;
indignant
41;61 12 (2)

慎
shèn
cautious
-
41;61 14 (3)

情
qíng
emotion; love;
favor; situation
41;61 11 (1)

悼
dào
mourn,
lament
41;61 11 (4)

惜
xī
cherish; pity;
begrudge
41;61 11 (3)

慌
huāng
flustered;
scared
41;61 12 (2)

懂
dǒng
understand
-
41;61 15 (1)

悦
yuè
pleased;
to please
41;61 10 (3)

恍
huǎng
sudden;
seemingly
41;61 9 (-)

悄
qiǎo qiāo
quiet;
softly
41;61 10 (2)

憎
zēng
hate,
detest
41;61 15 (-)

恒
恆 héng
permanent;
persist; usual
41;61 9 (4)

悟
wù
realize,
understand
41;61 10 (2)

怪
guài
strange; very;
monster; blame
41;61 8 (2)

悍
hàn
fierce,
brave
41;61 10 (-)

惕
tì
vigilant
-
41;61 11 (3)

慢
màn
slow; postpone;
haughty
41;61 14 (1)

愣
lèng
dazed;
reckless
41;61 12 (3)

惯
慣 guàn
habitual;
pamper
41;61 11 (1)

惧
懼 jù
fear,
dread
41;61 11 (4)

悔
huǐ
regret,
repent
41;61 10 (2)

惰
duò
lazy
-
41;61 12 (4)

憾
hàn
regret
-
41;61 16 (3)

怜
憐 lián
pity, sympathy;
pamper
41;61 8 (2)

恰
qià
suitable;
exactly
41;61 9 (3)

愉
yú
happy
-
41;61 12 (1)

怡
yí
happy
(literary)
41;61 8 (-)

惨
慘 cǎn
pitiful; cruel;
seriously
41;61 11 (3)

1	41
2	42
3	43
4	44
5	45
6	46
7	47
8	48
9	49
10	50
11	51
12	52
13	53
14	54
15	55
16	56
17	57
18	58
19	59
20	60
21	61
22	62
23	63
24	64
25	65
26	66
27	67
28	68
29	69
30	70
31	71
32	72
33	73
34	74
35	75
36	76
37	77
38	78
39	79
40	80

次
cì
sequence; 2nd;
next; inferior
8;76 6 (1)

冰 *冰 bīng
ice
-
8;15 6 (2)

决 *決 jué
decide, resolve;
definitely; &
8;15 6 (1)

冻 凍 dòng
freeze
-
8;15 7 (2)

冲 *沖 衝 chōng chòng
add water, rinse, flush;
rush; clash; vigorous; &
8;15 6 (2)

冯 馮 féng
(surname)
-
8;187 5 (4)

况 *況 kuàng
situation;
compare
8;15 7 (1)

凉 *涼 liáng liàng yě
cool, cold;
disappointed
8;15 10 (1)

冶 yě
smelt
-
8;15 7 (3)

冷 lěng
cold, frosty;
rare; deserted
8;15 7 (1)

凌 líng
approach; rise,
soar; insult
8;15 10 (4)

凄 *凄 悽 qī
chilly; sad;
bleak
8;15 10 (4)

凑 *湊 còu
get together;
luckily
8;15 11 (3)

净 *淨 jìng
completely; net
(profit); clean
8;15 8 (1)

凛 lǐn
cold; strict;
apprehensive
8;15 15 (-)

准 *準 zhǔn
allow; quasi-;
definitely; &
8;15 10 (1)

凝 níng
solidify;
concentrate
8;15 16 (3)

凋 diāo
wither;
fade
8;15 10 (-)

减 *減 jiǎn
subtract,
deduct, reduce
8;15 11 (2)

兆 zhào
omen; portend;
million, mega-
29;10 6 (4)

习 習 xí
practice; be
used to; habit
6;124 3 (1)

羽 yǔ
feather
-
183;124 6 (2)

疖 → 3

求 qiú
beg, request;
seek
1;85 7 (1)

录 錄 lù
record;
employ
70;167 8 (1)

隶 隸 lì
subordinate,
servant, slave
124;171 8 (3)

救 jiù
rescue,
aid
113;66 11 (2)

剥 剝 bāo bō
peel off
-
17;18 10 (3)

弱 ruò
weak; inferior;
a bit less
71;57 10 (2)

状 狀 zhuàng
form, condition;
certificate; &
42;94 7 (2)

壮 壯 zhuàng
strong, robust;
boost; grand
42;33 6 (3)

妆 妝 zhuāng
adorn;
apply make-up
42;38 6 (4)

将 將 jiāng jiàng
going to; about to; (preposition);
incite; commander; &
42;41 9 (1)

兆 zhào
omen; portend;
million, mega-
29;10 6 (4)

北 běi
north
-
39;21 5 (1)

乖 guāi
obedient;
quick-witted
4;4 8 (3)

乘 chéng shèng
ride; multiply;
make use of
149;4 10 (2)

■ 火

灶 zào
kitchen;
oven, stove
83;86 7 (4)

灿 燦càn
[magnificent,
bright]
83;86 7 (3)

烛 燭zhú
candle;
watt
83;86 10 (3)

炼 煉liàn
refine,
smelt, temper
83;86 9 (1)

灯 燈dēng
lamp, light,
lantern
83;86 6 (1)

炸 zhà zhá
explode; to
bomb; deep-fry
83;86 9 (3)

炊 chuī
to cook
-
83;86 8 (4)

烁 爍shuò
glittering;
sparkle
83;86 9 (3)

炉 爐lú
stove,
furnace
83;86 8 (3)

炕 kàng
to dry; kang,
heated bricks
83;86 8 (4)

炒 chǎo
fry, stir-fry;
heat up
83;86 8 (3)

熔 róng
melt, fuse,
smelt
83;86 14 (4)

煌 huáng
bright,
luminous
83;86 13 (3)

熄 xī
extinguish,
(fire) go out
83;86 14 (4)

烧 燒shāo
burn; fever;
to cook, heat
83;86 10 (1)

烂 爛làn
mushy; messy;
rotten; worn out
83;86 9 (2)

烘 hōng
bake;
to dry (at a fire)
83;86 10 (4)

煤 méi
coal
-
83;86 13 (2)

烦 煩fán
vexed; tired of;
bother, trouble
83;86 10 (1)

焊 hàn
weld,
solder
83;86 11 (3)

爆 bào
explode, burst;
quick-fry
83;86 19 (3)

燥 zào
dry,
arid
83;86 17 (2)

焰 yàn
flame,
blaze
83;86 12 (3)

焕 煥huàn
shining,
brilliant
83;86 11 (-)

燃 rán
burn,
ignite
83;86 16 (2)

烤 kǎo
bake,
roast
83;86 10 (2)

燧 suì
flint;
beacon fire
83;86 16 (-)

炮 pào páo bāo
artillery; to dry;
quick-fry
83;86 9 (2)

烟 *煙 菸 yān
smoke, mist;
tobacco; opium
83;86 10 (2)

1	41
2	42
3	43
4	44
5	45
6	46
7	47
8	48
9	49
10	50
11	51
12	52
13	53
14	54
15	55
16	56
17	57
18	58
19	59
20	60
21	61
22	62
23	63
24	64
25	65
26	66
27	67
28	68
29	69
30	70
31	71
32	72
33	73
34	74
35	75
36	76
37	77
38	78
39	79
40	80

讠

计 計 jì
compute; plan;
meter, gauge
10;149 4 (1)

让 讓 ràng
cede, allow;
invite; &
10;149 5 (1)

认 認 rèn
recognize,
admit; adopt
10;149 4 (1)

诀 訣 jué
farewell;
know-how
10;149 6 (-)

讲 講 jiǎng
speak, discuss,
tell, explain; &
10;149 6 (1)

许 許 xǔ
allow; promise;
praise; maybe
10;149 6 (1)

诈 詐 zhà
cheat, swindle;
feign; bluff
10;149 7 (4)

记 記 jì
recall; a mark;
note down
10;149 5 (1)

讥 譏 jī
ridicule
-
10;149 4 (4)

诅 詛 zǔ
[to curse]
-
10;149 7 (-)

课 課 kè
lesson, course,
class; tax
10;149 10 (1)

订 訂 dìng
fix; agree on;
book (seats); &
10;149 4 (2)

证 証 證 zhèng
prove; evidence;
certificate; &
10;149 7 (2)

讶 訝 yà
astonished
(literary)
10;149 6 (3)

评 評 píng
comment on,
appraise, judge
10;149 7 (1)

诬 誣 wū
falsely
accuse
10;149 9 (3)

讠

训 訓 xùn
teach, instruct;
model, example
10;149 5 (2)

诽 誹 fěi
slander
-
10;149 10 (4)

讹 訛 é
error; extort,
blackmail
10;149 6 (4)

谁 誰 shuí shéi
Who?;
anyone
10;149 10 (1)

谢 謝 xiè
thanks; politely
decline; wither
10;149 12 (1)

讠

讨 討 tǎo
discuss; incur;
demand; &
10;149 5 (1)

讯 訊 xùn
interrogate;
news, report
10;149 5 (2)

词 詞 cí
words,
speech
10;149 7 (1)

询 詢 xún
inquire
-
10;149 8 (3)

试 試 shì
try, attempt;
trial, test
10;149 8 (1)

诫 誡 jiè
warn,
admonish
10;149 9 (4)

诚 誠 chéng
sincere
-
10;149 8 (2)

讠

谜 謎 mí mèi
riddle,
puzzle
10;149 11 (3)

谴 譴 qiǎn
[condemn,
denounce]
10;149 15 (4)

诞 誕 dàn
birth; birthday;
fantastic
10;149 8 (3)

讠 / 讠

诉 訴 sù
inform; accuse;
complain
10;149 7 (1)

讽 諷 fěng
satire;
mock
10;149 6 (3)

调 調 tiáo diào
mix; fit in; mediate; provoke;
move, transfer; melody; &
10;149 10 (1)

■ 讠

议	访	谅	该	谊	诧
議 yì	訪 fǎng	諒 liàng	該 gāi	誼 yì	詫 chà
opinion;	visit; inquire,	forgive;	ought; deserve;	friendship	surprised
discuss	search for	guess, suppose	the aforesaid; &	-	-
10;149 5 (2)	10;149 6 (1)	10;149 10 (1)	10;149 8 (1)	10;149 10 (1)	10;149 8 (4)

诗	读	谈	请	诸	谤
詩 shī	讀 dú dòu	談 tán	請 qǐng	諸 zhū	謗 bàng
poetry	read, recite;	discuss;	please;	all, every;	slander
-	study	conversation	ask, invite	various	(literary)
10;149 8 (2)	10;149 10 (1)	10;149 10 (1)	10;149 10 (1)	10;149 10 (4)	10;149 12 (4)

详	谦	谱	说
詳 xiáng	謙 qiān	譜 pǔ	說 shuō shuì yuè
detailed;	modest	chart, register;	speak; explain;
fully known	-	melody; &	theory; scold; &
10;149 8 (2)	10;149 12 (3)	10;149 14 (4)	10;149 9 (1)

诺	谎	谋	谨
諾 nuò	謊 huǎng	謀 móu	謹 jǐn
promise;	lie,	plan; contrive;	cautious;
yes; consent	falsehood	consult	sincere
10;149 10 (-)	10;149 11 (4)	10;149 11 (3)	10;149 13 (3)

诵	译	语	设
誦 sòng	譯 yì	語 yǔ	設 shè
recite	translate,	language; say,	to found,
-	interpret	speak; words	establish; &
10;149 9 (3)	10;149 7 (1)	10;149 9 (1)	10;149 6 (1)

识	误	课	谓	谭
識 shí zhì	誤 wù	課 kè	謂 wèi	譚 tán
knowledge;	mistake; harm;	lesson, course,	say; to name;	(surname)
know; opinion	miss (train)	class; tax	meaning	-
10;149 7 (1)	10;149 9 (1)	10;149 10 (1)	10;149 11 (2)	10;149 14 (-)

话	谣	诱	诡	谗
話 huà	謠 yáo	誘 yòu	詭 guǐ	讒 chán
speech, word;	song, ballad;	guide, lead;	cunning,	slander
talk, talk about	rumor	entice	tricky; weird	-
10;149 8 (1)	10;149 12 (3)	10;149 9 (4)	10;149 8 (-)	10;149 11 (4)

论	诠	诊	讼	谐	谬
論 lùn lún	詮 quán	診 zhěn	訟 sòng	諧 xié	謬 miù
discuss; theory;	[annotate]	examine	dispute;	in accord;	mistaken;
decide; &	-	(a patient)	litigate	humorous	untrue
10;149 6 (1)	10;149 8 (-)	10;149 7 (3)	10;149 6 (4)	10;149 11 (4)	10;149 13 (4)

1	41
2	42
3	43
4	44
5	45
6	46
7	47
8	48
9	49
10	50
11	51
12	52
13	53
14	54
15	55
16	56
17	57
18	58
19	59
20	60
21	61
22	62
23	63
24	64
25	65
26	66
27	67
28	68
29	69
30	70
31	71
32	72
33	73
34	74
35	75
36	76
37	77
38	78
39	79
40	80

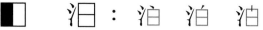

沪	泣	注	泳	泌	浅
滬 hù	qì	*註 zhù	yǒng	mì	淺 qiǎn
Shanghai	weep;	pour; pay heed;	swim	secrete	shallow; simple
-	tears	take notes; &	-	-	light (color); &
40;85 7 (4)	40;85 8 (4)	40;85 8 (1)	40;85 8 (1)	40;85 8 (3)	40;85 8 (1)

浪	泊	澳	浦	消	
làng	bó pō	澳 ào	pǔ	xiāo	
wave, billow;	anchor, moor;	bay, inlet;	river bank,	vanish; dispel;	
dissolute	lake, pool	harbor	river mouth	leisurely	
40;85 10 (2)	40;85 8 (4)	40;85 15 (4)	40;85 10 (-)	40;85 10 (1)	

淳	济	流	滚	潦	
chún	濟 jǐ jì	liú	滾 gǔn	liǎo lǎo	
honest	many (people);	stream, current;	tumble; boil;	sloppy, hasty;	
(literary)	aid, relief	flow; grade; &	Get lost!	unlucky; puddle	
40;85 11 (-)	40;85 9 (1)	40;85 10 (1)	40;85 13 (2)	40;85 15 (4)	

液	湾	滴			
yè	灣 wān	dī			
liquid,	gulf, bay,	drip, drop,			
fluid	bend in river	trickle			
40;85 11 (2)	40;85 12 (4)	40;85 14 (2)			

浓	淀	滨	演	溶	
濃 nóng	澱 diàn	濱 bīn	yǎn	róng	
dense,	sediment;	seashore,	develop;	dissolve	
thick	shallow lake	brink	perform; &	-	
40;85 9 (2)	40;85 11 (4)	40;85 13 (4)	40;85 14 (1)	40;85 13 (3)	

沾	洁	法	浩	洗	溃
zhān	潔 jié	fǎ	hào	xǐ	潰 kuì
wet; moisten;	clean,	law; method;	vast,	wash;	overflow; break
stain; touch	neat	model for	great	redress; to loot	through; ulcer
40;85 8 (3)	40;85 9 (3)	40;85 8 (1)	40;85 10 (4)	40;85 9 (1)	40;85 12 (4)

沙	涉	清	渣	漆	滞
shā	shè	qīng	zhā	qī	滯 zhì
sand; granules;	wade; involve;	clear; settle up;	shards; dregs,	paint,	stagnant
hoarse	to experience	quiet; fully; &	sediment	lacquer	-
40;85 7 (2)	40;85 10 (3)	40;85 11 (1)	40;85 12 (3)	40;85 14 (3)	40;85 12 (4)

浅	浇	淡	淹		
淺 qiǎn	澆 jiāo	dàn	yān		
shallow; simple;	to water,	insipid; pale;	inundate;		
light (color); &	irrigate	indifferent	drown; sweaty		
40;85 8 (1)	40;85 9 (3)	40;85 11 (2)	40;85 11 (3)		

■□ 氵 汩 ： 泊 泊

洋 涕 溢 滋 消

洋 yáng — ocean; foreign, Western; vast — 40;85 9 (2)

涕 tì — tears — - — 40;85 10 (4)

溢 yì — overflow — - — 40;85 13 (-)

滋 zī — grow, multiply — 40;85 12 (4)

消 xiāo — vanish; dispel; leisurely — 40;85 10 (1)

洪 淇 港

洪 hóng — flood; vast — 40;85 9 (3)

淇 qí — [ice cream] — - — 40;85 11 (4)

港 gǎng — port, harbor; [Hong Kong] — 40;85 12 (2)

澇 漠 潛 滿 瀟 灌

澇 lào — waterlogged, flooded — 40;85 10 (4)

漠 mò — desert; indifferent — 40;85 13 (2)

潛 qián — hidden; latent; secretly — 40;85 15 (4)

滿 mǎn — full; entirely; attain; satisfied — 40;85 13 (1)

瀟 xiāo — deep and clear (water) (literary) — 40;85 14 (-)

灌 guàn — irrigate; fill, pour in — 40;85 20 (3)

滯

滯 zhì — stagnant — - — 40;85 12 (4)

1	41
2	42
3	43
4	44
5	45
6	46
7	47
8	48
9	49
10	50
11	51
12	52
13	53
14	54
15	55
16	56
17	57
18	58
19	59
20	60
21	61
22	62
23	63
24	64
25	65
26	66
27	67
28	68
29	69
30	70
31	71
32	72
33	73
34	74
35	75
36	76
37	77
38	78
39	79
40	80

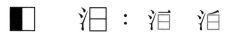

氵

污	添	泽	涌	涵
*汙 污 wū	tiān	澤 zé	湧 yǒng	hán
dirt, filth; smear; corrupt	add, increase	pond, marsh; damp; luster	gush, surge; emerge	contain; culvert
40;85 6 (2)	40;85 11 (2)	40;85 8 (3)	40;85 10 (3)	40;85 11 (-)

没	沿	沼	浸	涩
沒 méi mò	yán yàn	zhǎo	jìn	澀 sè
[not]; sink, submerge	along; follow; border, edge	pond, pool	soak, immerse	astringent; rough; difficult
40;85 7 (1)	40;85 8 (2)	40;85 8 (4)	40;85 10 (3)	40;85 10 (-)

涡	滑	澡	漂	潭
渦 wō	huá	zǎo	piāo piǎo piào	tán
eddy, whirlpool	slide; slippery, smooth; crafty	bath -	to float; rinse; beautiful; &	pond, pool
40;85 10 (-)	40;85 12 (2)	40;85 16 (1)	40;85 14 (1)	40;85 15 (4)

温	湿	混	渴	漫	瀑
wēn	濕 溼 shī	hùn hún	kě	màn	pù
warm; thermo-; review	wet, damp	mix up; pass for; &	thirsty -	overflow; freely; everywhere	waterfall -
40;85 12 (2)	40;85 12 (2)	40;85 11 (2)	40;85 12 (1)	40;85 14 (3)	40;85 18 (4)

泊

沃	泛	活
wò	*氾 汎 fàn	huó
irrigate; fertile	general, vague; to flood	alive; moving; work, labor; &
40;85 7 (4)	40;85 7 (2)	40;85 9 (1)

浮	淫	滔	溪	潘
fú	yín	tāo	xī	pān
to float; hollow; fleeting; &	excessive; lewd	flood; torrential	brook, small stream	(surname) -
40;85 10 (2)	40;85 11 (4)	40;85 13 (4)	40;85 13 (4)	40;85 15 (4)

沉 chén
to sink; lower; profound; heavy
40;85 7 (2)

泻 瀉 xiè
flow swiftly; torrent; diarrhea
40;85 8 (4)

浑 渾 hún
muddy; foolish; simple; entire
40;85 9 (3)

深 shēn
deep; very; late; intimate; &
40;85 11 (1)

汽 qì
vapor, steam
40;85 7 (1)

海 hǎi
sea; huge
40;85 10 (1)

净 *淨 jìng
completely; net (profit); clean
8;15 8 (1)

渔 漁 yú
fishing
-
40;85 11 (3)

洛 luò
(a river)
-
40;85 9 (-)

涤 滌 di
wash, cleanse (literary)
40;85 10 (4)

洽 qià
harmonious; discuss
40;85 9 (4)

沧 滄 cāng
deep blue (sea)
40;85 7 (-)

沦 淪 lún
sink; be reduced to
40;85 7 (-)

涂 塗 tú
rub on, smear; erase; scrawl
40;32 10 (2)

浴 yù
bath, bathe
40;85 10 (3)

治 zhì
control; peace; cure; study; &
40;85 8 (1)

渗 滲 shèn
seep, ooze, leak
40;85 11 (4)

淆 xiáo
confuse; mix up
40;85 11 (3)

滞 滯 zhì
stagnant
-
40;85 12 (4)

滥 濫 làn
excessive; overflow
40;85 13 (3)

澄 chéng
clear, transparent
40;85 15 (4)

涩 澀 sè
astringent; rough; difficult
40;85 10 (-)

溜 liū liù
glide; smooth; slip away; row of; flow of water; gutter; locality
40;85 13 (3)

1	41
2	42
3	43
4	44
5	45
6	46
7	47
8	48
9	49
10	50
11	51
12	52
13	53
14	54
15	55
16	56
17	57
18	58
19	59
20	60
21	61
22	62
23	63
24	64
25	65
26	66
27	67
28	68
29	69
30	70
31	71
32	72
33	73
34	74
35	75
36	76
37	77
38	78
39	79
40	80

汀

汁
zhī
juice
-
40;85 5 (4)

江
jiāng
river
-
40;85 6 (1)

汇 匯彙 huì
gather, meet;
remit (money)
40;22 5 (3)

汗 hàn hán
sweat
-
40;85 6 (2)

汪
wāng
form puddles;
(dog's) bark
40;85 7 (4)

沐
mù
wash (hair),
[bathe]
40;85 7 (-)

沫
mò
foam
-
40;85 8 (4)

沛
pèi
copious
-
40;85 7 (4)

池
chí
pond;
sunken area
40;85 6 (2)

泄 洩 xiè
release, let out,
to vent, to leak
40;85 8 (4)

浅 淺 qiǎn
shallow; simple
light (color); &
40;85 8 (1)

沃
wò
irrigate;
fertile
40;85 7 (4)

汰
tài
clean out;
discard
40;85 7 (4)

沈
shěn
(surname)
-
40;85 7 (3)

波
bō
a wave
-
40;85 8 (3)

泌
mì
secrete
-
40;85 8 (3)

汉 漢 hàn
Chinese (lang);
Han; man
40;85 5 (1)

汝
rǔ
you
(literary)
40;85 6 (-)

汤 湯 tāng
hot water;
soup
40;85 6 (1)

津
jīn
ferry; moist;
sweat; saliva
40;85 9 (4)

沸
fèi
boil (water)
-
40;85 8 (3)

浦
pǔ
river bank,
river mouth
40;85 10 (-)

浊 濁 zhuó
turbid, muddy;
chaotic
40;85 9 (4)

油
yóu
oil, grease, fat;
to paint
40;85 8 (2)

泪 淚 lèi
teardrop
-
40;85 8 (2)

沮
jǔ
dispirited;
prevent
40;85 8 (-)

洒 灑 sǎ
sprinkle;
spill
40;85 9 (2)

酒
jiǔ
wine,
liquor
40;164 10 (1)

洲 zhōu continent; shoals, islet 40;85 9 (4)	泌 mì secrete - 40;85 8 (3)	淮 huái [Huaihe river] - 40;85 11 (4)	滩 灘 tān beach, sands; shoals, rapids 40;85 13 (3)	涨 漲 zhǎng zhàng rise, go up; swell 40;85 10 (2)	
沏 qī infuse - 40;85 7 (4)	浙 zhè Zhejiang - 40;85 10 (3)	渐 漸 jiàn jiān gradually - 40;85 11 (2)	游 *遊 yóu swim; wander; reach (of river) 40;85 12 (1)	渊 淵 yuān deep; profound 40;85 11 (-)	润 潤 rùn moist; lubricate; adorn; profit 40;85 10 (3)
溯 sù go against flow; trace back 40;85 13 (-)	湖 hú lake - 40;85 12 (1)	潮 cháo tide, upsurge; damp 40;85 15 (3)	澎 pēng péng splash; sound of waves 40;85 15 (3)	淋 lín lìn drenched; filter 40;85 11 (3)	淑 shū virtuous (literary) 40;85 11 (3)
渺 miǎo vast (lake, sea); hazy; negligible 40;85 12 (4)	溉 gài [wash, irrigate] 40;85 12 (3)	激 jī violent; arouse; annoy: chill 40;85 16 (2)	鸿 鴻 hóng swan, goose; grand 40;196 11 (-)	测 測 cè to measure; predict, infer 40;85 9 (2)	溅 濺 jiàn splash - 40;85 12 (3)
沥 瀝 lì trickle, drip 40;85 7 (4)	涯 yá limit, margin; shoreline 40;85 11 (-)	源 yuán source - 40;85 13 (2)	渡 dù cross (a river); ferry 40;85 12 (2)	滤 濾 lù filter 40;85 13 (4)	
派 pài clan, faction; style; send 40;85 9 (1)	波 bō a wave - 40;85 8 (3)	泼 潑 pō sprinkle; unreasonable 40;85 8 (2)	涛 濤 tāo great waves, billows 40;85 10 (4)	泥 ní nì mashed (food); mud, plaster 40;85 8 (2)	漏 lòu omit; leak; divulge 40;85 14 (2)
汛 xùn flood - 40;85 6 (4)	河 hé river - 40;85 8 (1)	沟 溝 gōu ditch, ravine, channel, groove 40;85 7 (3)	泡 pào pāo bubble; soak; dawdle; spongy 40;85 8 (3)	淘 táo rinse, clean out; bothersome 40;85 11 (4)	
润 潤 rùn moist; lubricate; adorn; profit 40;85 10 (3)	洞 dòng hole, cave; thoroughly 40;85 9 (2)	汹 洶 xiōng [turbulent] - 40;85 7 (4)	涵 hán contain; culvert 40;85 11 (-)		

1 41 / 2 42 / 3 43 / 4 44 / 5 45 / 6 46 / **7** 47 / 8 48 / 9 49 / 10 50 / 11 51 / 12 52 / 13 53 / 14 54 / 15 55 / 16 56 / 17 57 / 18 58 / 19 59 / 20 60 / 21 61 / 22 62 / 23 63 / 24 64 / 25 65 / 26 66 / 27 67 / 28 68 / 29 69 / 30 70 / 31 71 / 32 72 / 33 73 / 34 74 / 35 75 / 36 76 / 37 77 / 38 78 / 39 79 / 40 80

□ 伯 ： 伯 伯 伯 伯 伯

伯
伯
伯

仪	代	伐	伏	优	伪
儀 yí	dài	fá	fú	優 yōu	偽 僞 wěi
apparatus; gift; rite; appearance	substitute for; era, generation	cut down (tree); attack	prostrate; hide; confess; &	excellent -	fake, bogus
21;9 5 (2)	21;9 5 (1)	21;9 6 (4)	21;9 6 (4)	21;9 6 (2)	21;9 6 (4)

仿	位	住	依	信	傅
倣 fǎng	wèi	zhù	yī	xìn	fù
imitate; resemble	place, seat, throne	live, reside; stay; cease	according to; comply; rely on	true; believe; letter, news; &	teach, teacher apply (paint)
21;9 6 (2)	21;9 7 (1)	21;9 7 (1)	21;9 8 (2)	21;9 9 (1)	21;9 12 (1)

伯	倍	停	傍	偏	傻
bó bǎi	bèi	tíng	bàng	piān	shǎ
uncle; earl	double; multiple	stop, halt; stay; park (car)	draw near; close to	leaning; biased; perverse	stupid, dumb; mechanically
21;9 7 (2)	21;9 10 (1)	21;9 11 (1)	21;9 12 (2)	21;9 11 (2)	21;9 13 (2)

估	侍	佳	债	值
gū	shì	jiā	債 zhài	zhí
to estimate -	attend, wait on	beautiful, fine	debt -	value, price; on duty; happen to
21;9 7 (2)	21;9 8 (4)	21;9 8 (3)	21;9 10 (3)	21;9 10 (2)

侦	催	倚	僚
偵 zhēn	cuī	yǐ	liáo
spy; scout; detect	to urge; expedite	lean on, rely on	official -
21;9 8 (4)	21;9 13 (2)	21;9 10 (3)	21;9 14 (3)

伯
伯

倦	僧	俏	倘	偿	伴
juàn	sēng	qiào	tǎng	償 cháng	bàn
tired -	Buddhist monk	handsome; in demand	if -	compensate; fulfil	partner; accompany
21;9 10 (3)	21;9 14 (-)	21;9 9 (3)	21;9 10 (3)	21;9 11 (3)	21;9 7 (3)

供	借
gōng gòng	*藉 jiè
supply; confess; &	borrow; lend; pretext
21;9 8 (2)	21;9 10 (1)

仁 rén	**侄** zhí
benevolence; kernel	nephew -
21;9 4 (4)	21;9 8 (4)

仁 rén
benevolence; kernel
21;9 4 (4)

侄 zhí
nephew
-
21;9 8 (4)

佰 bǎi
hundred
-
21;9 8 (-)

儒 rú
Confucian
-
21;9 16 (-)

僵 jiāng
numb; stiff, rigid; impasse
21;9 15 (3)

侯 hóu
marquis
-
21;9 9 (4)

侵 qīn
invade; intrude; approaching
21;9 9 (2)

侶 **侣** lǚ
companion, mate
21;9 8 (4)

保 bǎo
protect; ensure
21;9 9 (2)

促 cù
to urge; urgent; hurry
21;9 9 (2)

但 dàn
but, yet; merely
21;9 7 (1)

倡 chàng
initiate
-
21;9 10 (2)

俱 jù
all, complete
21;9 10 (2)

偶 ǒu
mate; in pairs; idol; by chance
21;9 11 (3)

仟 qiān
thousand
-
21;9 5 (-)

任 rèn rén
appoint; allow; despite; &
21;9 6 (1)

低 dī
low; to lower
21;9 7 (1)

僑 **侨** qiáo
live abroad, expatriot
21;9 8 (3)

俘 fú
capture; prisoner
21;9 9 (4)

傷 **伤** shāng
wound; harm, hurt; get sick of
21;9 6 (2)

侮 wǔ
to bully; to insult
21;9 9 (3)

侈 chǐ
extravagant; prattle (literary)
21;9 8 (4)

像 xiàng
shape; be like; (see Table 1)
21;9 13 (1)

*價 **价** jià jie jiè
value, price
21;9 6 (2)

倫 **伦** lún
series; peer; (feudal) ethics
21;9 6 (-)

伶 líng
actor (archaic); [clever; bereft]
21;9 7 (4)

儉 **俭** jiǎn
thrifty, frugal
21;9 9 (4)

偷 tōu
steal; stealthy
21;9 11 (2)

份 fèn
portion, share
21;9 6 (2)

俗 sú
custom, habit; popular; vulgar
21;9 9 (2)

俊 jùn
handsome; talented
21;9 9 (4)

倪 ní
[inkling]; (surname)
21;9 10 (-)

1 41
2 42
3 43
4 44
5 45
6 46
7 47
8 48
9 49
10 50
11 51
12 52
13 53
14 54
15 55
16 56
17 57
18 58
19 59
20 60
21 61
22 62
23 63
24 64
25 65
26 66
27 67
28 68
29 69
30 70
31 71
32 72
33 73
34 74
35 75
36 76
37 77
38 78
39 79
40 80

囗 囗

囗

仆
*僕 pú pū
servant;
fall prostrate
21;9 4 (4)

亿
億 yì
a hundred
million
21;9 3 (1)

化
huà huā
alter; -ise, -ify;
melt; spend; &
21;21 4 (1)

仅
僅 jǐn
merely;
barely
21;9 4 (2)

什
*甚 shén shí
[what?];
sundry; ten
21;9 4 (1)

仕
shì
an official
-
21;9 5 (-)

件
jiàn
thing; letter,
document
21;9 6 (1)

仟
qiān
thousand
-
21;9 5 (-)

任
rèn rén
appoint; allow;
despite; &
21;9 6 (1)

伍
wǔ
five;
5-man platoon
21;9 6 (2)

作
zuò zuō zuó
do, make, write; act as; pretend;
regard as; get up (from bed); &
21;9 7 (1)

仙
xiān
immortal being;
fairy
21;9 5 (4)

仗
zhàng
hold (weapon);
rely on; battle
21;9 5 (3)

仇
chóu
hatred;
enemy
21;9 4 (3)

仔
zǐ zī zǎi
young animal;
[careful]
21;9 5 (2)

仍
réng
still,
yet
21;9 4 (2)

伊
yī
he, she;
('i' sound)
21;9 6 (3)

休
xiū
to stop; to rest;
Don't!
21;9 6 (1)

体
體 tǐ tī
body; in person;
style; system
21;188 7 (1)

你
*妳 nǐ
you,
your
21;9 7 (1)

他
tā
he, him;
other, another
21;9 5 (1)

伟
偉 wěi
great
-
21;9 6 (1)

传
傳 chuán zhuàn
pass on,
transmit; &
21;9 6 (2)

付
fù
pay,
hand over
21;9 5 (2)

代
dài
substitute for;
era, generation
21;9 5 (1)

伐
fá
cut down (tree);
attack
21;9 6 (4)

伏
fú
prostrate; hide;
confess; &
21;9 6 (4)

优
優 yōu
excellent
-
21;9 6 (2)

伪
偽 僞 wěi
fake,
bogus
21;9 6 (4)

伴
bàn
partner;
accompany
21;9 7 (3)

侠
俠 xiá
[chivalrous]
-
21;9 8 (-)

佛
*佛 fó fú
Buddha
-
21;9 7 (2)

俩
倆 liǎ liǎng
two, both,
several (colloq)
21;9 9 (1)

俄
é
soon,
presently
21;9 9 (3)

仲
zhòng
go-between;
middle (of 3)
21;9 6 (-)

伸
shēn
stretch,
extend
21;9 7 (2)

使
shǐ
send; envoy;
use; enable; if
21;9 8 (1)

便
biàn pián
convenient;
informal; &
21;9 9 (1)

佣
*傭 yòng yōng
fee; servant,
hired labor
21;9 7 (4)

伙	似	仰
*夥 huǒ	sì shì	yǎng
partner; group; provisions	similar; seem; than	face up; admire; rely on
21;9 6 (2)	21;9 6 (2)	21;9 6 (2)

们	候	修
們 men	hòu	xiū
(plural suffix)	await; ask after; time, season	repair; amend; build; study; &
-		
21;9 5 (1)	21;9 10 (1)	21;9 9 (2)

例	俐	侧	倒
lì	lì	側 cè	dǎo dào
example; rules; precedent	[clever]	side; to lean, incline	topple, collapse; exchange; pour; invert; go back; &
	-		
21;9 8 (1)	21;9 9 (4)	21;9 8 (3)	21;9 10 (1)

做	傲	假	僻	倾	储
zuò	ào	jiǎ jià	pì	傾 qīng	儲 chǔ
make, do, write; be, become; &	defy; proud, arrogant	fake; borrow; vacation; &	secluded, eccentric	collapse; lean, incline; pour out	store up
					-
21;9 11 (1)	21;9 13 (2)	21;9 11 (1)	21;9 15 (4)	21;9 10 (3)	21;9 12 (4)

佐	佑	俯
zuǒ	*祐 yòu	fǔ
assist	help; protect; bless	condescend; bow one's head
-		
21;9 7 (-)	21;9 7 (-)	21;9 10 (3)

何	伺	付
hé	sì cì	fù
What?, Who? etc. (literary)	to watch; await; serve	pay, hand over
21;9 7 (1)	21;9 7 (3)	21;9 5 (2)

健
jiàn
healthy, strong; invigorate
21;9 10 (1)

佩	伪
pèi	偽 僞 wěi
admire; wear (sword, badge)	fake, bogus
21;9 8 (3)	21;9 6 (4)

1	41
2	42
3	43
4	44
5	45
6	46
7	47
8	48
9	49
10	50
11	51
12	52
13	53
14	54
15	55
16	56
17	57
18	58
19	59
20	60
21	61
22	62
23	63
24	64
25	65
26	66
27	67
28	68
29	69
30	70
31	71
32	72
33	73
34	74
35	75
36	76
37	77
38	78
39	79
40	80

彳

律	征	很	往	彷	彼
lǜ	*徵 zhēng	hěn	wàng wǎng	páng	bǐ
law, rule	travel; solicit; sign; evidence	very -	towards; go; previous	[hesitate, waver]	that; the other he, she
62;60 9 (2)	62;60 8 (2)	62;60 9 (1)	62;60 8 (1)	62;60 7 (-)	62;60 8 (3)

径	役	得	後	徐	
徑 jìng	yì	de dé děi	hòu	xú	
path; directly; diameter	compel; battle; service; servant	(particle); fit for; get; need; must	after (see Table 1)	slowly, gently	
62;60 8 (3)	62;60 7 (4)	62;60 11 (1)	62;60 9 (-)	62;60 10 (4)	

待	徒	德	循	徊	
dài dāi	tú	dé	xún	huái	
await; about to; to treat; stay; &	walk; merely; bare; in vain; &	virtue; kindness	follow; comply with	[hesitate, waver]	
62;60 9 (2)	62;60 10 (3)	62;60 15 (2)	62;60 12 (3)	62;60 9 (4)	

衍	銜	街	衡	行	
yǎn	衔 xián	jiē	héng	xíng háng	
redundant; spread (literary)	hold (in mouth); rank, title	street -	scales; weigh; measure	go; do, perform; capable; OK; for now; line; (business) firm	
62;144 9 (4)	62;167 11 (4)	62;144 12 (1)	62;144 16 (3)	62;144 6 (1)	

徘	彻	御	微	徽	
pái	徹 chè	*禦 yù	wēi	huī	
[hesitate, waver, linger]	thorough; penetrate	drive (vehicle); resist; imperial	micro-, tiny; wane; subtle	emblem -	
62;60 11 (4)	62;60 7 (2)	62;60 12 (3)	62;60 13 (2)	62;60 17 (4)	

忄

协	博
協 xié	bó
together, jointly; assist	plentiful; to gain, win
12;24 6 (3)	12;24 12 (3)

上

比	切	顷
bǐ	qiē qiè	頃 qǐng
compare; than; to gesture; &	slice; eager to; accord with; &	just now; (unit of land area)
123;81 4 (1)	27;18 4 (1)	39;181 8 (3)

止

此	歧	雌
cǐ	qí	cí
this -	fork (in road); diverge	female -
102;77 6 (2)	102;77 8 (4)	208;172 14 (4)

土

址	地	块	坡	坪	坏
zhǐ	dì de	塊 kuài	pō	píng	壞 huài
site, location	earth, soil; place; &	clod, lump; yuan (colloq)	slope -	level ground	bad, evil; spoil, ruin
49;32 7 (2)	49;32 6 (1)	49;32 7 (1)	49;32 8 (2)	49;32 8 (-)	49;32 7 (1)

坤	埔	埋	圾	场	
kūn	pǔ	mái mán	jī	場 chǎng cháng	
feminine -	[Huangpu] -	bury -	[garbage] -	site, spot, field; &	
49;32 8 (-)	49;32 10 (4)	49;32 10 (2)	49;32 6 (2)	49;32 6 (1)	

堆	圳	墩	疆		
duī	zhèn	dūn	jiāng		
heap, pile	irrigation ditch; [Shenzhen]	mound; block	boundary, frontier		
49;32 11 (2)	49;32 6 (-)	49;32 15 (-)	71;102 19 (3)		

垃	坟	坑	坊	埠	坯
lā	墳 fén	kēng	fáng fāng	bù	pī
[garbage] -	grave, tomb	hole, pit; tunnel; entrap	workshop, mill; lane, alley	jetty, port; city	semi-finished product
49;32 8 (2)	49;32 7 (3)	49;32 7 (3)	49;32 7 (4)	49;32 11 (4)	49;32 8 (4)

培	境	壤	填	堵	墙
péi	jìng	rǎng	tián	dǔ	牆 qiáng
cultivate, train, foster	boundary; place; situation	soil, earth, place	fill up; fill out (form)	block up, stifle, obstruct	wall -
49;32 11 (3)	49;32 14 (2)	49;32 20 (3)	49;32 13 (2)	49;32 11 (2)	49;90 14 (1)

垮	埃	堪	塔	增	坝
kuǎ	āi	kān	tā	zēng	壩 bà
collapse, break down	dirt, dust	able to; bear, sustain	tower, pagoda	increase, grow	dyke, dam, embankment
49;32 9 (3)	49;32 10 (4)	49;32 12 (4)	49;32 12 (2)	49;32 15 (1)	49;32 7 (3)

坦	堤	塌	埋	坛	
tǎn	dī	tā	mái mán	壇 壜 罎 潭 罈 tán	
level, smooth; calm; candid	dyke, dam, embankment	collapse, cave in; calm down	bury -	altar, platform; jar, jug	
49;32 8 (3)	49;32 12 (3)	49;32 13 (3)	49;32 10 (2)	49;32 7 (4)	

均	域	城	坡	塘	墟
jūn	yù	chéng	pō	táng	xū
equal, even, balanced; all	region, territory	(city) wall; city	slope -	embankment; pool, pond	ruins; mound; market
49;32 7 (2)	49;32 11 (3)	49;32 9 (1)	49;32 8 (2)	49;32 13 (4)	49;32 14 (3)

1	41
2	42
3	43
4	44
5	45
6	46
7	47
8	48
9	49
10	50
11	51
12	52
13	53
14	54
15	55
16	56
17	57
18	58
19	59
20	60
21	61
22	62
23	63
24	64
25	65
26	66
27	67
28	68
29	69
30	70
31	71
32	72
33	73
34	74
35	75
36	76
37	77
38	78
39	79
40	80

■□ 扌 ：拍 拍 拍

扌
拍
拍

拍 pāi	搗 搗 dǎo	扰 擾 rǎo	找 zhǎo	我 wǒ
clap, beat time; bat, racquet; & 55;64 8 (1)	to pound, beat; harass 55;64 10 (4)	harass, disturb; trouble 55;64 7 (2)	seek; call on; give change 55;64 7 (1)	I, me, my, we, our 101;62 7 (1)

护 護 hù	拄 zhǔ	捕 bǔ	搏 bó	
protect, guard 55;149 7 (2)	lean on (walking stick) 55;64 8 (4)	catch, seize, arrest 55;64 10 (2)	to fight; throb; pounce 55;64 13 (4)	

拉 lā lá lǎ	抗 kàng	挤 擠 jǐ	掠 lüè	
pull; lengthen; cut; chat; & 55;64 8 (1)	resist, defy, anti- 55;64 7 (2)	squeeze; jostle; crowded 55;64 9 (1)	plunder; sweep past 55;64 11 (3)	

摔 shuāi	搞 gǎo	接 jiē	摘 zhāi	撞 zhuàng	擅 shàn
fall, tumble; fling; break 55;64 14 (2)	make, do; set up; procure; & 55;64 13 (1)	receive; accept; catch; connect 55;64 11 (1)	pick, pluck, select 55;64 14 (2)	rush; collide, bump into 55;64 15 (2)	excel at; unilaterally 55;64 16 (4)

挖 wā	控 kòng	按 àn	擦 cā.	拧 擰 níng nǐng nìng
dig, excavate 55;64 9 (2)	accuse; control 55;64 11 (2)	push; restrain; according to; & 55;64 9 (2)	rub, wipe, erase; & 55;64 17 (1)	wring, screw; differ; mistake 55;64 8 (3)

技 jì	持 chí	挂 掛 guà	指 zhǐ zhī zhí	掉 diào
skill, ability, talent 55;64 7 (1)	hold, support, maintain; & 55;64 9 (1)	hang; to phone; worry; register 55;64 9 (1)	finger; point at; rely on 55;64 9 (1)	fall; drop, lose; swap; turn back 55;64 11 (1)

抄 chāo	搏 bó	摧 cuī	*蒐 sōu	携 攜 xié	捷 jié
copy; shortcut; confiscate; & 55;64 7 (2)	to fight; throb; pounce 55;64 13 (4)	break, destroy 55;64 14 (3)	search - 55;64 12 (3)	carry, bring, take along 55;64 13 (4)	victory; quick, nimble 55;64 11 (3)

挠 撓 náo	掩 yǎn	挎 kuà	揍 zòu	捧 pěng
scratch; hinder; disturb; yield 55;64 9 (4)	cover, conceal; shut 55;64 11 (3)	carry (on arm or shoulder) 55;64 9 (4)	hit, strike (colloq) 55;64 12 (4)	flatter; hold in both hands 55;64 11 (2)

拦
攔 lán
block,
obstruct
55;64 8 (2)

拼
*拼 pīn
piece together;
go all out
55;64 9 (2)

拌
bàn
mix
-
55;64 8 (4)

挡
擋 dǎng dàng
block, ward off;
gear (cars)
55;64 9 (2)

捎
shāo shào
take,
bring; &
55;64 10 (4)

撑
chēng
support, prop
up; fill; unfurl
55;64 15 (3)

搂
摟 lōu lǒu
extort; gather
up; embrace
55;64 12 (3)

搅
攪 jiǎo
stir, mix;
disturb
55;64 12 (3)

拱
gǒng
arch; encircle;
nudge; &
55;64 9 (4)

捞
撈 lāo
dredge, fish for;
get illicitly
55;64 10 (2)

措
cuò
arrange;
manage
55;64 11 (2)

搭
dā
build; join;
carry; travel; &
55;64 12 (2)

摸
mō
feel; grope for;
sound out
55;64 13 (2)

描
miáo
to trace, copy,
retouch
55;64 11 (2)

1	41
2	42
3	43
4	44
5	45
6	46
7	47
8	48
9	49
10	50
11	51
12	52
13	53
14	54
15	55
16	56
17	57
18	58
19	59
20	60
21	61
22	62
23	63
24	64
25	65
26	66
27	67
28	68
29	69
30	70
31	71
32	72
33	73
34	74
35	75
36	76
37	77
38	78
39	79
40	80

扌

择
擇 zé zhái
pick,
choose
55;64 8 (2)

投
tóu
fling; leap into;
send; deliver; &
55;64 7 (2)

招
zhāo
beckon; invite; recruit; incur;
provoke; confess; a trick
55;64 8 (2)

拯
zhěng
rescue,
save
55;64 9 (-)

抒
shū
express
(an opinion)
55;64 7 (-)

捅
tǒng
poke, stab;
disclose
55;64 10 (4)

揉
róu
rub,
knead
55;64 12 (3)

捉
zhuō
grasp; seize,
capture
55;64 10 (2)

拐
*拐 guǎi
to turn; abduct;
swindle; limp
55;64 8 (2)

损
損 sǔn
decrease; loss;
harm, damage
55;64 10 (2)

捐
juān
forsake;
donate; tax
55;64 10 (4)

操
cāo
grasp; operate;
exercise; &
55;64 16 (1)

担
擔 dān dàn
undertake;
burden
55;64 8 (2)

捍
hàn
defend,
guard
55;64 10 (4)

捏
niē
hold; knead;
fabricate (lie)
55;64 10 (3)

揭
jiē
remove;
uncover
55;64 12 (3)

提
tí dī
carry; lift, raise; to extract;
mention; put forward; &
55;64 12 (1)

摄
攝 shè
absorb; act for;
take (photo)
55;64 13 (3)

摆
擺 襬 bǎi
put, arrange;
sway, wave; &
55;64 13 (1)

扌

括
kuò
include;
to contract
55;64 9 (2)

插
chā
insert
-
55;64 12 (2)

捶
chuí
bang, thump;
to cudgel
55;64 11 (4)

抵
dǐ
resist; prop up;
compensate; &
55;64 8 (3)

摇
搖 yáo
shake, sway,
wave, flutter
55;64 13 (2)

授
shòu
give, confer;
teach
55;64 11 (2)

援
yuán
grasp;
help, aid; cite
55;64 12 (2)

播
bō
sow, scatter,
broadcast
55;64 15 (1)

拖 tuō pull, drag; delay 55;64 8 (2)	探 tàn explore, scout; visit; lean out 55;64 11 (2)	挥 揮 huī to wave, wield; wipe; scatter; & 55;64 9 (2)		
换 換 huàn exchange - 55;64 10 (1)	挽 wǎn pull; coil up; redeem; lament 55;64 10 (3)	搀 攙 chān support, help; mix, blend 55;64 12 (4)	掐 qiā nip, pinch, choke; sever 55;64 11 (4)	挣 掙 zhèng zhēng struggle free; earn 55;64 9 (3)
扮 bàn disguise, dress up as 55;64 7 (2)	抬 tái raise, lift 55;64 8 (1)	挨 āi ái abut; in turn; suffer; dawdle 55;64 10 (2)	掺 摻 chān mix, blend 55;64 11 (4)	
拾 shí pick up, collect; ten 55;64 9 (1)	抡 掄 lūn lún brandish; choose 55;64 7 (4)	捡 撿 jiǎn pick up, glean, collect 55;64 10 (2)	拴 shuān tie, fasten, to tether 55;64 9 (3)	抢 搶 qiǎng qiāng snatch; vie for; to rush; scrape 55;64 7 (2)
捻 撚 niǎn twist (with fingers) 55;64 11 (4)	擒 qín capture - 55;64 15 (-)	撼 hàn shake - 55;64 16 (-)	挫 cuò thwart; to lower 55;64 10 (3)	
携 攜 xié carry, bring, take along 55;64 13 (4)	揽 攬 lǎn clasp; tie rope to; to take over 55;64 12 (4)	撵 攆 niǎn drive out, expel 55;64 15 (4)	攒 攢 zǎn cuán save, hoard; assemble 55;64 19 (4)	撰 zhuàn write, compose 55;64 15 (-)

摺 zhé zhē shé
bend, fold; &
(see Table 1)
55;64 14 (-)

1	41
2	42
3	43
4	44
5	45
6	46
7	47
8	48
9	49
10	50
11	51
12	52
13	53
14	54
15	55
16	56
17	57
18	58
19	59
20	60
21	61
22	62
23	63
24	64
25	65
26	66
27	67
28	68
29	69
30	70
31	71
32	72
33	73
34	74
35	75
36	76
37	77
38	78
39	79
40	80

扣

扑 撲 pū	扶 fú	抹 mā mǒ mò	扯 chě	扎 *絷 紮 zhā zhá zā	
rush at, attack; to flap, flutter 55;64 5 (2)	hold on to; help 55;64 7 (2)	to plaster; wipe; erase; to skirt 55;64 8 (3)	pull, to tear; chat 55;64 7 (3)	prick, stab; encamp; tie up 55;64 4 (2)	
扩 擴 kuò	拙 zhuō	拌 bàn	扰 擾 rǎo	找 zhǎo	我 wǒ
expand, extend 55;64 6 (2)	clumsy; my (humble) 55;64 8 (4)	mix - 55;64 8 (4)	harass, disturb; trouble 55;64 7 (2)	seek; call on; give change 55;64 7 (1)	I, me, my, we, our 101;62 7 (2)
抉 jué	披 pī	挟 挾 xié	拣 揀 jiǎn	执 執 zhí	
pick, single out (literary) 55;64 7 (-)	drape over; unroll; split 55;64 8 (2)	coerce; hold (under the arm) 55;64 9 (4)	choose, select 55;64 8 (2)	hold; manage; persist; abide by; capture; receipt 55;32 6 (2)	
挫 cuò	拂 fú	抽 chōu	拽 zhuài zhuāi	捕 bǔ	
thwart; to lower 55;64 10 (3)	wipe, flick; brush away 55;64 8 (-)	to extract; to smoke; whip; & 55;64 8 (1)	pull, drag; hurl, fling 55;64 9 (4)	catch, seize, arrest 55;64 10 (2)	
扛 káng gāng	抚 撫 fǔ	拒 jù	打 dǎ dá		
to shoulder, lift, carry 55;64 6 (2)	pacify; caress; nurture 55;64 7 (4)	resist, reject, refuse 55;64 7 (2)	hit; make; tie up; send; fetch; buy; shoot; calculate; dozen; & 55;64 5 (1)		
托 *託 tuō	扔 rēng	扬 揚 yáng	扫 掃 sǎo sào	扭 niǔ	拇 mǔ
entrust; pretext; support; & 55;64 6 (2)	hurl; throw away 55;64 5 (2)	raise; winnow; publicize 55;64 6 (1)	clear away, sweep 55;64 6 (2)	turn round; roll; wrench; grapple 55;64 7 (2)	thumb; big toe 55;64 8 (4)
扣 kòu	押 yā	把 bǎ bà	报 報 bào	拥 擁 yōng	
arrest; fasten; knot; deduct; & 55;64 6 (2)	detain; escort; mortgage; & 55;64 8 (3)	to hold; control; a handle; & 55;64 7 (1)	report; reply; newspaper 55;32 7 (1)	swarm, crowd; embrace; & 55;64 8 (2)	

抠 抠 抠

拒 jù	抠 摳 kōu	抓 zhuā	搁 擱 gē gé	捆 kǔn
resist, reject, refuse 55;64 7 (2)	root out; carve; delve into 55;64 7 (4)	scratch; seize, arrest; & 55;64 7 (2)	put; put aside; endure 55;64 12 (2)	tie, bind; bundle 55;64 10 (2)

扒
bā pá
cling; to dig up,
rake; to stew; &
55;64 5 (3)

批
pī
slap; criticize;
batch
55;64 7 (1)

挑
tiāo tiǎo
choose; carry;
poke; stir up
55;64 9 (2)

排
pái pǎi
line up; row, line; platoon;
rehearse; raft; eject; push; pie
55;64 11 (1)

抑
yì
repress;
restrain
55;64 7 (3)

拟
擬 nǐ
draft; intend;
imitate
55;64 7 (4)

捌
bā
eight
-
55;64 10 (4)

推
tuī
push; grind; to clip; deduce;
shirk; postpone; elect; esteem
55;64 11 (1)

挪
nuó
move
-
55;64 9 (4)

掷
擲 zhì zhī
throw
-
55;64 11 (4)

揪
jiū
hold tight;
seize; pull
55;64 12 (3)

摊
攤 tān
spread out;
booth, stall; &
55;64 13 (3)

掀
xiān
lift
(lid or cover)
55;64 11 (2)

撕
sī
rip,
tear
55;64 15 (2)

搬
bān
move (house);
remove; &
55;64 13 (1)

撒
sā sǎ
let go; scatter,
spill, drop
55;64 15 (2)

撤
chè
remove,
withdraw
55;64 15 (3)

撇
piē piě
abandon, cast
off; fling; skim
55;64 14 (4)

扩
擴 kuò
expand,
extend
55;64 6 (2)

抓
zhuā
scratch; seize;
arrest; &
55;64 7 (2)

拆
chāi cā
tear apart,
dismantle
55;64 8 (2)

折
*摺 zhé zhē shé
bend; fold; break; lose; rebate;
be convinced; amount to; &
55;64 7 (2)

振
zhèn
shake, wave;
rouse; boost
55;64 10 (3)

扳
bān
pull;
to turn
55;64 7 (4)

披
pī
drape over;
unroll; split
55;64 8 (2)

拔
bá
root out; select;
seize; &
55;64 8 (2)

拨
撥 bō
stir, poke;
allocate; batch
55;64 8 (3)

拢
攏 lǒng
approach; sum;
tie up; comb
55;64 8 (3)

拓
tà tuò
make rubbing;
open up (land)
55;64 8 (4)

掂
diān
heft, weigh up
(in the hand)
55;64 11 (4)

搓
cuō
rub (with
the hands)
55;64 12 (3)

掘
jué
dig,
excavate
55;64 11 (4)

据
據 jù jū
seize, occupy;
according to; &
55;64 11 (2)

握
wò
grasp
-
55;64 12 (1)

拘
jū
arrest; restrict;
inflexible
55;64 8 (4)

抱
bào
cherish; adopt;
embrace; &
55;64 8 (1)

掏
tāo
pull out; scoop;
pick-pocket
55;64 11 (2)

抖
dǒu
tremble, shake;
rouse
55;64 7 (2)

抛
pāo
throw, fling;
leave behind
55;64 7 (3)

挺
tǐng
erect; stick out;
very; endure
55;64 9 (1)

1	41
2	42
3	43
4	44
5	45
6	46
7	47
8	48
9	49
10	50
11	51
12	52
13	53
14	54
15	55
16	56
17	57
18	58
19	59
20	60
21	61
22	62
23	63
24	64
25	65
26	66
27	67
28	68
29	69
30	70
31	71
32	72
33	73
34	74
35	75
36	76
37	77
38	78
39	79
40	80

犭 豸

犭

狂 kuáng	犯 fàn	独 獨 dú	狸 lí	狠 hěn	狼 láng
crazy; violent; wild; arrogant	offense; attack; criminal	single, alone; only	raccoon, wild cat	ruthless; resolute	wolf
69;94 7 (3)	69;94 5 (2)	69;94 9 (2)	69;94 10 (4)	69;94 9 (3)	- 69;94 10 (2)

犹 猶 yóu	狭 狹 xiá	狡 jiǎo	猿 yuán
still, yet	narrow	crafty, sly	ape
69;94 7 (3)	- 69;94 9 (4)	- 69;94 9 (3)	- 69;94 13 (3)

狄 dí	狱 獄 yù	猴 hóu	狮 獅 shī
(surname)	prison, jail; lawsuit	monkey	lion
- 69;94 7 (-)	69;94 9 (3)	- 69;94 12 (2)	- 69;94 9 (2)

猜 cāi	猪 豬 zhū	猎 獵 liè	猫 貓 māo máo	猛 měng
guess, suspect	pig, swine	hunt	cat	fierce, violent; brave; abrupt
69;94 11 (2)	69;152 11 (1)	- 69;94 11 (3)	- 69;153 11 (2)	69;94 11 (3)

狸 lí	猩 xīng	猖 chāng	猾 huá
raccoon, wild cat	orangutan, chimpanzee	[wild, savage, rampant]	sly, cunning
69;94 10 (4)	69;94 12 (-)	69;94 11 (4)	69;94 12 (3)

狗 gǒu	狈 狽 bèi	狐 hú
dog	[legendary wolf; dire straits]	fox
- 69;94 8 (2)	69;94 7 (4)	- 69;94 8 (4)

豸

豹 bào	貌 mào
leopard, panther	view; face, appearance
198;153 10 (-)	198;153 14 (2)

■ □ 子 弓 巾 山

1	41
2	42
3	43
4	44
5	45
6	46
7	47
8	48
9	49
10	50
11	51
12	52
13	53
14	54
15	55
16	56
17	57
18	58
19	59
20	60
21	61
22	62
23	63
24	64
25	65
26	66
27	67
28	68
29	69
30	70
31	71
32	72
33	73
34	74
35	75
36	76
37	77
38	78
39	79
40	80

孔 kǒng
hole, aperture
74;39 4 (2)

孙 孫 sūn
grandchild -
74;39 6 (3)

孩 hái
child -
74;39 9 (1)

孤 gū
orphan; alone; lonely
74;39 8 (3)

引 yǐn
to guide, lead; lure; cite; &
71;57 4 (2)

弘 hóng
great, grand; enlarge
71;57 5 (-)

弥 彌 瀰 mí
full; more; redeem
71;57 8 (4)

张 張 zhāng
open; expand; display; look
71;57 7 (1)

强 *強 彊 qiáng qiǎng jiàng
strong; better; force; stubborn
71;57 12 (2)

弦 xián
string (of bow, musical inst.)
71;57 8 (4)

弹 彈 tán dàn
shoot; flick; pluck; rebound; bullet
71;57 11 (2)

粥 zhōu
gruel, porridge
71;119 12 (3)

弱 ruò
weak; inferior; a bit less
71;57 10 (2)

疆 jiāng
boundary, frontier
71;102 19 (3)

帐 帳 賬 zhàng
canopy, curtain; accounts
57;50 7 (3)

帕 pà
handkerchief; turban
57;50 8 (-)

帖 tiē tiě tiè
docile; fitting; note, card
57;50 8 (4)

帆 fān
a sail; canvas
57;50 6 (4)

帜 幟 zhì
flag, banner (literary)
57;50 8 (3)

帽 mào
hat, cap
57;50 12 (1)

幅 fú
size, width (e.g. of cloth)
57;50 12 (2)

幢 chuáng zhuàng
stone pillar; pennant
57;50 15 (3)

屿 嶼 yǔ
small island
60;46 6 (3)

峡 峽 xiá
gorge, ravine
60;46 9 (3)

崎 qí
[rugged, uneven]
60;46 11 (-)

岭 嶺 lǐng
mountain peak, ridge, range
60;46 8 (4)

峻 jùn
high; steep; stern, severe
60;46 10 (4)

峰 fēng
peak, summit; hump
60;46 10 (3)

纠 纠 jiū
entangle; rectify
77;120 5 (2)

纪 纪 jì
discipline; age, era; chronicle
77;120 6 (1)

红 红 hóng gōng
red; bonus
77;120 6 (1)

纯 純 chún
pure, simple; skilful
77;120 7 (3)

纤 纖 縴 xiān qiàn
tiny, slender; tow-rope
77;120 6 (2)

练 練 liàn
silk; practice; experienced
77;120 8 (1)

纬 緯 wěi
latitude, weft
77;120 7 (-)

线 綫 線 xiàn
thread; route, line; brink; clue
77;120 8 (2)

纸 紙 zhǐ
paper
-
77;120 7 (1)

级 級 jí
rank, grade; step
77;120 6 (1)

纳 納 nà
receive; accep
pay; enjoy; se
77;120 7 (4)

细 細 xì
tiny, slender; delicate; careful
77;120 8 (1)

组 組 zǔ
organize; group
77;120 8 (1)

纽 紐 niǔ
handle, button, knob; fasten
77;120 7 (4)

绅 紳 shēn
gentry
-
77;120 8 (4)

维 維 wéi
hold together; maintain; &
77;120 11 (2)

纵 縱 zòng
leap; vertical; indulge; release
77;120 7 (3)

绑 綁 bǎng
bind, tie
77;120 9 (3)

缴 繳 jiǎo
pay, hand over; capture
77;120 16 (4)

缎 緞 duàn
satin
-
77;120 12 (4)

绷 繃 bēng bèng běng
stretch taut; rebound; crack
77;120 11 (4)

缠 纏 chán
entwine, tangle; pester
77;120 13 (4)

编 編 biān
weave; arrange; compile, edit
77;120 12 (2)

绒 絨 róng
soft cloth, velvet, flannel
77;120 9 (4)

约 約 yuē yāo
make appointment; agreement; restrict; approx; brief; frugal; &
77;120 6 (2)

继 繼 jì
follow on; afterwards
77;120 10 (1)

缝 縫 féng fèng
sew, stitch; seam, fissure
77;120 13 (3)

绸 綢 chóu
silk
-
77;120 11 (4)

纲 綱 gāng
nub; precis; category
77;120 7 (3)

纳 納 nà
receive; accept; pay; enjoy; sew
77;120 7 (4)

◧ 纟

纹 紋 wén wrinkles; grain (of wood) 77;120 7 (3)	绞 絞 jiǎo twist; wring; hang (by neck) 77;120 9 (4)

纹 紋 wén
wrinkles;
grain (of wood)
77;120 7 (3)

绞 絞 jiǎo
twist; wring;
hang (by neck)
77;120 9 (4)

纺 紡 fǎng
spin (cotton);
reel
77;120 7 (2)

统 統 tǒng
unify; all;
system
77;120 9 (2)

缔 締 dì
bind, join;
contract
77;120 12 (4)

综 綜 zōng zèng
sum up;
put together
77;120 11 (2)

缩 縮 suō
withdraw;
shrink
77;120 14 (2)

绪 緒 xù
thread; task;
emotion
77;120 11 (2)

结 結 jié jiē
tie; knot; settle
up; congeal; &
77;120 9 (1)

续 續 xù
continue;
add more
77;120 11 (1)

绩 績 jī
meritorious
achievement
77;120 11 (1)

绵 綿 mián
silk floss; soft;
continuous
77;120 11 (4)

缚 縛 fù
tie up
-
77;120 13 (3)

线 綫 線 xiàn
thread; route,
line; brink; clue
77;120 8 (2)

绕 繞 rào rǎo
go round; coil,
wind; confuse
77;120 9 (2)

纱 紗 shā
yarn,
gauze
77;120 7 (3)

缕 縷 lǚ
thread; wisp;
detailed
77;120 12 (-)

缘 緣 yuán
reason, cause;
edge; along
77;120 12 (3)

绿 綠 lǜ lù
green
-
77;120 11 (1)

绍 紹 shào
continue
-
77;120 8 (1)

经 經 jīng jìng
go through; manage; constant;
scriptures; longitude; &
77;120 8 (1)

织 織 zhī
weave,
knit
77;120 8 (1)

绢 絹 juàn
silk
-
77;120 10 (2)

缉 緝 jī qī
seize, arrest;
stitch
77;120 12 (-)

绳 繩 shéng
rope, string;
restrain
77;120 11 (2)

缅 緬 miǎn
remote;
far back
77;120 12 (-)

缓 緩 huǎn
slow, relaxed;
delay; revive
77;120 12 (3)

绣 繡 繡 xiù
embroider
-
77;120 10 (3)

终 終 zhōng
end, finish;
death; entire
77;120 8 (2)

络 絡 luò
to coil up;
keep in a net
77;120 9 (3)

绝 絕 jué
absolutely; sever;
use up; hopeless; &
77;120 9 (2)

纷 紛 fēn
in profusion;
confused
77;120 7 (2)

绘 繪 huì
draw,
paint
77;120 9 (4)

给 給 gěi jǐ
give; for (someone);
allow; supply; ample
77;120 9 (1)

缀 綴 zhuì
sew, stitch; put
together; adorn
77;120 11 (4)

幻 huàn
unreal;
changeable
76;52 4 (3)

幼 yòu
young;
child
76;52 5 (3)

丝 絲 sī
silk; thread;
tiny amount
2;120 5 (2)

1	41
2	42
3	43
4	44
5	45
6	46
7	47
8	48
9	49
10	50
11	51
12	52
13	53
14	54
15	55
16	56
17	57
18	58
19	59
20	60
21	61
22	62
23	63
24	64
25	65
26	66
27	67
28	68
29	69
30	70
31	71
32	72
33	73
34	74
35	75
36	76
37	77
38	78
39	79
40	80

■ 柏 ： 柏 柏 柏 榃 柑

柏
柏
柏

榃
柑

柱	柏	棉	槐	栈
zhù	bǎi bò bó	mián	huái	棧 zhàn
pillar, column	cypress, cedar	cotton	acacia, locust tree	storehouse; stable; inn
94;75 9 (3)	94;75 9 (3)	94;75 12 (2)	94;75 13 (4)	94;75 9 (-)

杭	校	梳	核	榜
háng	xiào jiào	shū	hé hú	bǎng
Hangzhou	school; check, collate; &	comb	nucleus, kernel; examine	announcement; list of names
94;75 8 (-)	94;75 10 (1)	94;75 11 (3)	94;75 10 (3)	94;75 14 (2)

柠	榨	棕	棺	榷
檸 níng	zhà	zōng	guān	què
[lemon]	squeeze, wring	palm (tree)	coffin	discuss
94;75 9 (4)	94;75 14 (4)	94;75 12 (4)	94;75 12 (4)	94;75 14 (4)

枯	枝	桂
kū	zhī	guì
withered, dried up; boring	branch, twig	laurel, cassia, cinnamon tree
94;75 9 (3)	94;75 8 (3)	94;75 10 (4)

桔	柿	棱	植
*橘 jú jié	shì	*稜楞 léng	zhí
tangerine	persimmon	edge; ridge	to plant, grow, set up
94;75 10 (1)	94;75 9 (2)	94;75 12 (4)	94;75 12 (2)

棒	椅
bàng	yǐ
stick, cudgel; good, capable	chair
94;75 12 (3)	94;75 12 (1)

栏	样	梯	档	梢	楼
欄 lán	樣 yàng	tī	檔 dàng	shāo	樓 lóu
railing; column (in newspaper)	sample; shape; appearance; &	ladder, stairs; terracing	files; shelves; grade	tip (of twig, branch)	floor, story; tower
94;75 9 (4)	94;75 10 (1)	94;75 11 (2)	94;75 10 (3)	94;75 11 (4)	94;75 13 (1)

棋	横	模	槽	檬
qí	橫 héng hèng	mó mú	cáo	méng
chess, board game	horizontal; harsh; &	pattern, mold, template	trough; groove, slot	[lemon]
94;75 12 (3)	94;75 15 (3)	94;75 14 (2)	94;75 15 (4)	94;75 17 (4)

标	梧	棍	棵	桶	橘
標 biāo	wú	gùn	kē	tǒng	jú
label, sign, symptom; prize	[phoenix tree, parasol tree]	cudgel; rascal	(measure word) -	bucket, barrel	tangerine -
94;75 9 (2)	94;75 11 (4)	94;75 12 (3)	94;75 12 (1)	94;75 11 (2)	94;75 16 (1)

桥	杉
橋 qiáo	shān shā
bridge -	China fir tree
94;75 10 (1)	94;75 7 (-)

梅	格	桅	橡
méi	gé	wéi	xiàng
plum -	grid; standard; subdivision	mast -	oak; rubber tree
94;75 11 (3)	94;75 10 (2)	94;75 10 (4)	94;75 15 (4)

枪	检	榆	松
槍 qiāng	檢 jiǎn	yú	*鬆 sōng
gun; spear, lance	check, inspect; act correctly	[elm] -	pine tree; loose; relaxed; &
94;75 8 (2)	94;75 11 (1)	94;75 13 (4)	94;75 8 (2)

榴	樱
liú	櫻 yīng
pomegranate -	cherry -
94;75 14 (4)	94;75 15 (4)

1	41
2	42
3	43
4	44
5	45
6	46
7	47
8	48
9	49
10	50
11	51
12	52
13	53
14	54
15	55
16	56
17	57
18	58
19	59
20	60
21	61
22	62
23	63
24	64
25	65
26	66
27	67
28	68
29	69
30	70
31	71
32	72
33	73
34	74
35	75
36	76
37	77
38	78
39	79
40	80

木

杜	材	林	株	朴
dù	cái	lín	zhū	*樸 pǔ pō pò piáo
prevent, shut out	materials; timber; ability	forest, grove; group	tree trunk; a plant	plain, simple
94;75 7 (4)	94;75 7 (2)	94;75 8 (2)	94;75 10 (2)	94;75 6 (2)

枚	杖	枕	栈	栋
méi	zhàng	zhěn	棧 zhàn	棟 dòng
(measure word)	cane, crutch, walking stick	pillow; block	storehouse; stable; inn	supporting beam, ridgepole
-				
94;75 8 (4)	94;75 7 (-)	94;75 8 (3)	94;75 9 (-)	94;75 9 (4)

权	机	杨	极
權 quán	機 jī	楊 yáng	極 jí
rights; power, authority; &	machine; opportunity; &	poplar	extreme, pole, polar
		-	
94;75 6 (3)	94;75 6 (1)	94;75 7 (4)	94;75 7 (1)

杠	朽	杯	杆	枉
gàng	xiǔ	*盃 bēi	桿 gān gǎn	wǎng
bar, pole; delete	decayed, rotten; senile	cup	pole, shaft	crooked; to wrong; in vain
		-		
94;75 7 (4)	94;75 6 (3)	94;75 8 (1)	94;75 7 (2)	94;75 8 (3)

柄	栖	梗	棵
bǐng	棲 qī	gěng	kē
stem, handle	stay; perch (birds)	stalk, stem; obstruct; &	(measure word)
			-
94;75 9 (3)	94;75 10 (-)	94;75 11 (4)	94;75 12 (1)

柜	相	根	栅
*櫃 guì jǔ	xiāng xiàng	gēn	柵 zhà shān
cupboard; (shop) counter	mutual; looks; photo; &	root; basis; thoroughly	railings, fence
94;75 8 (3)	94;109 9 (1)	94;75 10 (1)	94;75 9 (-)

桃	柳	树	彬	
táo	liǔ	樹 shù	bīn	
peach	willow	tree; to plant,	[urbane,	
-	-	set up; uphold	refined]	
94;75 10 (3)	94;75 9 (3)	94;75 9 (1)	94;59 11 (-)	

椒	棚	椰	概	椭
jiāo	péng	yē	gài	橢 tuǒ
spice plant,	shed, shack;	coconut	general,	[oval,
pepper, chili	awning	-	in summary; &	ellipse]
94;75 12 (3)	94;75 12 (3)	94;75 12 (-)	94;75 13 (1)	94;75 12 (4)

桩	板	析	橱	
樁 zhuāng	* 闆 bǎn	xī	櫥 chú	
stake	board, plank;	divide, dissect,	wardrobe,	
(in the ground)	hard, stiff	discriminate	cabinet, closet	
94;75 10 (3)	94;75 8 (1)	94;75 8 (2)	94;75 16 (-)	

村	柯	构	械	
cūn	kē	構 gòu	xiè	
village	stalk; handle	construct,	tool, weapon,	
-	(literary)	compose	instrument	
94;75 7 (1)	94;75 9 (-)	94;75 8 (2)	94;75 11 (2)	

枢	柜	框	
樞 shū	* 櫃 guì jū	kuāng kuàng	
axis, pivot,	cupboard;	frame,	
hub	(shop) counter	rim	
94;75 8 (-)	94;75 8 (3)	94;75 10 (4)	

枫	桐	
楓 fēng	tóng	
maple	tung tree,	
-	paulowina tree	
94;75 8 (-)	94;75 10 (4)	

1	41
2	42
3	43
4	44
5	45
6	46
7	47
8	48
9	49
10	50
11	51
12	52
13	53
14	54
15	55
16	56
17	57
18	58
19	59
20	60
21	61
22	62
23	63
24	64
25	65
26	66
27	67
28	68
29	69
30	70
31	71
32	72
33	73
34	74
35	75
36	76
37	77
38	78
39	79
40	80

私	秆 秆gǎn	秤	科	称 稱chēng chèn
sī	gǎn	chèng	kē	chēng chèn
private; selfish; secret, illicit	stalk, stem	steelyard, weighing scales	area of study; section; branch	call, name; weigh; suitable
149;115 7 (2)	149;115 8 (4)	149;115 10 (4)	149;115 9 (1)	149;115 10 (2)

秩	租	和	秧	种 種zhǒng zhòng
zhì	zū	hé hè huó huò	yāng	zhǒng zhòng
decade; in good order (literary)	rent, hire, lease	harmony; mild; with; sum; mix	seedling; small fry; vine	seed; species, type; cultivate
149;115 10 (2)	149;115 10 (1)	149;30 8 (1)	149;115 10 (3)	149;115 9 (1)

利	秋	秘 *祕mì bì	稚
lì	qiū	mì bì	zhì
profit, benefit; sharp	fall, autumn; period, year	secret -	young, infantile
149;18 7 (1)	149;115 9 (1)	149;115 10 (2)	149;115 13 (3)

秒	秘 *祕mì bì	秽 穢huì	穆	税	稍
miǎo	mì bì	huì	mù	shuì	shāo
second (of time, arc)	secret -	dirty; ugly; weeds	solemn -	tax -	slightly -
149;115 9 (2)	149;115 10 (2)	149;115 11 (4)	149;115 16 (4)	149;115 12 (3)	149;115 12 (

稼	稿	穗
jià	gǎo	suì
sow (grain); crops	manuscript, draft; straw	ear (of grain); tassel; Guangzhou
149;115 15 (2)	149;115 15 (3)	149;115 17 (4)

积 積jī	程
jī	chéng
amass, store; long-standing	regulation; journey; &
149;115 10 (2)	149;115 12 (2)

稻	移	稳 穩wěn	稀
dào	yí	wěn	xī
rice; paddy field	move, change	steady, certain, reliable	sparse, scarce, dilute
149;115 15 (2)	149;115 11 (2)	149;115 14 (2)	149;115 12 (3)

科	稠
kē	chóu
area of study; section; branch	dense, thick, crowded
149;115 9 (1)	149;115 13 (4)

释	彩
釋 shì	cǎi
explain; resolve; release	color; variety; acclaim; prize
197;165 12 (2)	63;59 11 (1)

籽	料	粗	粒	粹	粮
zǐ	liào	cū	lì	cuì	糧 liáng
seed	raw materials; grain; expect	thick, coarse, rough; careless	grain, granule	pure; essence	grain, provisions
-					
159;119 9 (4)	159;68 10 (2)	159;119 11 (2)	159;119 11 (2)	159;119 14 (4)	159;119 13 (2)

粉	粘	精	糟	糕
fěn	*黏 zhān nián	jīng	zāo	gāo
dust, powder; white; pink	glue; sticky; paste up	splendid; spirit; fine; clever; &	rotten; a mess; grain; dregs	cake
				-
159;119 10 (2)	159;119 11 (2)	159;119 14 (1)	159;119 17 (2)	159;119 16 (2)

糊	糖	糠
hú hū hù	táng	kāng
paste, gum; plaster	sugar; candy	husk, chaff
159;119 15 (2)	159;119 16 (1)	159;119 17 (4)

辉	耀
輝 huī	yào
radiance; shine	dazzle; honor; boast
172;159 12 (2)	172;124 20 (3)

耗	耕
hào	*畊 gēng
use up; dawdle; bad news	plow -
176;127 10 (3)	176;127 10 (3)

1	41
2	42
3	43
4	44
5	45
6	46
7	47
8	48
9	49
10	50
11	51
12	52
13	53
14	54
15	55
16	56
17	57
18	58
19	59
20	60
21	61
22	62
23	63
24	64
25	65
26	66
27	67
28	68
29	69
30	70
31	71
32	72
33	73
34	74
35	75
36	76
37	77
38	78
39	79
40	80

■□　牛　车　片

牛

牡	牲	牧	物	特	牺
mǔ	shēng	mù	wù	tè	犧 xī
male (animal)	livestock; animal sacrifice	to herd, tend (animals)	thing; content, substance	special; particular; spy	animal sacrifice (literary)
110;93 7 (-)	110;93 9 (2)	110;93 8 (3)	110;93 8 (1)	110;93 10 (1)	110;93 10 (2

车

轧	轨	轩	软	斩
軋 yà zhá gá	軌 guǐ	軒 xuān	軟 ruǎn	斬 zhǎn
grind, crush; squeeze out	rail, track; path, orbit	balcony; ancient carriage	soft, pliable; inferior; weak	chop, cut; behead
100;159 5 (4)	100;159 6 (3)	100;159 7 (-)	100;159 8 (2)	100;69 8 (4)

轴	辅	辆	转
軸 zhóu	輔 fǔ	輛 liàng	轉 zhuǎn zhuàn
axis, axle; spool, reel	assist -	(measure word) -	revolve; change; to forward; stroll
100;159 9 (-)	100;159 11 (1)	100;159 11 (1)	100;159 8 (2)

较	辖	轮	输
較 jiào	轄 xiá	輪 lún	輸 shū
compare; evident; dispute	linchpin; govern	wheel; take turns	to transport; be defeated
100;159 10 (1)	100;159 14 (4)	100;159 8 (2)	100;159 13 (1)

辐	轿	轻	辑	辙
輻 fú	轎 jiào	輕 qīng	輯 jí	轍 zhé
spoke (of wheel)	sedan chair	light, slight, minor; gently	collect, edit, precis	(wheel) track, rut; rhyme
100;159 13 (4)	100;159 10 (4)	100;159 9 (1)	100;159 13 (3)	100;159 16 (4)

片

版	牌	鼎
bǎn	pái	dǐng
printing; edition, page	card, tablet; brand (goods)	cauldron; tripod, tripartite
114;91 8 (2)	114;91 12 (2)	141;206 12 (-)

1	41
2	42
3	43
4	44
5	45
6	46
7	47
8	48
9	49
10	50
11	51
12	52
13	53
14	54
15	55
16	56
17	57
18	58
19	59
20	60
21	61
22	62
23	63
24	64
25	65
26	66
27	67
28	68
29	69
30	70
31	71
32	72
33	73
34	74
35	75
36	76
37	77
38	78
39	79
40	80

顶　竹

顶 頂 dǐng
stand up to; top; utmost; &
170;181 8 (2)

竹 zhú
bamboo
-
178;118 6 (2)

巧　功　攻　巩　项　式

巧 qiǎo
skilful; cunning; happily, luckily
48;48 5 (2)

功 gōng
merit; achieve; effect; skill
48;19 5 (2)

攻 gōng
attack; accuse; study
48;66 7 (2)

巩 鞏 gǒng
consolidate; stable, strong
48;177 6 (2)

项 項 xiàng
item; nape of neck
48;181 9 (2)

式 shì
formula; format, style; ceremony
56;56 6 (2)

珠　球　珑　环　琢　玻

珠 zhū
pearl, bead, (water) drop
88;96 10 (2)

球 qiú
ball, sphere, globe
88;96 11 (1)

珑 瓏 lóng
[exquisite, deft]
-
88;96 9 (4)

环 環 huán
ring, hoop; surround
88;96 8 (4)

琢 zhuó zuó
chisel, carve
88;96 12 (4)

玻 bō
[glass]
-
88;96 9 (2)

玖　玫　玛　现　珊

玖 jiǔ
nine
-
88;96 7 (4)

玫 méi
[rose]
-
88;96 8 (4)

玛 瑪 mǎ
[agate]
-
88;96 7 (-)

现 現 xiàn
present, now, modern; appear
88;96 8 (1)

珊 珊 shān
[coral]
88;96 9 (4)

琼　琦　璃　瑰　理

琼 瓊 qióng
jade; palace (literary)
88;96 12 (-)

琦 qí
jade; admirable (literary)
88;96 12 (-)

璃 lí
[glass, glaze]
88;96 14 (2)

瑰 guī
marvelous (literary)
88;96 13 (4)

理 lǐ
reason, logic; science; texture; manage; pay heed to; tidy up
88;96 11 (1)

玩　瑞　瑾　珍　玲　瑜

玩 wán
play; trifle with; enjoy; resort to
88;96 8 (1)

瑞 ruì
auspicious, lucky
88;96 13 (4)

瑾 jǐn
fine jade; lustrous
88;96 15 (-)

珍 zhēn
treasure; precious
88;96 9 (3)

玲 líng
[tinkling of jade; exquisite, deft]
88;96 9 (4)

瑜 yú
fine jade; luster; virtues
88;96 13 (-)

班　斑　瑚　琳

班 bān
team; duty; scheduled
88;96 10 (1)

斑 bān
spots; stripes; speckled
88;67 12 (4)

瑚 hú
[coral]
-
88;96 13 (4)

琳 lín
jade; valuables (literary)
88;96 12 (-)

刑　形

刑 xíng
punishment; torture
17;18 6 (4)

形 xíng
appearance, shape, form; &
63;59 7 (2)

飠 矢 缶 立

飠

饥 饑 jī
hunger, famine
68;184 5 (3)

饮 飲 yǐn yìn
drink
-
68;184 7 (3)

饪 飪 rèn
[cooking]
-
68;184 7 (4)

蚀 蝕 shí
lose; erode; eclipse
68;142 9 (3)

饿 餓 è
hunger, starve
68;184 10 (1)

饭 飯 fàn
food, meal, cooked rice
68;184 7 (1)

饲 飼 sì
fodder; to rear (animals)
68;184 8 (3)

饱 飽 bǎo
full, satisfied, eat one's fill
68;184 8 (1)

饺 餃 jiǎo
dumpling
-
68;184 9 (1)

馆 館 guǎn
hall, inn, shop, public building
68;184 11 (1)

饶 饒 ráo
plentiful; forgive; &
68;184 9 (3)

馈 饋 kuì
to present (a gift)
68;184 12 (4)

饼 餅 bǐng
cake
-
68;184 9 (2)

饰 飾 shì
adorn; cover u
play (role)
68;184 8 (3)

馒 饅 mán
steamed bread
68;184 14 (2)

馀 餘 yú
surplus; after (see Table 1)
68;184 10 (-)

馅 餡 xiàn
filling, stuffing (of food)
68;184 11 (4)

馋 饞 chán
greedy
68;184 12 (4)

矢

知 zhī
know; inform; administer
148;111 8 (1)

矩 jǔ
rules; square, rectangle
148;111 9 (3)

短 duǎn
brief; lacking; weak point
148;111 12 (1)

矫 矯 jiǎo jiáo
rectify; pretend; strong, brave
148;111 11 (-)

矮 ǎi
short; low rank
148;111 13 (1)

缶

缸 gāng
jar
-
175;121 9 (3)

缺 quē
to lack; absent; defect; vacancy
175;121 10 (2)

罐 guàn
tin, jar, pot
175;121 23 (2)

立

站 zhàn
station; (bus) stop; to stand
126;117 10 (1)

端 duān
tip, end; cause; carry; proper
126;117 14 (2)

靖 jìng
tranquillity; pacify
126;174 13 (-)

竭 jié
exhaust, use up
126;117 14 (3)

放	旅	族	施	旋
fàng	lǚ	zú	shī	xuán xuàn
set free; expel; put; adjust; &	travel; brigade	clan, race; group, family	carry out; use; bestow; impose	revolve; return; whorl; lathe
85;66 8 (1)	85;70 10 (1)	85;70 11 (1)	85;70 9 (2)	85;70 11 (3)

旗	於
qí	yú
flag, banner	in, to, at, of (see Table 1)
85;70 14 (2)	85;70 8 (-)

礼	社	祈	祷
禮 lǐ	shè	qí	禱 dǎo
ceremony; etiquette; gift	society; agency; &	worship, pray, beg	pray -
87;113 5 (1)	87;113 7 (1)	87;113 8 (-)	87;113 11 (-)

祖	神	祥	禅
zǔ	shén	xiáng	禪 chán shàn
ancestor; grandparent	gods; magical; spirit; &	good luck, auspicious	meditation; Buddhist
87;113 9 (1)	87;113 9 (1)	87;113 10 (4)	87;113 12 (-)

祝	视	祸	福	禧
zhù	視 shì	禍 huò	fú	xǐ
best wishes -	look at, regard, inspect	disaster; bring misfortune	good fortune, blessing	blessings; happy occasion
87;113 9 (1)	87;147 8 (1)	87;113 11 (4)	87;113 13 (1)	87;113 16 (-)

补	初	袄	袜	衬	衫
補 bǔ	chū	襖 ǎo	襪 wà	襯 chèn	shān
mend; use; fill; replace; nourish	beginning; first, original	coat, jacket	socks, stockings	lining; serve as contrast	shirt, vest
129;145 7 (2)	129;18 7 (1)	129;145 9 (4)	129;145 10 (1)	129;145 8 (2)	129;145 8 (2)

袖	被	裤	袱	裙	袍
xiù	bèi	褲 kù	fú	qún	páo
sleeve -	quilt; (particle; passive verbs)	pants, trousers	[bundle of cloth]	a skirt -	robe, gown
129;145 10 (2)	129;145 10 (1)	129;145 12 (2)	129;145 11 (3)	129;145 12 (2)	129;145 10 (3)

裕	裸	襟
yù	luǒ	jīn
plentiful; affluent	naked, exposed	brother in law; front of garment
129;145 12 (3)	129;145 13 (-)	129;145 18 (-)

1	41
2	42
3	43
4	44
5	45
6	46
7	47
8	48
9	49
10	50
11	51
12	52
13	53
14	54
15	55
16	56
17	57
18	58
19	59
20	60
21	61
22	62
23	63
24	64
25	65
26	66
27	67
28	68
29	69
30	70
31	71
32	72
33	73
34	74
35	75
36	76
37	77
38	78
39	79
40	80

钅◻

针	钉	钝	钦	铁	钱
針 zhēn	釘 dīng dìng	鈍 dùn	欽 qīn	鐵 tiě	錢 qián
needle; stitch	nail; sew on; press, urge	blunt; dull, stupid	respect; imperial	iron; weapons	money, cash, coin
147;167 7 (2)	147;167 7 (3)	147;167 9 (-)	147;76 9 (4)	147;167 10 (2)	147;167 10 (

钟	钥	钮	钳	钙
鐘 鍾 zhōng	鑰 yuè yào	鈕 niǔ	鉗 拑 qián	鈣 gài
bell, clock, o'clock; &	key -	knob, button; to tie, fasten	pincers, pliers; clamp; restrain	calcium -
147;167 9 (1)	147;167 9 (3)	147;167 9 (4)	147;167 10 (4)	147;167 9 (4)

铀	银	锤	铺
鈾 yóu	銀 yín	錘 chuí	鋪 pū pù
uranium -	silver -	hammer; a weight	spread; pave; store, shop
147;167 10 (4)	147;167 11 (1)	147;167 13 (4)	147;167 12 (2)

钅◻

锹	锄	锻
鍬 qiāo	鋤 chú	鍛 duàn
spade, shovel	hoe; uproot	forge, temper (metals)
147;167 14 (4)	147;167 12 (4)	147;167 14 (1)

钅◻

锯	铸	镀	镰
鋸 jù	鑄 zhù	鍍 dù	鐮 lián
saw -	cast (metal) -	gilding, (gold) plating	sickle, scythe
147;167 13 (4)	147;167 12 (3)	147;167 14 (4)	147;167 18 (4)

钅◻

钓	钩
釣 diào	鉤 gōu
to fish; bait	hook -
147;167 8 (2)	147;167 9 (3)

钅◻

链	键
鏈 鍊 liàn	鍵 jiàn
chain -	key (on keyboard)
147;167 12 (4)	147;167 13 (2)

钅◻

钢	铜
鋼 gāng gàng	銅 tóng
steel; sharpen	copper, brass, bronze
147;167 9 (1)	147;167 11 (2)

■◻ 钅◻

钞
钞 chāo
banknote,
paper money
147;167 9 (3)

锦
锦 jǐn
brocade;
splendid
147;167 13 (4)

铺
铺 pū pù
spread; pave;
store, shop
147;167 12 (2)

镇
镇 zhèn
calm, quell;
iced; town; &
147;167 15 (3)

钻
鑽 zuān zuàn
penetrate, bore,
drill; diamond
147;167 10 (2)

钱
錢 qián
money,
cash, coin
147;167 10 (1)

铲
鏟 chǎn
shovel,
spade
147;167 11 (3)

锌
鋅 xīn
zinc
-
147;167 12 (4)

镜
鏡 jìng
mirror;
lens
147;167 16 (2)

镑
鎊 bàng
pound sterling
(UK money)
147;167 15 (-)

镶
鑲 xiāng
inlay;
edge
147;167 22 (4)

锐
鋭 ruì
sharp;
vigor
147;167 12 (2)

销
銷 xiāo
to fuse; sell;
cancel; spend
147;167 12 (4)

锁
鎖 suǒ
lock,
padlock
147;167 12 (3)

镁
鎂 měi
magnesium
-
147;167 14 (4)

错
錯 cuò
mistake; fault;
alternating; &
147;167 13 (1)

铅
鉛 qiān
lead
(the metal)
147;167 10 (1)

铝
鋁 lǚ
aluminum
-
147;167 11 (3)

锅
鍋 guō
pot, pan,
cauldron
147;167 12 (2)

锡
錫 xī
tin
(the metal)
147;167 13 (3)

锣
鑼 luó
gong
-
147;167 13 (3)

镖
鏢 biāo
an old dart-like
weapon
147;167 16 (-)

锤
錘 chuí
hammer;
a weight
147;167 13 (4)

锈
銹 鏽 xiù
rust
-
147;167 12 (3)

铃
鈴 líng
bell
-
147;167 10 (2)

铭
銘 míng
inscription;
engrave
147;167 11 (4)

锋
鋒 fēng
point, edge
(of blade)
147;167 12 (4)

1	41
2	42
3	43
4	44
5	45
6	46
7	47
8	48
9	49
10	50
11	51
12	52
13	53
14	54
15	55
16	56
17	57
18	58
19	59
20	60
21	61
22	62
23	63
24	64
25	65
26	66
27	67
28	68
29	69
30	70
31	71
32	72
33	73
34	74
35	75
36	76
37	77
38	78
39	79
40	80

奸	奴	妹	姓	好
*姦 jiān	nú	mèi	xìng	hǎo hào
evil; traitor; crafty; illicit	slave	younger sister	surname, family name	good; be well; easy; so that; very; to like, love; be prone to
73;38 6 (4)	73;38 5 (3)	73;38 8 (1)	73;38 8 (1)	73;38 6 (1)

妇	妖	妊	她	姊	姨
婦 fù	yāo	*姙 rèn	tā	zǐ	yí
woman; wife	monster, devil; charming	conceive, be pregnant	she, her	elder sister	aunt; sister in law
73;38 6 (2)	73;38 7 (4)	73;38 7 (-)	73;38 6 (1)	73;38 7 (-)	73;38 9 (2)

如	妞	姐	奶	妈	姆
rú	niū	jiě	*妳 嬭 nǎi	媽 mā	mǔ
such as; as if, if; as...as...; &	girl (colloq)	elder sister	breast; milk; suckle	mother, mum; aunt (colloq)	[nanny; housekeeper]
73;38 6 (1)	73;38 7 (-)	73;38 8 (1)	73;38 5 (1)	73;38 6 (1)	73;38 8 (4)

姚	娴	娜	嫩
yáo	嫻 嫺 xián	nuó	nèn
(surname)	refined; adept (literary)	[fascinating; courteous]	tender; rookie; light (color)
73;38 9 (-)	73;38 10 (-)	73;38 9 (-)	73;38 14 (3)

妙	妨	娘	妒	姑	妓
miào	fáng fāng	孃 niáng	dù	gū	jì
wonderful; subtle	hinder, impede; harm	mother; aunt; young lady	jealous	aunt; nun; sister in law	prostitute
73;38 7 (2)	73;38 7 (3)	73;38 10 (1)	73;38 7 (4)	73;38 8 (1)	73;38 7 (-)

媳	嫁	婶	婉	娃	嫂
xí	jià	嬸 shěn	wǎn	wá	sǎo
daughter in law	marry (a man); transfer	aunt	graceful; gracious	baby	sister in law
73;38 13 (3)	73;38 13 (3)	73;38 11 (3)	73;38 11 (-)	73;38 9 (3)	73;38 12 (2)

始	娱	娇	婚	嫌	媒
shǐ	娛 yú	嬌 jiāo	hūn	xián	méi
beginning	joy; happy; amuse	lovely; delicate; pamper	marriage; to marry	suspicion; grudge; dislike	matchmaker; go-between
73;38 8 (1)	73;38 10 (3)	73;38 9 (4)	73;38 11 (2)	73;38 13 (3)	73;38 12 (4)

姥	嫉	妮	媚	姻
lǎo	jí	nī	mèi	yīn
[grandmother]	jealousy; dislike	[girl]	flatter; charming	marriage; in-laws
73;38 9 (3)	73;38 13 (4)	73;38 8 (-)	73;38 12 (-)	73;38 9 (2)

▌ 阝

队 隊 duì
squad, team
33;170 4 (2)

阵 陣 zhèn
formation, array; period
33;170 6 (2)

陈 陳 chén
exhibit, explain; old, stale
33;170 7 (3)

陕 陝 shǎn
Shaanxi
-
33;170 8 (3)

阳 陽 yáng
yang, positive; sun; overt; &
33;170 6 (1)

阻 zǔ
hinder, block, obstruct
33;170 7 (3)

限 xiàn
limit
-
33;170 8 (2)

阴 陰 陰 yīn
yin, negative; occult; shade; cloudy; moon; &
33;170 6 (1)

防 fáng
dyke; defend; guard against
33;170 6 (2)

陪 péi
accompany
-
33;170 10 (2)

障 zhàng
obstruct, hinder; barrier
33;170 13 (3)

陀 tuó
[(spinning) top]
-
33;170 7 (-)

院 yuàn
institute; courtyard
33;170 9 (1)

陆 陸 liù lù
six; (dry) land
33;170 7 (2)

陡 dǒu
precipitous; abruptly
33;170 9 (3)

陵 líng
hill, mound; tomb
33;170 10 (3)

隙 *郤 隟 xì
crevice, gap, rift; discord
33;170 12 (4)

隘 ài
narrow; mountain pass
33;170 12 (4)

际 際 jì
border; inter-; occasion; &
33;170 7 (2)

陌 mò
path, road
33;170 8 (3)

隔 gé
separate, apart; cut off
33;170 12 (2)

降 jiàng xiáng
fall, drop, lower; give in; subdue
33;170 8 (2)

隆 lóng lōng
grand; thriving; intense; bulge
33;170 11 (4)

陷 xiàn
bogged down; pitfall; flaw; &
33;170 10 (3)

隐 隱 yīn
hidden, latent
33;170 11 (3)

阶 階 jiē
steps, stairs; rank
33;170 6 (2)

险 險 xiǎn
danger; risky; sinister; almost
33;170 9 (1)

除 chú
get rid of; divide by; except
33;170 9 (1)

附 fù
append; agree; near to
33;170 7 (1)

阿 ā ē
('a' sound); pander to
33;170 7 (2)

陶 táo
earthenware; nurture; happy
33;170 10 (4)

随 隨 suí
follow; comply; allow; &
33;170 11 (2)

隧 suì
[tunnel]
-
33;170 14 (4)

陋 lòu
vulgar, humble; ugly; shallow
33;170 8 (4)

1	41
2	42
3	43
4	44
5	45
6	46
7	47
8	48
9	49
10	50
11	51
12	52
13	53
14	54
15	55
16	56
17	57
18	58
19	59
20	60
21	61
22	62
23	63
24	64
25	65
26	66
27	67
28	68
29	69
30	70
31	71
32	72
33	73
34	74
35	75
36	76
37	77
38	78
39	79
40	80

▐ 口日 ： 咱 咱 咱 啹 啹

咱					
咱	**嗅**	**噢**	**啤**	**鸣**	**鸣**
zán zan	xiù	噢ō	pí	嗚wū	鳴míng
we	sniff	(exclamation:	[beer]	hoot,	chirp; to voice
(including you)	-	Oh!)	-	toot	make a soun◁
58;30 9 (1)	58;30 13 (4)	58;30 15 (3)	58;30 11 (1)	58;30 7 (4)	58;196 8 (3⨯

响	**咏**	**哦**	**喧**
響xiǎng	詠yǒng	ó ò é	xuān
sound, noise;	chant	(exclamation:	noise,
loud	-	What?, Oh!)	clamor
58;180 9 (1)	58;149 8 (4)	58;30 10 (3)	58;30 12 (4)

吭	咬	咳	哼	啼	嚷
háng kēng	yǎo	hāi ké	hēng hng	tí	rǎng rāng
throat;	bite; snap at;	Doh!;	moan; groan;	weep, wail;	shout,
make a sound	pronounce; &	cough	hum; Humph!	to crow, caw	make an upr◁
58;30 7 (-)	58;30 9 (2)	58;30 9 (1)	58;30 10 (2)	58;30 12 (-)	58;30 20 (2)⨯

咕	哇	嗦	喷	喃	嘻
gū	wā wa	suo	噴pēn pèn	nán	xī
cluck,	cry, wail;	[tremble;	squirt, spray;	[mutter,	laugh,
coo	(particle)	wordy]	in season	chatter]	giggle
58;30 8 (-)	58;30 9 (2)	58;30 13 (3)	58;30 12 (2)	58;30 12 (-)	58;30 15 (-)

吵	啃	喘	嗤	啸
chǎo chāo	kěn	chuǎn	chī	嘯xiào
quarrel, make	nibble,	gasp, pant,	sneer	whistle; roar
noise, disturb	gnaw	breathe hard	-	(of animal)
58;30 7 (2)	58;30 11 (4)	58;30 12 (3)	58;30 13 (-)	58;30 11 (4)

啹		
哨	**咪**	**喽**
shào	mī	嘍lóu lou
sentry, guard;	[mew, miaow;	[underling];
whistle; chirp	smiling]	(particle)
58;30 10 (3)	58;30 9 (-)	58;30 12 (3)

哎	喵	唠	哄
āi	miāo	嘮láo	hōng hŏng hòng
Ah!; Hey!;	miaow	[chatter]	deceive; coax;
Look out!	-	-	hubbub
58;30 8 (2)	58;30 11 (-)	58;30 10 (4)	58;30 9 (4)

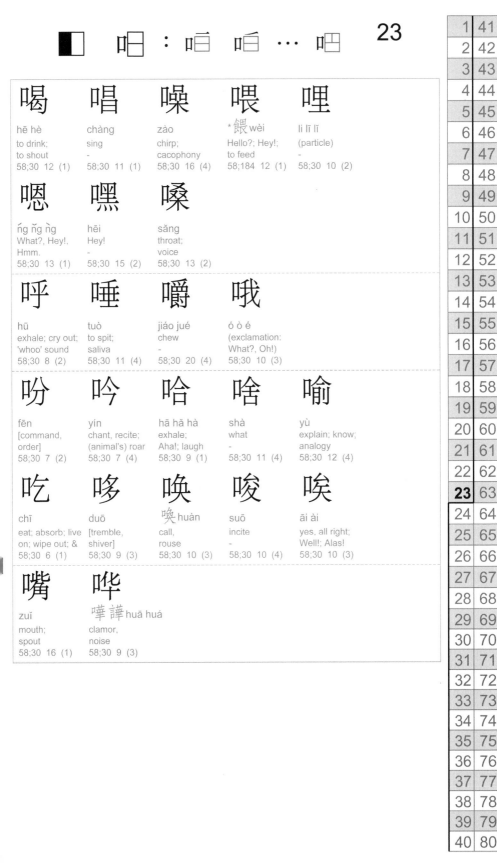

喝　唱　噪　喂　哩

喝	**唱**	**噪**	**喂**	**哩**
hē hè	chàng	zào	*餵 wèi	li lī lǐ
to drink; to shout	sing -	chirp; cacophony	Hello?; Hey!; to feed	(particle) -
58;30 12 (1)	58;30 11 (1)	58;30 16 (4)	58;184 12 (1)	58;30 10 (2)

嗯	**嘿**	**嗓**
ńg ňg ǹg	hēi	sǎng
What?, Hey!, Hmm.	Hey!	throat; voice
58;30 13 (1)	58;30 15 (2)	58;30 13 (2)

呼	**唾**	**嚼**	**哦**
hū	tuò	jiáo jué	ó ò é
exhale; cry out; 'whoo' sound	to spit; saliva	chew -	(exclamation: What?, Oh!)
58;30 8 (2)	58;30 11 (4)	58;30 20 (4)	58;30 10 (3)

吩	**吟**	**哈**	**啥**	**喻**
fēn	yín	hā hǎ hà	shà	yù
[command, order]	chant, recite; (animal's) roar	exhale; Aha!; laugh	what -	explain; know; analogy
58;30 7 (2)	58;30 7 (4)	58;30 9 (1)	58;30 11 (4)	58;30 12 (4)

吃	**哆**	**唤**	**唆**	**唉**
chī	duō	喚 huàn	suō	āi ài
eat; absorb; live on; wipe out; &	[tremble, shiver]	call, rouse	incite -	yes, all right; Well!!; Alas!
58;30 6 (1)	58;30 9 (3)	58;30 10 (3)	58;30 10 (4)	58;30 10 (3)

嘴	**哗**
zuǐ	嘩 譁 huā huá
mouth; spout	clamor, noise
58;30 16 (1)	58;30 9 (3)

1	41
2	42
3	43
4	44
5	45
6	46
7	47
8	48
9	49
10	50
11	51
12	52
13	53
14	54
15	55
16	56
17	57
18	58
19	59
20	60
21	61
22	62
23	63
24	64
25	65
26	66
27	67
28	68
29	69
30	70
31	71
32	72
33	73
34	74
35	75
36	76
37	77
38	78
39	79
40	80

口

叶
*葉 yè
leaf;
period, epoch
58;30 5 (2)

吐
tū tù
spit; vent;
vomit; disgorge
58;30 6 (2)

吨
噸 dūn
ton
-
58;30 7 (2)

味
wèi
taste; smell;
interest
58;30 8 (2)

咪
mī
[mew, miaow;
smiling]
58;30 9 (-)

呐
nà
[shout]
-
58;30 7 (1)

呻
shēn
[groan]
-
58;30 8 (4)

啸
嘯 xiào
whistle; roar
(of animal)
58;30 11 (4)

叫
*呌 jiào
cry, call; tell;
be called
58;30 5 (1)

吹
chuī
blow, puff;
brag; failure
58;30 7 (1)

咋
zǎ zhā zhà
Why?, How?;
[boast]; bite
58;30 8 (4)

吻
wěn
lips; kiss;
animal's mouth
58;30 7 (3)

呼
hū
exhale; cry out;
'whoo' sound
58;30 8 (2)

唾
tuò
to spit;
saliva
58;30 11 (4)

哦
ó ò é
(exclamation:
What?, Oh!)
58;30 10 (3)

叮
dīng
sting;
make sure
58;30 5 (4)

吓
嚇 hè xià
intimidate;
Pah! (annoyed)
58;30 6 (2)

吁
*籲 yù xū
plead;
groan; Oh!
58;30 6 (4)

呀
ya yā
(particle);
Oh!
58;30 7 (1)

啄
zhuó
peck at
-
58;30 11 (4)

吧
ba bā
(particle);
'crack' sound
58;30 7 (1)

叽
嘰 jī
chirp,
twitter
58;30 5 (-)

叨
tāo dāo
obliged;
[chatter]
58;30 5 (4)

叹
嘆 歎 tàn
sigh; admire;
acclaim
58;30 5 (3)

吸
xī
inhale, absorb;
attract
58;30 6 (2)

吗
嗎 ma má mǎ
(question
particle)
58;30 6 (1)

哩
li lǐ lǐ
(particle)
-
58;30 10 (2)

叭
bā
'bang'
sound
58;30 5 (3)

哑
啞 yǎ yā
dumb; hoarse;
Oh!
58;30 9 (4)

啡
fēi
('fi' sound);
[coffee]
58;30 11 (1)

啦
la lā
(particle)
-
58;30 11 (1)

啪
pā
'bang'
sound
58;30 11 (-)

咐
fu
[instruct;
exhort]
58;30 8 (2)

唯
wéi wěi
solely;
[yes-man]
58;30 11 (4)

喉
hóu
throat,
larynx
58;30 12 (3)

咧
liě liē
[grin;
careless]
58;30 9 (-)

喇
lǎ lá lā
trumpet,
horn
58;30 12 (3)

嗽
sòu
cough
-
58;30 14 (1)

吼
hǒu
roar,
bellow
58;30 7 (3)

哟
喲 yo yō
(particle);
Oh!
58;30 9 (3)

咖
kā gā
('ka' sound);
[coffee]
58;30 8 (1)

啊
ā á ǎ à a
(exclamation:
Eh?, Oh!, etc.)
58;30 10 (1)

嘲
cháo
to ridicule,
mock
58;30 15 (4)

哪
na nǎ něi
(particle);
Which?, What?
58;30 9 (1)

嘟
dū
toot, honk;
pout
58;30 13 (-)

咙
嚨 lóng
[throat]
-
58;30 8 (3)

听
聽 tīng
listen; obey;
allow
58;128 7 (1)

呢
ne ní
(particle);
woollen
58;30 8 (1)

喔
wō ō
cock's crow;
Oh!
58;30 12 (-)

嘱
囑 zhǔ
urge,
advise
58;30 15 (3)

嘛
ma
(particle)
-
58;30 14 (1)

叼
diāo
hold (in the
mouth)
58;30 5 (4)

呵
hē
scold;
exhale; Oh!
58;30 8 (3)

吗
嗎 ma má mǎ
(question
particle)
58;30 6 (1)

呜
嗚 wū
hoot,
toot
58;30 7 (4)

鸣
鳴 míng
chirp; to voice;
make a sound
58;196 8 (3)

喊
hǎn
shout, cry,
call
58;30 12 (1)

呕
嘔 ǒu
vomit;
spit out
58;30 7 (4)

咽
嚥 yàn yān yè
swallow, gulp;
throat
58;30 9 (2)

1	41
2	42
3	43
4	44
5	45
6	46
7	47
8	48
9	49
10	50
11	51
12	52
13	53
14	54
15	55
16	56
17	57
18	58
19	59
20	60
21	61
22	62
23	63
24	64
25	65
26	66
27	67
28	68
29	69
30	70
31	71
32	72
33	73
34	74
35	75
36	76
37	77
38	78
39	79
40	80

日

旷 曠 kuàng
spacious;
carefree; &
103;72 7 (4)

昨 zuó
yesterday
-
103;72 9 (1)

昧 mèi
conceal;
ignorant of
103;72 9 (4)

旺 wàng
flourishing;
brisk
103;72 8 (4)

时 時 shí
time; hour; season; opportunity
present, current; now and then
103;72 7 (1)

明 míng
bright; clear;
overt; next; &
103;72 8 (1)

映 yìng
reflect;
shine
103;72 9 (2)

晒 曬 shài
to shine (sun);
sunbathe
103;72 10 (2)

晌 shǎng
midday;
part of the day
103;72 10 (4)

晖 暉 huī
sunshine
-
103;72 10 (-)

晾 liàng
to air,
dry in the sun
103;72 12 (4)

暗 àn
dark; dim;
hidden, secret
103;72 13 (2)

昭 zhāo
clear,
evident
103;72 9 (-)

晤 wù
meet,
interview
103;72 11 (4)

晓 曉 xiǎo
dawn;
know; tell
103;72 10 (2)

晚 wǎn
evening, night
late; junior
103;72 11 (1

晴 qíng
fine
(weather)
103;72 12 (1)

暖 nuǎn
warm,
genial
103;72 13 (1)

曝 pù bào
expose to the
sun (literary)
103;72 19 (-)

晰 xī
clear,
distinct
103;72 12 (3)

暇 xiá
leisure
-
103;72 13 (-)

白

的 de dí dì
(particle);
bull's eye
150;106 8 (1)

魄 pò bó tuò
soul, spirit,
vigor
150;194 14 (4)

酉

配 pèi
mix; match up;
deserve; &
193;164 10 (2)

酌 zhuó
pour out (wine),
drink; consider
193;164 10 (4)

酗 xù
[get drunk]
-
193;164 11 (4)

酬 chóu
reward; fulfil;
entertain friends
193;164 13 (3)

醉 zuì
be drunk
-
193;164 15 (2)

醇 chún
alcohol;
good wine
193;164 15 (-)

酵 jiào
ferment,
leaven
193;164 14 (-)

酷 kù
cruel, harsh;
extremely
193;164 14 (3)

酿 釀 niàng niáng
brew, ferment;
lead to; wine
193;164 14 (4)

酝 醞 yùn
[brew]
-
193;164 11 (4)

酶 méi
ferment, yeast;
enzyme
193;164 14 (4)

醋 cù
vinegar;
jealousy
193;164 15 (2)

酸 suān
acid; sour;
ache; grief; &
193;164 14 (1)

醒 xǐng
revive, wake up;
awake; &
193;164 16 (2)

盯
dīng
observe,
gaze at
141;109 7 (3)

眯
*眯 mī mī
squint; get
(dust) in eyes
141;109 11 (3)

眼
yǎn
eye;
key point
141;109 11 (1)

眠
mián
sleep
-
141;109 10 (3)

助
zhù
help,
assist
28;19 7 (1)

睦
mù
harmonious
-
141;109 13 (4)

睹
dǔ
see
-
141;109 13 (4)

瞎
xiā
blind;
senseless
141;109 15 (3)

睛
jīng
eyeball
-
141;109 13 (1)

瞒
瞞 mán
deceive
141;109 15 (3)

眨
zhǎ
wink,
blink
141;109 9 (4)

睬
cǎi
take note
-
141;109 13 (4)

睡
shuì
sleep
-
141;109 13 (1)

瞬
shùn
blink,
wink
141;109 17 (-)

盼
pàn
hope for;
look
141;109 9 (2)

睁
睜 zhēng
open
(eyes)
141;109 11 (2)

瞻
zhān
look ahead,
look up
141;109 18 (4)

瞧
qiáo
look, see
(colloq)
141;109 17 (2)

瞪
dèng
stare,
glare
141;109 17 (3)

瞩
矚 zhǔ
gaze,
look at
141;109 17 (4)

眶
kuàng
eyesocket
-
141;109 11 (4)

耻
*恥 chǐ
shame,
disgrace
163;128 10 (4)

取
qǔ
take; obtain;
choose; &
163;29 8 (1)

耶
yē yé
('je' sound)
-
34;128 8 (-)

耽
dān
delay;
indulge in
163;128 10 (3)

耿
gěng
honest, just;
dedicated
163;128 10 (4)

聊
liáo
merely;
slightly; chat
163;128 11 (2)

聘
pìn
employ,
engage
163;128 13 (4)

联
聯 lián
unite, join;
link up
163;128 12 (1)

聪
聰 cōng
acute hearing;
intelligent
163;128 15 (2)

职
職 zhí
duty, job,
post
163;128 11 (2)

敢
gǎn
bold; dare;
be sure
113;66 11 (1)

畔
pàn
side, border,
(river) bank
142;102 10 (3)

略
lüè
slightly; omit;
plan; seize; &
142;102 11 (2)

畴
疇 chóu
category;
farmland
142;102 12 (4)

邮
郵 yóu
post,
mail
143;163 7 (1)

1	41
2	42
3	43
4	44
5	45
6	46
7	47
8	48
9	49
10	50
11	51
12	52
13	53
14	54
15	55
16	56
17	57
18	58
19	59
20	60
21	61
22	62
23	63
24	64
25	65
26	66
27	67
28	68
29	69
30	70
31	71
32	72
33	73
34	74
35	75
36	76
37	77
38	78
39	79
40	80

石

矿	砍	矽	破	砖	础
礦 kuàng	kǎn	xī	pò	磚 zhuān	礎 chǔ
ore, mine	chop, hack	silicon -	destroy; split; broken; torn; &	brick -	plinth, base
136;112 8 (2)	136;112 9 (2)	136;112 8 (-)	136;112 10 (1)	136;112 9 (3)	136;112 10

砰	研	硬	硕	码	
pēng	yán	yìng	碩 shuò	碼 mǎ	
bang, thump	grind; study, research	hard, tough; with difficulty; &	huge -	numeral; wharf; yard (3 ft)	
136;112 10 (-)	136;112 9 (1)	136;112 12 (2)	136;112 11 (-)	136;112 8 (2)	

砂	碎	硫	磅	碗	辟
shā	suì	liú	bàng páng	wǎn	*闢 pì bì
sand, grit	smash; broken; garrulous	sulfur -	weigh; scales; pound (16 oz)	a bowl -	open up (land); incisive; refut
136;112 9 (4)	136;112 13 (2)	136;112 12 (4)	136;112 15 (3)	136;112 13 (1)	186;160 13

碑	硅	磕	碳	碟	确
bēi	guī	kē	tàn	dié	確 què
stele (upright stone tablet)	silicon -	knock against -	carbon -	small dish, small plate	true, real; firmly (believe
136;112 13 (2)	136;112 11 (4)	136;112 15 (4)	136;112 14 (4)	136;112 14 (4)	136;112 12

碰	磁	磋	磷	碌	碍
pèng	cí	cuō	lín	碌 lù liù	礙 ài
bump; meet; try one's luck	magnet; porcelain	to polish; consult	phosphorus -	busy; ordinary	obstruct, impede
136;112 13 (1)	136;112 14 (1)	136;112 14 (4)	136;112 17 (4)	136;112 13 (4)	136;112 13

砌	砸	破	碱		
qì	zá	pò	jiǎn		
lay (bricks); steps	break, smash, pound, crush	destroy; split; broken; torn; &	alkali, (caustic) soda		
136;112 9 (4)	136;112 10 (3)	136;112 10 (1)	136;112 14 (3)		

歹

列	歼	殊	殃	残	殖
liè	殲 jiān	shū	yāng	殘 cán	zhí
arrange, line up; rank, file; list; &	annihilate -	different; special; very	disaster; bring misfortune	incomplete; injure; savage	breed, reproduce
97;18 6 (2)	97;78 7 (3)	97;78 10 (2)	97;78 9 (4)	97;78 9 (3)	97;78 12 (3)

死	外
sǐ	wài
die; death; rigid	outside; foreign; besides; &
97;78 6 (1)	64;36 5 (1)

邪 xié evil; heretical 34;163 6 (4)	鸦 鴉 yā a crow 99;196 9 (4)	雅 yǎ proper; elegant; your (polite) 99;172 12 (4)		
乱 亂 luàn confused; riot; random; & 177;5 7 (1)	敌 敵 dí foe; oppose 177;66 10 (2)	辞 辭 cí depart; decline; dismiss; & 177;160 13 (3)	甜 tián sweet; (sleep) soundly 177;99 11 (2)	刮 guā scrape; extort; to blow; & 177;18 8 (1)
跃 躍 yuè leap, jump 196;157 11 (2)	跌 diē fall, decline 196;157 12 (2)	践 踐 jiàn trample; carry out 196;157 12 (1)	跟 gēn heel; follow; with 196;157 13 (1)	距 jù distance (from, apart) 196;157 11 (2)
趴 pā bend over; lie prone 196;157 9 (3)	跳 tiào jump, leap; omit; throb 196;157 13 (1)	踌 躊 chóu [hesitate] - 196;157 14 (4)	跑 pǎo run; flee; away 196;157 12 (1)	
踪 蹤 zōng tracks, footprint 196;157 15 (4)	蹄 tí hoof - 196;157 16 (3)	踏 tà tā tread, trample; on the spot 196;157 15 (3)	跨 kuà stride; bestride; straddle 196;157 13 (2)	蹦 bèng jump, leap, hop 196;157 18 (4)
蹲 dūn crouch, squat 196;157 19 (2)	蹭 cèng rub; loiter 196;157 19 (4)	蹰 chú [hesitate] - 196;157 18 (4)		
跺 duò stamp (foot) - 196;157 13 (4)	蹋 tà [trample on] - 196;157 17 (4)	踢 tī kick - 196;157 15 (1)	躁 zào impetuous; restless 196;157 20 (3)	踊 踴 yǒng jump up, leap up 196;157 14 (3)
蹈 dǎo skip; tread, trample 196;157 17 (3)	踩 cǎi step on, tread 196;157 15 (2)	跪 guì kneel - 196;157 13 (2)	路 lù road, route; way; region; & 196;157 13 (1)	蹬 dēng dèng step on, trample 196;157 19 (3)

1	41
2	42
3	43
4	44
5	45
6	46
7	47
8	48
9	49
10	50
11	51
12	52
13	53
14	54
15	55
16	56
17	57
18	58
19	59
20	60
21	61
22	62
23	63
24	64
25	65
26	66
27	67
28	68
29	69
30	70
31	71
32	72
33	73
34	74
35	75
36	76
37	77
38	78
39	79
40	80

肚 dù dǔ
belly, abdomen; tripe
118;130 7 (2)

胜 勝 shèng
victory; superb; surpass; &
118;19 9 (1)

肤 膚 fū
skin; [superficial]
118;130 8 (2)

胖 pàng pán
fat, plump; contented
118;130 9 (2)

胀 脹 zhàng
expand, swell; bloated
118;130 8 (3)

肿 腫 zhǒng
swollen
-
118;130 8 (3

肝 gān
liver
-
118;130 7 (2)

肌 jī
muscle
-
118;130 6 (3)

肠 腸 cháng
intestines
-
118;130 7 (2)

豚 tún
pig, piglet
118;152 11 (-)

肥 féi
fat; baggy; fertile; fertilizer
118;130 8 (2)

朋 péng
friend
-
118;74 8 (1)

服 fú
clothes; serve; obey; &
118;74 8 (1)

那 nà nèi nè nā
that; in that case
34;163 6 (1)

胁 脅 xié
upper body, ribs; coerce
118;130 8 (3)

膨 péng
[inflate, expand; swollen]
118;130 16 (3)

脚 腳 jiǎo
foot, base; leg
118;130 11 (1)

鹏 鵬 péng
roc (fabled giant bird)
152;196 13 (-)

脏 臟 髒 zàng zāng
viscera; dirty
118;130 10 (1)

肘 zhǒu
elbow
-
118;130 7 (-)

胸 xiōng
chest, thorax; at heart
118;130 10 (2)

胞 bāo
placenta; siblings
118;130 9 (3)

腻 膩 nì
greasy; tired of; dirt; meticulous
118;130 13 (-)

腿 tuǐ
leg; thigh; ham
118;130 13 (1)

冂　　　肭

脉	腺	脾	膊	彤
脈 mài mò	xiàn	pí	bó	tóng
vein; pulse; lovingly	gland	spleen	arm	red (literary)
-	-	-	-	
118;130　9　(2)	118;130　13　(-)	118;130　12　(2)	118;130　14　(2)	63;59　7　(-)

肺	肪	胶	脑	膀
fèi	fáng	膠 jiāo	腦 nǎo	bǎng pāng páng
lungs	[animal fat]	glue; sticky; rubber	brain	upper arm; swell; bladder
-	-		-	
118;130　8　(2)	118;130　8　(4)	118;130　10　(3)	118;130　10　(2)	118;130　14　(2)

腔	腕
qiāng	wàn
cavity; tune; accent	wrist
	-
118;130　12　(3)	118;130　12　(-)

肢	脖	膝	脂
zhī	bó	xī	zhī
limb	neck	knee	grease, fat; rouge
-	-	-	
118;130　8　(4)	118;130　11　(2)	118;130　15　(4)	118;130　10　(4)

脱	腾	膛	腊	膜	朦
tuō	騰 téng tēng	táng	臘 là xī	mó	méng
cast off, shed; omit; escape	jump, ascend; make room	chest, thorax; hollow chamber	cured (meat); December	membrane	[dim, hazy]
				-	
118;130　11　(1)	118;187　13　(3)	118;130　15　(4)	118;130　12　(4)	118;130　14　(4)	118;74　17　(-)

股	胆	腥	腰	腮
gǔ	膽 dǎn	xīng	yāo	sāi
thigh; section; strand; a share	courage, guts; gall bladder	raw meat, fish; fishy	waist; pocket; halfway up	cheeks
118;130　8　(3)	118;130　9　(2)	118;130　13　(4)	118;130　13　(2)	118;130　13　(4)

腹	胳	脆
fù	gē gé	cuì
belly, abdomen	[arm]	crisp; brittle
	-	
118;130　13　(4)	118;130　10　(2)	118;130　10　(2)

脸	胎
臉 liǎn	tāi
face, countenance	embryo; birth; a tire; padding
118;130　11　(1)	118;130　9　(-)

1	41
2	42
3	43
4	44
5	45
6	46
7	47
8	48
9	49
10	50
11	51
12	52
13	53
14	54
15	55
16	56
17	57
18	58
19	59
20	60
21	61
22	62
23	63
24	64
25	65
26	66
27	67
28	68
29	69
30	70
31	71
32	72
33	73
34	74
35	75
36	76
37	77
38	78
39	79
40	80

舟

舶 bó
(sea-going) ship
182;137 11 (4)

航 háng
boat, ship;
to sail, fly
182;137 10 (2)

舵 duò
rudder,
helm
182;137 11 (4)

舱 艙 cāng
cabin, hold
(on ship)
182;137 10 (3)

彤 tóng
red
(literary)
63;59 7 (-)

舰 艦 jiàn
warship
-
182;137 10 (3)

船 chuán
boat,
ship
182;137 11 (1)

般 bān
sort, kind;
manner
182;137 10 (1)

艘 sōu
(measure word)
-
182;137 15 (3)

艇 tǐng
boat
-
182;137 12 (4)

身

躬 gōng
to bend, bow;
in person
200;158 10 (4)

射 shè
shoot (gun);
radiate; allude
200;41 10 (2)

躯 軀 qū
human
body
200;158 11 (-)

躲 duǒ
hide oneself;
avoid
200;158 13 (2)

躺 tǎng
lie down,
recline
200;158 15 (1)

良

朗 lǎng
bright;
loud and clear
118;74 10 (2)

郎 láng
man, person;
darling
34;163 8 (2)

艮

即 jí
right away;
approach; i.e.
184;26 7 (2)

既 jì
already; since;
as well as
184;71 9 (2)

欧	殴	鸥
歐 ōu	毆 ōu	鷗 ōu
Europe; (surname)	beat, strike	gull
120;76 8 (3)	119;79 8 (4)	152;196 9 (-)

财	败	账	贱	则
財 cái	敗 bài	賬 zhàng	賤 jiàn	則 zé
wealth, property	defeated; fail; defeat; spoil; &	accounts, credit	cheap; lowly; my (humble)	rules; norm, model; then; &
106;154 7 (3)	106;66 8 (2)	106;154 8 (-)	106;154 9 (3)	106;18 6 (2)

贴	赔	赎	赠	赚
貼 tiē	賠 péi	贖 shú	贈 zèng	賺 zhuàn zuàn
paste; nestle; subsidize	compensate; suffer a loss	redeem, ransom, atone	give (as gift) -	make a profit -
106;154 9 (2)	106;154 12 (2)	106;154 12 (-)	106;154 16 (3)	106;154 14 (3)

贬	赐	赂
貶 biǎn	賜 cì	賂 lù
demote; censure	bestow, grant	[bribe] -
106;154 8 (4)	106;154 12 (-)	106;154 10 (4)

贩	贿	赌	购	贼	赋
販 fàn	賄 huì	賭 dǔ	購 gòu	賊 zéi	賦 fù
buy and sell; dealer	bribe -	gamble, bet	buy -	thief; traitor; furtive; cunning	bestow; compose poem
106;154 8 (4)	106;154 10 (4)	106;154 12 (4)	106;154 8 (2)	106;154 10 (4)	106;154 12 (4)

驮	驰	驶	驱	驴	驻
馱 tuó duò	馳 chí	駛 shǐ	驅 qū	驢 lǘ	駐 zhù
carry (on back, of animals)	gallop, go fast; far and wide	(of a vehicle) to go; to speed	drive (vehicle); expel; run fast	donkey -	stay; halt; be stationed
75;187 6 (3)	75;187 6 (4)	75;187 8 (3)	75;187 7 (4)	75;187 7 (3)	75;187 8 (3)

驼	骇	骗	骑	驳	骏
駝 tuó	駭 hài	騙 piàn	騎 qí	駁 bó	駿 jùn
camel; hump-backed	startled, astonished	deceive, swindle	ride (animal, bicycle)	refute; a barge	fine horse, steed
75;187 8 (3)	75;187 9 (-)	75;187 12 (2)	75;187 11 (1)	75;187 7 (4)	75;187 10 (-)

验	骄	骆	骚	骡	骤
驗 yàn	驕 jiāo	駱 luò	騷 sāo	騾 luó	驟 zhòu
examine; effective	arrogant -	[camel] -	disturb, upset; literary; &	mule -	sudden; trot (horse)
75;187 10 (1)	75;187 9 (2)	75;187 9 (3)	75;187 12 (3)	75;187 14 (4)	75;187 17 (3)

1	41
2	42
3	43
4	44
5	45
6	46
7	47
8	48
9	49
10	50
11	51
12	52
13	53
14	54
15	55
16	56
17	57
18	58
19	59
20	60
21	61
22	62
23	63
24	64
25	65
26	66
27	67
28	68
29	69
30	70
31	71
32	72
33	73
34	74
35	75
36	76
37	77
38	78
39	79
40	80

虫

虹	虾	蚁	蛛	蚂	蛾
hóng	蝦 xiā	蟻 yǐ	zhū	螞 mǎ mà	é
rainbow	shrimp	ant	spider	[ant; locust]	moth
-	-	-	-	-	-
174;142 9 (4)	174;142 9 (3)	174;142 9 (4)	174;142 12 (4)	174;142 9 (4)	174;142 13 (

蜘	蝴	螂
zhī	hú	láng
[spider]	[butterfly]	[mantis, cockroach]
-	-	-
174;142 14 (4)	174;142 15 (3)	174;142 14 (-)

蚊	蛇	蟑	螃	蝗	蝉
wén	shé yí	zhāng	páng	huáng	蟬 chán
mosquito	snake	[cockroach]	[crab]	locust	cicada
-	-	-	-	-	-
174;142 10 (3)	174;142 11 (2)	174;142 17 (-)	174;142 16 (-)	174;142 15 (4)	174;142 14 (

蛙	蜻	蜡	蝶
wā	qīng	蠟 là	dié
frog	[dragonfly]	wax, polish; candle	butterfly
-	-	-	-
174;142 12 (3)	174;142 14 (4)	174;142 14 (3)	174;142 15 (3)

蝇	螺	蜂
蠅 yíng	luó	fēng
a fly	snail, conch; spiral	bee, wasp; swarm
-	-	-
174;142 14 (3)	174;142 17 (4)	174;142 13 (2)

蜓
tíng
[dragonfly]
-
174;142 12 (4)

鱼

稣	鲜	鲸	鲍
穌 sū	鮮 xiān xiǎn	鯨 jīng	鮑 bào
revive	fresh; colorful; tasty; seafood	whale	[abalone]; (surname)
-		-	
210;115 13 (-)	210;195 14 (2)	210;195 16 (3)	210;195 13 (-)

角

触	解
觸 chù	jiě jiè xiè
touch	untie; explain; solve; dispel; &
-	
201;148 13 (2)	201;148 13 (1)

韩	朝	乾	翰	
韓 hán	cháo zhāo	qián	hàn	
(surname)	facing; dynasty;	male (archaic)	writing brush;	
-	morning; day; &	(see Table 1)	writing (literary)	
203;178 12 (-)	203;74 12 (1)	203;5 11 (-)	203;124 16 (-)	

辣	辨	辩	辫	瓣
là	biàn	辯 biàn	辮 biàn	bàn
spicy, acrid;	differentiate,	dispute,	plait, braid;	petal, segment,
vicious	distinguish	debate	pigtail	piece; valve
186;160 14 (3)	186;160 16 (4)	186;160 16 (3)	186;120 17 (4)	186;97 19 (3)

勒	鞋	鞠	靴	鞭
lēi lè	xié	jū	xuē	biān
tighten, rein in;	shoe	to rear, bring	boot	whip
compel	-	up; nourish	-	-
212;19 11 (4)	212;177 15 (1)	212;177 17 (4)	212;177 13 (4)	212;177 18 (4)

欺	斯	期		
qī	sī	qī jī		
deceive;	this; thus;	expect; period;		
bully	('si' sound)	appointed time		
120;76 12 (2)	115;69 12 (3)	118;74 12 (1)		

1	41
2	42
3	43
4	44
5	45
6	46
7	47
8	48
9	49
10	50
11	51
12	52
13	53
14	54
15	55
16	56
17	57
18	58
19	59
20	60
21	61
22	62
23	63
24	64
25	65
26	66
27	67
28	68
29	69
30	70
31	71
32	72
33	73
34	74
35	75
36	76
37	77
38	78
39	79
40	80

以	北	乖	乘	剩
yǐ	běi	guāi	chéng shèng	shèng
using; so as to; according to; &	north -	obedient; quick-witted	ride; multiply; make use of	surplus; residue
23;9 4 (1)	39;21 5 (1)	4;4 8 (3)	149;4 10 (2)	17;18 12 (1)

丨丆

赖	救	颊	顿	颇
賴 lài	jiù	頰 jiá	頓 dùn	頗 pō
rely; linger; deny; shirk	rescue; aid	cheeks -	pause; arrange; suddenly; &	quite, rather
192;154 13 (4)	113;66 11 (2)	170;181 12 (4)	170;181 10 (1)	153;181 11 (

朿 求 来 屯 皮

鹤	叔	疑	鼎
鶴 hè	shū	yí	dǐng
crane (bird) -	uncle; brother in law	doubt -	cauldron; tripod, tripartite
152;196 15 (-)	35;29 8 (2)	39;103 14 (2)	141;206 12 (-)

隹 朮 𠂤 ㇇

衅	邮	畅	氓	刘
釁 xìn	郵 yóu	暢 chàng	méng máng	劉 liú
quarrel -	post, mail	smooth, fluent; uninhibited	the common people	(surname) -
181;164 11 (4)	143;163 7 (1)	144;72 8 (3)	43;83 8 (3)	84;18 6 (3)

血 由 申 亡 文

邦	韧	艳
bāng	韌 靭 rèn	艷 豔 豊 yàn
nation, state	tough; pliable yet strong	gorgeous; romantic
34;163 6 (4)	91;178 7 (4)	27;139 10 (3)

丯 韦 丰

韵	新	毅	就
*韻 yùn	xīn	yì	jiù
rhyme; melodic tone; charming	new -	firm, resolute	right away; only, just; even if; then; precisely; concerning; &
211;180 13 (4)	115;69 13 (1)	119;79 15 (3)	9;43 12 (1)

音 亲 豖 京

战	故	胡	封	鼓
戰 zhàn	gù	*鬍 hú	fēng	gǔ
war, battle; tremble	former; to die; on purpose; &	reckless; beard; &	seal up; bestow	drum; rouse; bellows; bulge
101;62 9 (2)	113;66 9 (1)	118;130 9 (2)	54;41 9 (1)	224;207 13 (

占 古 圭 壴

赫	兢	静	豁
hè	jīng	靜 jìng	huō huò
impressive -	[conscientious] -	still, calm, quiet	crack; forsake; open; exempt
190;155 14 (4)	12;10 14 (4)	202;174 14 (1)	199;150 17 (4)

赤 克 青 害

幺 左 夫

肙

齿 昔

并

句 个 刍

加	幻	幼	雄	规
jiā	huàn	yòu	xióng	規 guī
plus; add, augment	unreal; changeable	young; child	male; mighty, grand; hero	rule, law; plan; admonish
28;19 5 (1)	76;52 4 (3)	76;52 5 (3)	208;172 12 (2)	107;147 8 (2)

从	巫	能
從 cóng cōng	wū	néng
from; to follow; secondary; &	witch, wizard	able to; energy; capability
23;60 4 (1)	48;48 7 (4)	37;130 10 (1)

收	龄	鹊
shōu	齡 líng	鵲 què
receive; collect up; cease; &	age, years, duration	magpie -
113;66 6 (1)	206;211 13 (2)	152;196 13 (4)

翔	瓶
xiáng	píng
soar, hover	bottle, vase, jug
157;124 12 (4)	98;98 10 (1)

外	够	竹	皱
wài	*夠 gòu	zhú	皺 zhòu
outside; foreign; besides; &	enough; attain; rather, quite	bamboo -	crease, wrinkle
64;36 5 (1)	64;36 11 (1)	178;118 6 (2)	153;107 10 (3)

1	41
2	42
3	43
4	44
5	45
6	46
7	47
8	48
9	49
10	50
11	51
12	52
13	53
14	54
15	55
16	56
17	57
18	58
19	59
20	60
21	61
22	62
23	63
24	64
25	65
26	66
27	67
28	68
29	69
30	70
31	71
32	72
33	73
34	74
35	75
36	76
37	77
38	78
39	79
40	80

丁 干 正 而	顶 顶dǐng stand up to; top; utmost; & 170;181 8 (2)	刊 kān print; publication 17;18 5 (3)	政 zhèng politics; administration 113;66 9 (1)	耐 nài endure, bear 169;126 9 (2)	
艮 甲 里 果	既 jì already; since; as well as 184;71 9 (2)	即 jí right away; approach; i.e. 184;26 7 (2)	鸭 鴨yā a duck - 152;196 10 (3)	野 yě countryside; wild; limit; & 195;166 11 (2)	夥 huǒ many (literary) (see Table 1) 142;36 15 (-)
厉 厄 镸 臣 臣	励 勵lì encourage - 28;19 7 (2)	顾 顧gù look around; look after; visit 170;181 10 (1)	肆 sì reckless; unbridled; four 124;129 13 (4)	颐 頤yí cheeks; keep fit (literary) 170;181 13 (-)	卧 臥wò lie down; berth, sleeper 164;131 8 (
习 予 圣 歪	羽 yǔ feather - 183;124 6 (2)	预 預yù in advance - 170;181 10 (1)	豫 yù pleased; Henan (literary) 31;152 15 (3)	颈 頸jīng gěng neck - 170;181 11 (4)	疏 shū sparse; negle unfamiliar; & 31;103 12 (
己 弓 弔 君	改 gǎi change, alter, rectify 113;66 7 (1)	弱 ruò weak; inferior; a bit less 71;57 10 (2)	疆 jiāng boundary, frontier 71;102 19 (3)	群 qún crowd, group, herd 157;123 13 (2)	
云 兀 豆	动 動dòng move, act; use; alter; arouse 28;19 6 (1)	魂 hún soul, spirit 216;194 13 (3)	顽 頑wán stupid; naughty; stubborn 170;181 10 (3)	豌 wān [pea] - 191;151 15 (4)	
后 周 骨	辟 *闢 pì bì open up (land); incisive; refute 186;160 13 (2)	雕 diāo carve, engrave; vulture, eagle 208;172 16 (3)	髓 髓suǐ (bone) marrow; pith 214;188 21 (-)		

手

拜	掰	我	鹅
bài	bāi	wǒ	鵝 é
pay a visit; bow to	break (with the fingers)	I, me, my, we, our	goose
-	-	-	-
111;64 9 (2)	111;64 12 (4)	101;62 7 (1)	152;196 12 (2)

斤戶委

卯	卿	欣	所	魏
mǎo	qīng	xīn	suǒ	wèi
EB; mortise	minister (archaic)	happy, joyful	place; building; (particle)	(old kingdom; surname)
32;26 5 (-)	32;26 10 (-)	115;76 8 (3)	115;63 8 (1)	216;194 18 (4)

臣耳月

卵	印	段	殷
luǎn	yìn	duàn	yīn yān
egg	print, stamp, seal; tally with	section, segment	ardent; cordial; rich; & (literary)
-			
227;26 7 (3)	32;26 6 (2)	119;79 9 (1)	119;79 10 (4)

令

斜	叙	邻	领
xié	*敘 敍 xù	鄰 lín	領 lǐng
slanting, oblique	chat; narrate; assess; &	neighbor	neck, collar; to lead, guide; get (award); outline; &
82;68 11 (2)	35;29 9 (3)	34;163 7 (2)	170;181 11 (1)

舍分公

鸽	舒	颁	颂
鴿 gē	shū	頒 bān	頌 sòng
dove, pigeon	stretch, unfold; leisurely	publish; to issue, send out	praise; song, eulogy
152;196 11 (3)	23;135 12 (1)	170;181 10 (4)	170;181 10 (3)

望

删	毁
*刪 shān	huǐ
delete, omit	destroy; defame
17;18 7 (3)	119;79 13 (3)

1	41
2	42
3	43
4	44
5	45
6	46
7	47
8	48
9	49
10	50
11	51
12	52
13	53
14	54
15	55
16	56
17	57
18	58
19	59
20	60
21	61
22	62
23	63
24	64
25	65
26	66
27	67
28	68
29	69
30	70
31	71
32	72
33	73
34	74
35	75
36	76
37	77
38	78
39	79
40	80

厂

厅 廳 tīng	厉 厲 lì	历 曆歷 lì	厌 厭 yàn	压 壓 yā yà	厂 廠 chǎng
hall; office; department	stern, strict; sharpen	undergo; all of; chronicle	detest, dislike; fed up; sated	press, crush; suppress; &	factory, depot
13;53 4 (2)	13;27 5 (2)	13;72 4 (1)	13;27 6 (2)	13;32 6 (2)	13;53 2 (1)

厄	辰	厘 釐 lí	石		
è	chén		shí dàn		
adversity; nub (literary)	stars; EB; time, occasion	fraction, centi-, %; li (Chin unit)	stone, rock; inscription		
13;27 4 (-)	187;161 7 (4)	13;166 9 (2)	136;112 5 (2)		

雁	厢 廂 xiāng	厕 廁 cè si	厨 廚 chú		
yàn					
wild goose	side; side room; (house) wing; &	toilet, washroom	kitchen		
-			-		
13;172 12 (4)	13;53 11 (3)	13;53 8 (2)	13;53 12 (2)		

厚	原	愿 願 yuàn	厦 廈 shà xià	唇 唇 chún	辱
hòu	yuán	* willing; wish, desire; vow	tall building; mansion	* lips	rǔ
thick; generous; deep; to stress	original, raw; a plain; excuse				disgrace; to insult
13;27 9 (2)	13;27 10 (1)	81;61 14 (1)	13;53 12 (4)	187;30 10 (3)	187;161 10 (

厂

斤	斥	反	后 後 hòu	爪	瓜
jīn	chì	fǎn	*	zhǎo zhuǎ	guā
(unit of weight: 1/2 kilogram)	denounce; exclude	contrary; anti-, counter-	back, behind, after; empress	claw, talon	melon, gourd
115;69 4 (1)	115;69 5 (3)	22;29 4 (1)	22;30 6 (1)	116;87 4 (4)	151;97 5 (2)

盾	质 質 zhì				
dùn					
shield	quality, nature; simple; query				
-					
22;109 9 (2)	22;154 8 (2)				

ナ

右	左	友	灰	布 佈 bù	有
yòu	zuǒ	yǒu	huī	*	yǒu yòu
right (hand)	left (hand); different; wrong	friend	ash, dust; gray; disheartened	cloth; spread; deploy; declare	have, possess there is / are; &
-		-			
14;30 5 (1)	14;48 5 (1)	14;29 4 (1)	14;86 6 (2)	14;50 5 (1)	14;74 6 (1)

在	存	龙 龍 lóng	尤	寿 壽 shòu
zài	cún		yóu	
exist; be -ing; at; depends; &	exist; preserve; deposit; &	dragon; imperial	especially; blame, fault	longevity; age; birthday; funeral
14;32 6 (1)	14;39 6 (2)	137;212 5 (2)	53;43 4 (1)	54;33 7 (3)

老	**考**	**孝**	**者**	**煮**
lǎo	kǎo	xiào	zhě	zhǔ
old; longtime; always; &	inspect, test, examine	filial piety; mourning	person, -er, -ist; this	to cook, boil
92;125 6 (1)	92;125 6 (1)	92;39 7 (4)	92;125 8 (1)	80;86 12 (2)

尼	**屎**	**尿**	**屈**	**尾**	**屏**
ní	shǐ	niào suī	qū	wěi	bǐng píng
Buddhist nun; ('ni' sound)	excrement; secretion	urine; urinate	bend; yield, submit; wrong	tail; end	reject; screen; hold (breath); &
67;44 5 (4)	67;44 9 (4)	67;44 7 (4)	67;44 8 (3)	67;44 7 (2)	67;44 9 (4)

屜	**屆**	**居**	**屑**
*屜 tì	届 jiè	jū	xiè
drawer; food steamer	appointed time	reside; house; to claim; &	fragments, scraps; trivial
67;44 8 (4)	67;44 8 (2)	67;44 8 (2)	67;44 10 (4)

展	**屋**	**屠**	**層**	**屬**	**屢**
zhǎn	wū	tú	层 céng	属 shǔ zhǔ	屡 lǚ
unfold; display; postpone	a room; house	massacre; to butcher	layer, tier, story, floor	category; belong to	repeatedly -
67;44 10 (1)	67;44 9 (1)	67;44 11 (4)	67;44 7 (1)	67;44 12 (2)	67;44 12 (4)

屁	**履**	**局**	**尺**	**盡**
pì	lǚ	jú	chǐ	尽 儘 jìn jǐn
break wind, fart	shoe; tread, footstep; fulfil	office; situation; trap; part; &	ruler, foot (12 inches)	used up; entire; utmost; &
67;44 7 (3)	67;44 15 (4)	67;44 7 (1)	117;44 4 (2)	117;108 6 (2)

尸	**晝**	**民**	**眉**
屍 shī	画 zhòu	mín	méi
corpse -	daytime	the people; folk, popular; civilian	eyebrow
67;44 3 (4)	117;72 9 (4)	227;83 5 (1)	141;109 9 (3)

启	**肩**	**房**	**扁**	**雇**	**扇**
啓 qǐ	jiān	fáng	biǎn piān	gù	shàn shān
open, begin; enlighten	shoulder -	house; building; a room	flat, flatten	hire, employ	fan -
86;30 7 (2)	86;130 8 (2)	86;63 8 (1)	86;63 9 (2)	86;172 12 (3)	86;63 10 (2)

户
hù
door; family; bank account
86;63 4 (1)

1	41
2	42
3	43
4	44
5	45
6	46
7	47
8	48
9	49
10	50
11	51
12	52
13	53
14	54
15	55
16	56
17	57
18	58
19	59
20	60
21	61
22	62
23	63
24	64
25	65
26	66
27	67
28	68
29	69
30	70
31	71
32	72
33	73
34	74
35	75
36	76
37	77
38	78
39	79
40	80

广　卢

广

庄	庆	床	应	皮	广
莊 zhuāng	慶 qìng	chuáng	應 yīng yìng	pí	廣 guǎng
village; solemn; premises	celebration; congratulate	bed -	should; agree; respond; cope	skin, leather; outer layer; &	wide, broad; spread; many
44;140 6 (2)	44;53 6 (2)	44;53 7 (1)	44;61 7 (1)	153;107 5 (2)	44;53 3 (1)

庙	库	座	庐	序	底
廟 miào	庫 kù	zuò	廬 lú	xù	dǐ
temple -	warehouse -	seat, place; pedestal	hut, cottage	sequence; preface	bottom, base; end; rough co
44;53 8 (2)	44;53 7 (3)	44;53 10 (1)	44;53 7 (-)	44;53 7 (2)	44;53 8 (2)

店	庚	康	唐	庸	廉
diàn	gēng	kāng	táng	yōng	lián
shop, store; inn	age; 7th; HS	health -	Tang (dynasty)	ordinary; inferior	cheap; honest
44;53 8 (1)	44;53 8 (-)	44;53 11 (1)	44;30 10 (4)	44;53 11 (4)	44;53 13 (4)

度	席	鹿	腐	鹰
dù duó	xí	lù	fǔ	鷹 yīng
degrees; times; spend (time); &	seat, place; mat; banquet	deer -	bean curd; rotten, decayed	eagle, hawk
44;53 9 (1)	44;50 10 (2)	222;198 11 (4)	44;130 14 (2)	152;196 18 (4)

座	麽	摩	魔	磨
zuò	mó	mó mā	mó	mó mò
seat, place; pedestal	[petty, clown] (see Table 1)	rub; scrape; contemplate	demon; magical	rub, grind; sharpen; wear down; pester; dawdle, kill time; mill; &
44;53 10 (1)	221;200 14 (-)	221;64 15 (3)	221;194 20 (4)	221;112 16 (2)

府	麻	廊	廓
fǔ	má mā	láng	kuò
government; mansion; &	rough, coarse; hemp; &	veranda, porch, corridor	wide; outline
44;53 8 (1)	221;200 11 (1)	44;53 11 (3)	44;53 13 (3)

庞	废	庭	座
龐 páng	廢 fèi	tíng	zuò
huge; a face; disorderly	abandon; junk; waste; disabled	courtyard; law court	seat, place; pedestal
44;53 8 (4)	44;53 8 (3)	44;53 9 (1)	44;53 10 (1)

卢

虎	虐	虏	虑	虚
hǔ	nüè	虜 lǔ	慮 lǜ	xū
tiger -	tyrannical, cruel	captive, capture	ponder; anxiety	empty; modest; feeble; sham; &
173;141 8 (2)	173;141 9 (-)	173;141 8 (4)	173;61 10 (2)	173;141 11 (2)

疗 療 liáo cure, heal 127;104 7 (3)	疾 jí illness; to hate; hardship; quick 127;104 10 (3)	疲 pí weary, tired out 127;104 10 (2)	症 zhèng zhēng disease, illness 127;104 10 (3)	病 bìng disease; ill; fault, defect 127;104 10 (1)	疤 bā scar - 127;104 9 (4)
疟 瘧 nüè yào malaria - 127;104 8 (-)	痕 hén scar; mark, stain 127;104 11 (3)	疯 瘋 fēng mad, insane 127;104 9 (3)	痴 *癡 chī stupid, silly; crazy about 127;104 13 (4)	瘫 癱 tān paralysis - 127;104 15 (4)	瘾 癮 yǐn addiction; mad about (pastime) 127;104 16 (-)
瘦 shòu thin, lean, weak, meager 127;104 14 (2)	痰 tán phlegm, spit 127;104 13 (4)	痒 癢 yǎng itch - 127;104 11 (4)	瘩 dá da [pimple; tangle] 127;104 14 (4)	痛 tòng pain, ache; sorrow; deeply 127;104 12 (1)	
疮 瘡 chuāng a sore; a wound 127;104 9 (4)	疹 zhěn rash (on skin) 127;104 10 (-)	疫 yì epidemic, plague 127;104 9 (4)	癌 ái cancer - 127;104 17 (3)	瘟 wēn (contagious, acute) disease 127;104 14 (4)	痹 痺 bì numb; rheumatism 127;104 13 (4)
疙 gē swelling, pimple; knot 127;104 8 (4)	疼 téng ache, pain; to love 127;104 10 (1)	痪 瘓 huàn [paralysis] 127;104 12 (4)	瘤 liú tumor 127;104 15 (4)	瘸 qué lame; limp (colloq) 127;104 16 (4)	
在 zài exist; be -ing; at; depends; & 14;32 6 (1)	存 cún exist; preserve; deposit; & 14;39 6 (2)	彦 yàn a good man (literary) 63;59 9 (-)	危 wēi danger; near death 27;26 6 (1)	眉 méi eyebrow 141;109 9 (3)	
龙 龍 lóng dragon; imperial 137;212 5 (2)	发 發 髮 fā fà emit; become; develop; hair; & 35;105 5 (1)	寿 壽 shòu longevity; age; birthday; funeral 54;33 7 (3)	皮 pí skin, leather; outer layer; & 153;107 5 (2)	看 kàn kān watch; look at; look after; & 141;109 9 (1)	
无 無 wú without; not; nothing; & 53;86 4 (2)	死 sǐ die; death; rigid 97;78 6 (1)	石 shí dàn stone, rock; inscription 136;112 5 (2)	名 míng name; renown; famous 64;30 6 (1)	君 jūn monarch; gentleman; Mr. 58;30 7 (4)	羌 → 58 旆 → 20

辶口

辽
遼 liáo
distant
-
47;162 5 (4)

迈
邁 mài
stride;
old (in years)
47;162 6 (2)

还
還 hái huán
still, yet; fairly;
also; return
47;162 7 (1)

迁
遷 qiān
move;
change
47;162 6 (4)

达
達 dá
reach, attain;
notify; &
47;162 6 (2)

边
邊 biān bia
side; rim; lim
border; close
47;162 5 (1

违
違 wéi
disobey;
be separated
47;162 7 (2)

连
連 lián
in succession;
link; include; &
47;162 7 (1)

进
進 jìn
proceed; enter;
take in; into
47;162 7 (1)

述
shù
narrate,
tell
47;162 8 (2)

迷
mí
lost, confused;
fascinated by
47;162 9 (2)

逮
dǎi dài
catch, arrest
reach
47;162 11 (

迭
dié
repeatedly;
to alternate
47;162 8 (-)

逐
zhú
chase; expel;
bit by bit
47;162 10 (2)

迟
遲 chí
late,
delayed
47;162 7 (1)

退
tuì
retreat; wane;
quit; give back
47;162 9 (1)

迪
dí
initiate; to
guide (literary)
47;162 8 (-)

速
sù
fast, rapid;
speed
47;162 10 (

迎口

迎
yíng
meet; greet,
welcome
47;162 7 (1)

逃
táo
flee; evade,
escape
47;162 9 (2)

巡
xún
patrol; round
(of drinks)
47;47 6 (4)

避
bì
avoid, evade;
repel
47;162 16 (2)

逛
guàng
stroll,
wander, roam
47;162 10 (2)

逝
shì
pass away,
die
47;162 10 (3)

逊
遜 xùn
abdicate;
modest
47;162 9 (4)

邀
yāo
invite; ask for;
intercept
47;162 16 (2)

迴口

近
jìn
near, close;
intimate; recent
47;162 7 (1)

返
fǎn
to return
-
47;162 7 (3)

遮
zhē
cover, conceal;
block, impede
47;162 14 (3)

迴口

迅
xùn
swift,
fast
47;162 6 (2)

过
過 guò guo guō
to cross; exceed; after, over;
very, too (much); (particle)
47;162 6 (1)

迫　　追　　述　　这　　迹　　遍

迫 pò pǎi
compel; urgent;
approach
47;162 8 (2)

追 zhuī
pursue; recall;
look into; &
47;162 9 (2)

述 shù
narrate,
tell
47;162 8 (2)

这 這 zhè zhèi
this;
here; now
47;162 7 (1)

迹 *跡 蹟 jī
tracks, traces,
vestige; a sign
47;162 9 (2)

遍 biàn
everywhere;
(no. of) times
47;162 12 (1)

递　　送　　逆　　遂　　道　　遵

递 遞 dì
hand over;
successively
47;162 10 (2)

送 sòng
carry; escort;
deliver; give
47;162 9 (1)

逆 nì
disobey; rebel;
inverse, contra-
47;162 9 (4)

遂 suì suí
succeed,
fulfil
47;162 12 (-)

道 dào
road, way; line;
Taoist; say; &
47;162 12 (1)

遵 zūn
abide by,
obey
47;162 15 (2)

逍　　迷

逍 xiāo
[unrestrained]
-
47;162 10 (-)

迷 mí
lost, confused;
fascinated by
47;162 9 (2)

选　　造　　逮　　遗　　遣　　遭

选 選 xuǎn
select,
elect
47;162 9 (2)

造 zào
make, build; to
train; concoct
47;162 10 (2)

逮 dǎi dài
catch, arrest;
reach
47;162 11 (3)

遗 遺 yí wèi
lose; omit;
bequeath
47;162 12 (3)

遣 qiǎn
send;
dispel
47;162 13 (4)

遭 zāo
suffer
mishap
47;162 14 (2)

远　　运　　逗　　逼　　通

远 遠 yuǎn
distant
-
47;162 7 (1)

运 運 yùn
move, transport;
luck; to use
47;162 7 (1)

逗 dòu
stay; amusing;
tease
47;162 10 (2)

逼 bī
compel; press
for; close in on
47;162 12 (2)

通 tōng tòng
go through, passable; connect;
know; expert; common; whole
47;162 10 (1)

适　　透　　遥　　逻　　遇

适 適 shì
suitable;
proceed
47;162 9 (1)

透 tòu
penetrate;
thoroughly; &
47;162 10 (2)

遥 遙 yáo
distant
(literary)
47;162 13 (3)

逻 邏 luó
patrol
-
47;162 11 (3)

遇 yù
meet; chance;
behave towards
47;162 12 (1)

迄　　逸　　逢　　途　　逾

迄 qì
up to, until;
up to now
47;162 6 (-)

逸 yì
leisure; flee;
gone; excel
47;162 11 (-)

逢 féng
meet,
encounter
47;162 10 (2)

途 tú
way,
route
47;162 10 (2)

逾 yú
exceed
-
47;162 12 (-)

莲　　蓬

莲 蓮 lián
lotus
-
50;140 10 (4)

蓬 péng
disheveled;
fluffy
50;140 13 (3)

1	41
2	42
3	43
4	44
5	45
6	46
7	47
8	48
9	49
10	50
11	51
12	52
13	53
14	54
15	55
16	56
17	57
18	58
19	59
20	60
21	61
22	62
23	63
24	64
25	65
26	66
27	67
28	68
29	69
30	70
31	71
32	72
33	73
34	74
35	75
36	76
37	77
38	78
39	79
40	80

走

赴 fù
go to; attend
189;156　9　(4)

赵 趙 zhào
(surname)
-
189;156　9　(3)

赶 趕 gǎn
hurry; catch up; catch (bus); &
189;156　10　(2)

起 qǐ qi
raise, rise; up; begin; able to
189;156　10　(1)

趋 趨 qū
hurry; tendency
189;156　12　(4)

趁 chèn
take advantage of; whilst
189;156　12　(2)

越 yuè
surmount; overstep; &
189;156　12　(2)

趟 tàng
(measure word)
-
189;156　15　(2)

超 chāo
exceed, ultra-, super-
189;156　12　(2)

趣 qù
interest, liking delight
189;156　15　(

又

廷 tíng
(imperial or feudal) court
36;54　6　(-)

延 yán
prolong, extend; delay; send for
36;54　7　(2)

建 jiàn
build; establish; suggest
36;54　8　(1)

是

匙 chí shi
spoon
-
213;21　11　(3)

题 題 tí
topic, subject; inscribe
213;181　15　(1)

鬼

魁 kuí
head, chief; outstanding
216;194　13　(-)

魅 mèi
demon
-
216;194　15　(-)

鬼 guǐ
ghost; stealthy; sinister; &
216;194　9　(2)

处
處 chǔ chù
manage; deal
with; place; &
65;141 5 (1)

翅
chì
wing,
fin
183;124 10 (2)

爬
pá
crawl;
climb
116;87 8 (1)

毯
tǎn
blanket;
carpet, rug
112;82 12 (2)

勉
miǎn
strive;
encourage
28;19 9 (3)

翘
翹 qiào qiáo
lift up, raise;
bend upwards
183;124 12 (3)

彪
biāo
young tiger
(literary)
63;59 11 (-)

1	41
2	42
3	43
4	44
5	45
6	46
7	47
8	48
9	49
10	50
11	51
12	52
13	53
14	54
15	55
16	56
17	57
18	58
19	59
20	60
21	61
22	62
23	63
24	64
25	65
26	66
27	67
28	68
29	69
30	70
31	71
32	72
33	73
34	74
35	75
36	76
37	77
38	78
39	79
40	80

⎰少 ➔ 4

斗
*鬥 dòu dǒu
fight; dovetail;
dipper; &
82;68 4 (2)

头
頭 tóu tou
head; top; first,
chief; end; &
52;181 5 (1)

少
shǎo shào
few; lacking;
Stop!; young; &
79;42 4 (1)

以
yǐ
using; so as to;
according to; &
23;9 4 (1)

寸
cùn
very small;
inch
54;41 3 (2)

习
diāo
cunning
-
6;18 2 (4)

习
習 xí
practice; be
used to; habit
6;124 3 (1)

可
kě
approve; indeed;
can, may; &
58;30 5 (1)

司
sī
attend to;
department
6;30 5 (2)

飞
飛 fēi
to fly;
swiftly; &
7;183 3 (1)

勺
sháo
spoon,
ladle
26;20 3 (2)

匀
yún
evenly;
to spare
26;20 4 (3)

勾
gōu gòu
cancel; collude;
sketch; &
26;20 4 (3)

句
jù
sentence,
line of verse
26;30 5 (1)

旬
xún
10-day period;
decade (of life)
26;72 6 (3)

包
bāo
wrap; package;
hire; assure; &
26;20 5 (1)

匈
xiōng
('hun' sound)
-
26;20 6 (4)

与
與 yǔ yù yú
and; with; to;
help; give; &
2;134 3 (2)

马
馬 mǎ
horse
-
75;187 3 (1)

乌
烏 wū
crow;
black, dark
4;86 4 (4)

鸟
鳥 niǎo
bird
-
152;196 5 (2)

式
shì
formula; format,
style; ceremony
56;56 6 (2)

武
wǔ
military,
martial; brave
102;77 8 (2)

戒
jiè
on guard; warn;
quit (habit); &
101;62 7 (4)

或
huò
or; either;
perhaps
101;62 8 (1)

贰
貳 èr
two
-
56;154 9 (4)

戊
wù
5th;
HS
138;62 5 (-)

戌
xū
EB
-
138;62 6 (-)

咸
*鹹 xián
salty
-
138;30 9 (3)

成
chéng
to become;
succeed; &
138;62 6 (1)

威
wēi
strength; might;
coerce
138;38 9 (3)

戚
qī
relatives;
sorrow
138;62 11 (2)

哉
zāi
Alas!; Why?
(literary)
165;30 9 (-)

栽
zāi
to plant; insert;
impose; to fall
165;75 10 (3)

裁
cái
cut out; reduce;
to judge; &
165;145 12 (3)

载
載 zǎi zài
year; to record;
carry
165;159 10 (3)

截
jié
cut, sever;
intercept; up to
165;62 14 (2)

戴
dài
wear (hat etc.)
honor
165;62 17 (1)

同
tóng tòng
same, equal;
together, with
19;30 6 (1)

向
*嚮 xiàng
facing; towards;
direction; &
4;30 6 (1)

网
網 wǎng
net; catch with
a net; network
19;120 6 (2)

冈
岡 gāng
ridge
(of hill)
19;46 4 (4)

内
nèi
inside, inner;
one's wife
19;11 4 (1)

肉
ròu
meat, flesh;
pulp
19;130 6 (1)

尚
shàng
esteem,
respect; yet
79;42 8 (3)

周
*週 zhōu
circuit; week;
thoughtful; &
19;30 8 (1)

丹
dān
red,
cinnabar
19;3 4 (4)

舟
zhōu
boat
(literary)
182;137 6 (4)

为
為 wéi wèi
do, act, act as; become;
be equal to; for the sake of
1;86 4 (1)

贝
貝 bèi
sea shell
-
106;154 4 (4)

见
見 jiàn
see; meet, visit;
evident; opinion
107;147 4 (4)

尽
盡 儘 jìn jǐn
used up; entire;
utmost; &
117;108 6 (2)

冒
mào
emit; take risk;
bold; fraud
104;13 9 (1)

参
參 cān cēn shēn
join in; consult,
refer; ginseng
37;28 8 (1)

凡
fán
common,
ordinary; every
30;16 3 (2)

风
風 fēng
wind; scenery;
habits; news
121;182 4 (1)

凤
鳳 fèng
phoenix
-
30;196 4 (4)

凰
huáng
[phoenix]
-
30;16 11 (4)

爪
zhǎo zhuǎ
claw,
talon
116;87 4 (4)

瓜
guā
melon,
gourd
151;97 5 (2)

闪
閃 shǎn
flash; lightning;
dodge; sprain
46;169 5 (2)

闭
閉 bì
shut;
close
46;169 6 (2)

闲
閑 閒 xián
unused, idle;
leisure
46;169 7 (2)

闺
閨 guī
small door;
boudoir
46;169 9 (4)

闰
閏 rùn
leap (year)
-
46;169 7 (-)

闹
鬧 nào
noisy; to vent;
suffer from; &
46;191 8 (2)

问
問 wèn
ask; ask after;
interrogate
46;30 6 (1)

间
間 jiān jiàn
between; room;
to separate; &
46;169 7 (1)

闻
聞 wén
hear; smell;
news; fame
46;128 9 (1)

闯
闖 chuǎng
rush;
break through
46;169 6 (2)

闸
閘 zhá
brake;
sluice
46;169 8 (4)

阐
闡 chǎn
explain,
enlighten
46;169 11 (4)

闷
悶 mēn mèn
stuffy; sealed;
airtight; bored
46;61 7 (3)

阀
閥 fá
valve;
powerful person
46;169 9 (4)

阂
閡 hé
barrier;
cut off from
46;169 9 (3)

阅
閱 yuè
read; review;
to experience
46;169 10 (2)

阔
闊 kuò
wide, vast;
wealthy
46;169 12 (2)

阁
閣 gé
pavilion;
Excellency; &
46;169 9 (4)

门
門 mén
gate, door;
family; sect; &
46;169 3 (1)

1	41
2	42
3	43
4	44
5	45
6	46
7	47
8	48
9	49
10	50
11	51
12	52
13	53
14	54
15	55
16	56
17	57
18	58
19	59
20	60
21	61
22	62
23	63
24	64
25	65
26	66
27	67
28	68
29	69
30	70
31	71
32	72
33	73
34	74
35	75
36	76
37	77
38	78
39	79
40	80

凶 *兇 xiōng	画 畫 huà	函 hán	齿 齒 chǐ	凿 鑿 záo zuò
ominous; ferocious; &	picture; (of Ch char) stroke	letter, mail	tooth -	chisel; mortise; make a hole
38;17 4 (3)	38;102 8 (1)	38;17 8 (4)	206;211 8 (3)	140;167 12 (3)

鼎 dǐng	幽 yōu	凹 āo	凸 tū	义 義 yì	以 yǐ
cauldron; tripod, tripartite	secluded; quiet; gloomy; Hades	concave, hollow	protruding, raised; convex	justice; meaning; &	using; so as t according to;
141;206 12 (-)	60;52 9 (4)	227;17 5 (4)	227;17 5 (4)	25;123 3 (1)	23;9 4 (1)

区 區 qū ōu	巨 jù	臣 chén	匠 jiàng	医 醫 yī
area, district; classify	huge, gigantic	vassal; courtier, minister	craftsman -	doctor; heal; medical
15;23 4 (2)	15;48 4 (2)	164;131 6 (4)	15;22 6 (4)	15;164 7 (1)

匹 pǐ	匪 fěi	匣 xiá
equal to; a match for	bandit, robber	small box, casket
15;23 4 (2)	15;22 10 (4)	15;22 7 (-)

囚 qiú	四 sì	因 yīn	困 kùn	团 團 糰 tuán	围 圍 wéi
prisoner, imprison	four -	cause, reason; because of	surround; hard pressed; weary	group; unite; ball; dumpling	surround, enclose; arou
59;31 5 (-)	59;31 5 (1)	59;31 6 (1)	59;31 7 (1)	59;31 6 (1)	59;31 7 (1)

回 *迴 huí	国 國 guó	园 園 yuán	圆 圓 yuán	圈 quān juān juàn
return; reply; re-; times	nation; national; Chinese	garden, park	circle; tactful; yuan; justify; &	circle, ring; encircle, pen in
59;31 6 (1)	59;31 8 (1)	59;31 7 (1)	59;31 10 (1)	59;31 11 (2)

固 gù	图 圖 tú	囱 cōng	田 tián	曰 yuē
solid, sturdy, firm; strengthen	picture, map; plan; seek	[chimney] -	field, farmland	say (literary)
59;31 8 (2)	59;31 8 (1)	4;31 7 (3)	142;102 5 (2)	104;73 4 (4)

日 rì	目 mù	叉 chā chǎ chá	丹 dān	瓦 wǎ wà	母 mǔ
sun; day, daily; time	eye; item; catalog	fork; cross ('x' mark)	red, cinnabar	(roof) tile; earthenware	mother; female (animal)
103;72 4 (1)	141;109 5 (1)	35;29 3 (2)	19;3 4 (4)	98;98 4 (3)	2;80 5 (1)

衍	衔	街	衡	行
yǎn	銜 xián	jiē	héng	xíng háng
redundant; spread (literary)	hold (in mouth); rank, title	street	scales; weigh, measure	go; do, perform; capable; OK; for now; line; (business) firm
62;144 9 (4)	62;167 11 (4)	62;144 12 (1)	62;144 16 (3)	62;144 6 (1)
辨	辩	瓣	辫	
biàn	辯 biàn	bàn	辮 biàn	
differentiate, distinguish	dispute, debate	petal, segment, piece; valve	plait, braid, pigtail	
186;160 16 (4)	186;160 16 (3)	186;97 19 (3)	186;120 17 (4)	
班	斑			
bān	bān			
team; duty; scheduled	spots; stripes; speckled			
88;96 10 (1)	88;67 12 (4)			
承	鼎	掰		
chéng	dǐng	bāi		
undertake; indebted; &	cauldron; tripod, tripartite	break (with the fingers)		
5;64 8 (2)	141;206 12 (-)	111;64 12 (4)		

能	疑	毁	毅
néng	yí	huǐ	yì
able to; energy; capability	doubt	destroy; defame	firm, resolute
37;130 10 (1)	39;103 14 (2)	119;79 13 (3)	119;79 15 (3)
赫	兢	鼓	
hè	jīng	gǔ	
impressive	[conscientious]	drum; rouse; bellows; bulge	
190;155 14 (4)	12;10 14 (4)	224;207 13 (2)	
豁	舒	静	龄	聚
huō huò	shū	靜 jìng	齡 líng	jù
crack; forsake; open; exempt	stretch, unfold; leisurely	still, calm, quiet	age, years, duration	assemble, get together
199;150 17 (4)	23;135 12 (1)	202;174 14 (1)	206;211 13 (2)	163;128 14 (3)

1	41
2	42
3	43
4	44
5	45
6	46
7	47
8	48
9	49
10	50
11	51
12	52
13	53
14	54
15	55
16	56
17	57
18	58
19	59
20	60
21	61
22	62
23	63
24	64
25	65
26	66
27	67
28	68
29	69
30	70
31	71
32	72
33	73
34	74
35	75
36	76
37	77
38	78
39	79
40	80

卜
*薥 bǔ bo
divination;
foretell
16;25 2 (2)

上
shàng shang shǎng
above, on, up; ascend; go to;
previous; first; put in position; &
16;1 3 (1)

止
zhǐ
stop, halt;
until; limited to
102;77 4 (2)

土
tǔ
soil, ground;
local, native; &
49;32 3 (2)

士
shì
person; knight;
scholar; &
49;33 3 (2)

生
shēng
give birth; grow; life; livelihood;
raw, unripe, un-; student; &
4;100 5 (1)

十
shí
ten
-
12;24 2 (1)

牛
niú
cow, ox,
cattle
110;93 4 (1)

半
bàn
half, semi-;
partly
3;24 5 (1)

丰
*豐 fēng
abundant;
handsome
3;2 4 (1)

韦
韋 wéi
leather,
hide
91;178 4 (-)

书
書 shū
write; letter,
book, docum
3;73 4 (1)

巾
jīn
towel,
(piece of) cloth
57;50 3 (2)

山
shān
mountain
-
60;46 3 (1)

击
擊 jī
strike, hit,
attack
38;64 5 (2)

出
chū
exit; go out; to issue, produce,
vent; exceed; occur; expenditure
61;17 5 (1)

木
mù
tree, timber,
wood; numb; &
94;75 4 (2)

未
wèi
not yet,
not; EB
94;75 5 (2)

末
mò
tip, end; trivia;
dust, powder
94;75 5 (3)

朱
zhū
vermilion,
bright red
4;75 6 (3)

术
*術 shù zhú
art, technique,
skill; method
94;75 5 (1)

本
běn
root, base; this;
book, edition; &
94;75 5 (1)

米
mǐ
rice;
meter (length)
159;119 6 (1)

来
來 lái lai
come, arrive; do; bring;
future; during; approx.; &
94;9 7 (1)

虫
*蟲 chóng
insect;
worm
174;142 6 (2)

柬
jiǎn
card, note,
letter
192;75 9 (4)

束
shù
bind, tie;
bundle; restrain
192;75 7 (1)

串
chuàn
get mixed up;
gang up; &
3;2 7 (3)

中
zhōng zhòng
middle, mid-; among; Chinese;
in progress; fit for; hit, be hit by
105;2 4 (1)

申
shēn
explain, state;
EB; Shanghai
144;102 5 (3)

电
電 diàn
electric,
electricity
104;173 5 (1)

由
yóu
by; from; allow;
due to; obey; &
143;102 5 (2)

事
shì
affair, matter;
do; job; &
2;6 8 (1)

甫
fǔ
just now
(literary)
1;101 7 (-)

七 qī qí
seven
-
2;1 2 (1)

屯 tún
village; collect; station (troops)
227;45 4 (4)

长 長 cháng zhǎng
long; long-term; steadily; forte; grow; senior, chief; get, acquire
4;168 4 (1)

广 廣 guǎng
wide, broad; spread; many
44;53 3 (1)

才 *纔 cái
ability, talent; only, just
2;64 3 (1)

水 shuǐ
water; liquid; river, lake
125;85 4 (1)

求 qiú
beg, request; seek
1;85 7 (1)

隶 隸 lì
subordinate, servant, slave
124;171 8 (3)

肃 肅 sù
solemn; respectful
124;129 8 (2)

人 rén
person, people; others; &
23;9 2 (1)

入 rù
enter; income; conform
23;11 2 (2)

火 huǒ
fire
-
83;86 4 (1)

尤 yóu
especially; blame, fault
53;43 4 (1)

内 nèi
inside, inner; one's wife
19;11 4 (1)

肉 ròu
meat, flesh; pulp
19;130 6 (1)

大 dà dài
big; great; strong; fully; &
52;37 3 (1)

犬 quǎn
dog
-
96;94 4 (4)

太 tài
excessive, too, over-; utmost
52;37 4 (1)

夫 fū fú
husband; man
52;37 4 (1)

失 shī
lose; fail to; error; deviate
4;37 5 (2)

央 yāng
center; implore
52;37 5 (2)

丈 zhàng
(unit of length: 10 feet); &
2;1 3 (2)

史 shǐ
history
-
58;30 5 (1)

头 頭 tóu tou
head; top; first, chief; end; &
52;181 5 (1)

夹 夾 jiā jiá gā
squeeze; mix; pincers; clip; &
52;37 6 (2)

爽 shuǎng
clear; forthright; be well; deviate
52;89 11 (4)

夷 yí
safety; wipe out (literary)
52;37 6 (-)

专 專 zhuān
specialized; expert
11;41 4 (2)

车 車 chē jū
car, vehicle, machine
100;159 4 (1)

东 東 dōng
east; master, host
227;75 5 (1)

幺 yāo
one (on dice); when speaking)
76;52 3 (-)

乡 鄉 xiāng
country, rural; hometown
227;163 3 (2)

片 piàn piān
sheet, slice; fragment; film
114;91 4 (1)

九 jiǔ
nine; many
7;5 2 (1)

丸 wán
ball; pellet, pill
66;3 3 (3)

方 fāng
direction; place; square; &
85;70 4 (1)

力 lì
strength, force, power; strive
28;19 2 (1)

为 為 wéi wèi
do, act, act as; become; be equal to; for the sake of
1;86 4 (1)

女 nǚ
woman; female; daughter, girl
73;38 3 (1)

戈 gē
lance, spear, (an old weapon)
101;62 4 (4)

戊 wù
5th; HS
138;62 5 (-)

成 chéng
to become; succeed; &
138;62 6 (1)

农 農 nóng
agriculture; peasant
18;161 6 (1)

皮 pí
skin, leather; outer layer; &
153;107 5 (2)

1	41
2	42
3	43
4	44
5	45
6	46
7	47
8	48
9	49
10	50
11	51
12	52
13	53
14	54
15	55
16	56
17	57
18	58
19	59
20	60
21	61
22	62
23	63
24	64
25	65
26	66
27	67
28	68
29	69
30	70
31	71
32	72
33	73
34	74
35	75
36	76
37	77
38	78
39	79
40	80

■ □

□

一
yī yí yì
one; a; once;
each; whole; &
2;1 1 (1)

厂 廠 chǎng
factory,
depot
13;53 2 (1)

丁 dīng zhēng
4th; HS; man,
population
2;1 2 (3)

下 xià xia
below, down; descend; unload;
next; inferior; send; decide; &
16;1 3 (1)

不 bù bú
no, not, un-;
can't
95;1 4 (1)

平 píng
flat, even, level;
calm; average
2;51 5 (1)

于 *於 yú
in, at, to,
from, than
11;7 3 (2)

干 *乾 幹 gān gàn
dry; futile; adopt (child);
main part, trunk; do, work; fight
11;51 3 (1)

开 開 kāi kai
open; start;
operate; &
51;169 4 (1)

牙 yá
tooth;
ivory
99;92 4 (2)

无 無 wú
without; not;
nothing; &
53;86 4 (2)

天 tiān
sky, Heaven; God; day; season;
weather; nature, natural
90;37 4 (1)

工 gōng
to work, worker;
industry; skill
48;48 3 (1)

王 wáng
king
-
88;96 4 (2)

玉 yù
jade;
your (polite)
131;96 5 (2)

丐 gài
beg; beggar
(literary)
2;1 4 (-)

正 zhèng zhēng
correct, straight, upright, prope
exactly; main, chief; January; &
102;77 5 (1)

万 *萬 wàn mò
ten thousand;
many; utterly
2;1 3 (1)

歹 dǎi
bad,
evil
97;78 4 (4)

互 hù
mutual
-
2;7 4 (1)

五 wǔ
five
-
2;7 4 (1)

瓦 wǎ wà
(roof) tile;
earthenware
98;98 4 (3)

巫 wū
witch,
wizard
48;48 7 (4)

雨 yǔ
rain
-
204;173 8 (1)

而 ér
and; due to;
but; (from …) to
169;126 6 (1)

丙 bǐng
3rd;
HS
2;1 5 (3)

两 兩 liǎng
two, a couple;
both; a few; &
2;11 7 (1)

百 bǎi
a hundred;
numerous
150;106 6 (1)

面 *麵 麪 miàn
face; surface;
extent; flour; &
2;176 9 (1)

再 zài
again; further;
more; before; &
2;13 6 (1)

更 gèng gēng
even more;
to change
2;73 7 (1)

西 xī
west
-
166;146 6 (1)

酉 yǒu
EB
-
193;164 7 (-

耳 ěr
ear;
on each side
163;128 6 (2)

亚 亞 yà
inferior;
Asia
168;7 6 (3)

严 嚴 yán
tight;
strict, severe
168;30 7 (2)

■   冖

几	**又**	**叉**	**尸**	**尺**	**民**
*幾 jǐ jī	yòu	chā chǎ chá	屍 shī	chǐ	mín
a few, several; how many	again; further; and, but; &	fork; cross ('x' mark)	corpse -	ruler, foot (12 inches)	the people; folk, popular; civilian
30;16 2 (1)	35;29 2 (1)	35;29 3 (2)	67;44 3 (4)	117;44 4 (2)	227;83 5 (1)

己	**已**	**巳**	**巴**	
jǐ	yǐ	sì	bā	
self;	already; to end, cease	EB -	hope for; stick to; next to	
6th; HS				
72;49 3 (1)	72;49 3 (1)	72;49 3 (-)	227;49 4 (2)	

弓	**了**	**乙**	**飞**	**子**
gōng	*瞭 le liǎo liào	yǐ	飛 fēi	zǐ zi
(stringed) bow; arch, bend	(particle); finish; know; observe	2nd; HS	to fly; swiftly; &	child; son; egg, seed; person; thing; EB
71;57 3 (3)	5;6 2 (1)	7;5 1 (3)	7;183 3 (1)	74;39 3 (1)

刀	**刃**	**乃**	**及**	**卫**
dāo	rèn	nǎi	jí	衛 wèi
knife; razor; sword	blade; sword, knife; kill	be; then; your (literary)	attain; timely, on time; and	protect, defend, guard
27;18 2 (1)	27;18 3 (4)	4;4 2 (4)	4;29 3 (2)	32;144 3 (2)

口	**日**	**曰**	**丑**	**且**	**目**
kǒu	rì	yuē	*醜 chǒu	qiě	mù
mouth; opening; &	sun; day, daily; time	say (literary)	ugly; disgraceful; EB	as well as; for a while	eye; item; catalog
58;30 3 (1)	103;72 4 (1)	104;73 4 (4)	2;1 4 (3)	2;1 5 (1)	141;109 5 (1)

凸	**凹**	**田**	**甲**	**果**	**里**
tū	āo	tián	jiǎ	guǒ	*裹 裡 lǐ li
protruding, raised; convex	concave, hollow	field, farmland	1st; HS; shell, armor	fruit; result; sure enough; &	in, inside; mile, 1/2 km; &
227;17 5 (4)	227;17 5 (4)	142;102 5 (2)	104;102 5 (3)	94;75 8 (1)	195;166 7 (1)

月	**用**	**甩**	**毋**
yuè	yòng	shuǎi	wú
moon; month	use, using; (don't) need; &	cast off; toss; swing to and fro	Don't! (literary)
118;74 4 (1)	19;101 5 (1)	19;101 5 (2)	2;80 4 (-)

丹	**母**	**册**
dān	mǔ	*冊 cè
red, cinnabar	mother; female (animal)	copy, volume (books)
19;3 4 (4)	2;80 5 (1)	2;13 5 (2)

1	41
2	42
3	43
4	44
5	45
6	46
7	47
8	48
9	49
10	50
11	51
12	52
13	53
14	54
15	55
16	56
17	57
18	58
19	59
20	60
21	61
22	62
23	63
24	64
25	65
26	66
27	67
28	68
29	69
30	70
31	71
32	72
33	73
34	74
35	75
36	76
37	77
38	78
39	79
40	80

甘	甘	井	弗	曲	革
niàn	gān	jǐng	fú	qū qǔ	gé
twenty	sweet;	a well, pit;	not	a bend; bent;	leather, hide
-	willing	neat, orderly	(literary)	wrong; melody	change; exp
93;55 3 (-)	135;99 5 (3)	11;7 4 (2)	71;57 5 (-)	104;73 6 (3)	212;177 9

业	止	也	世	片	
業 yè	zhǐ	yě	shì	piàn piān	
business;	stop, halt;	also;	life; generation;	sheet, slice;	
already	until; limited to	still, even so	era; world	fragment; film	
140;75 5 (1)	102;77 4 (2)	5;5 3 (1)	2;1 5 (1)	114;91 4 (1)	

千	币	禾	手	毛	
qiān	幣 bì	hé	shǒu	máo	
thousand;	money	grain, cereal;	hand; by hand;	fur, hair, wool; scared; rough;	
numerous	-	rice	hold; person	gross (profit); 1/10 yuan; &	
12;24 3 (1)	57;50 4 (2)	149;115 5 (4)	111;64 4 (1)	112;82 4 (1)	

壬	乎	舌	升	我	
rén	hū	shé	*昇 shēng	wǒ	
9th;	(suffix;	tongue	rise, raise;	I, me, my,	
HS	particle)	-	promote; liter	we, our	
49;33 4 (-)	2;4 5 (2)	177;135 6 (2)	4;24 4 (2)	101;62 7 (1)	

斤	斥	丘	氏	乐	爪
jīn	chì	qiū	shì	樂 yuè lè	zhǎo zhuǎ
(unit of weight:	denounce;	mound,	family name;	music;	claw,
1/2 kilogram)	exclude	grave	surname; née	enjoy; happy	talon
115;69 4 (1)	115;69 5 (3)	4;1 5 (3)	122;83 4 (3)	4;75 5 (1)	116;87 4 (4

系	乖	乘	秉	垂	重
*係 繫 xì	guāi	chéng shèng	bǐng	chuí	chóng zhò
fasten; system;	obedient;	ride; multiply;	grasp; control	droop;	repeat; heav
department; &	quick-witted	make use of	(literary)	hang down	to stress; &
77;120 7 (1)	4;4 8 (3)	149;4 10 (2)	149;115 8 (4)	4;32 8 (3)	4;166 9 (1)

■　　凵　　…

夕
xī
dusk, sunset,
evening
64;36　3　(4)

久
jiǔ
long time;
lasting
4;4　3　(1)

欠
qiàn
lacking; owe;
yawn; &
120;76　4　(2)

矢
shǐ
arrow;
vow
148;111　5　(-)

尔
爾 ěr
you; like that,
that (literary)
79;89　5　(3)

午
wǔ
noon;
EB
20;24　4　(1)

乍
zhà
suddenly;
at first; extend
20;4　5　(-)

年
nián
year; annual;
age; New Year
20;51　6　(1)

勿
wù
must not,
Don't!
26;20　4　(4)

匆
* 怱 cōng
hasty
-
26;20　5　(3)

争
爭 zhēng
compete (for),
argue (about)
27;87　6　(2)

丫
yā
fork (in tree),
bifurcation
24;2　3　(-)

○
líng
zero
-
227;0　1　(-)

1	41
2	42
3	43
4	44
5	45
6	46
7	47
8	48
9	49
10	50
11	51
12	52
13	53
14	54
15	55
16	56
17	57
18	58
19	59
20	60
21	61
22	62
23	63
24	64
25	65
26	66
27	67
28	68
29	69
30	70
31	71
32	72
33	73
34	74
35	75
36	76
37	77
38	78
39	79
40	80

▮ 、 卜

、

卜	小	尔	不	下
*蔔 bǔ bo	xiǎo	爾 ěr	bù bú	xià xia
divination; foretell	small; young; petty	you; like that; that (literary)	no, not, un-; can't	below, down; descend; unload next; inferior; send; decide; &
16;25 2 (2)	79;42 3 (1)	79;89 5 (3)	95;1 4 (1)	16;1 3 (1)
心	必	办	亦	玉
xīn	bì	辦 bàn	yì	yù
heart; core; feelings	necessarily; certainly	manage; set up; punish	also, too (literary)	jade; your (polite)
81;61 4 (1)	1;61 5 (1)	28;160 4 (1)	162;8 6 (4)	131;96 5 (2)
犬	尤	术	书	甫
quǎn	yóu	*術 shù zhú	書 shū	fǔ
dog	especially; blame, fault	art, technique, skill; method	write; letter, book, document	just now (literary)
96;94 4 (4)	53;43 4 (1)	94;75 5 (1)	3;73 4 (1)	1;101 7 (-)
戈	戊	成	我	求
gē	wù	chéng	wǒ	qiú
lance, spear, (an old weapon)	5th; HS	to become; succeed; &	I, me, my, we, our	beg, request; seek
101;62 4 (4)	138;62 5 (-)	138;62 6 (1)	101;62 7 (1)	1;85 7 (1)
发	泼	拨	拔	球
發 髮 fā fà	潑 pō	撥 bō	bá	qiú
emit; become; develop; hair; &	sprinkle; unreasonable	stir, poke; allocate; batch	root out; select; seize; &	ball, sphere, globe
35;105 5 (1)	40;85 8 (2)	55;64 8 (3)	55;64 8 (2)	88;96 11 (1)
孙	秘	泌	协	胁	苏
孫 sūn	*祕 mì bì	mi	協 xié	脅 xié	蘇 嘛 sū
grandchild	secret	secrete	together, jointly; assist	upper body, ribs; coerce	revive; ('su' sound)
74;39 6 (3)	149;115 10 (2)	149;115 10 (2) wait	40;85 8 (3)	12;24 6 (3)	118;130 8 (3)	50;140 7 (4)

代 →
戈 →
戋 →
少 →
尤 →
龙 →
人 →
伏 →
下 →
不 →
尔 →
甫 →

卜

外	扑	补	卦	朴
wài	撲 pū	補 bǔ	guà	*樸 pǔ pō pò piáo
outside; foreign; besides; &	rush at, attack; to flap, flutter	mend; use; fill, replace; nourish	divination	plain, simple
64;36 5 (1)	55;64 5 (2)	129;145 7 (2)	16;25 8 (-)	94;75 6 (2)
卧	处	赴		
臥 wò	處 chǔ chù	fù		
lie down; berth, sleeper	manage; deal with; place; &	go to; attend		
164;131 8 (3)	65;141 5 (1)	189;156 9 (4)		

火	业	亚	哑	碰	⬚比 → 42
huǒ	業 yè	亞 yà	啞 yǎ yā	pèng	⬚长 → 43
fire	business; already	inferior; Asia	dumb; hoarse; Oh!	bump; meet; try one's luck	⬚火 → 46
-	140;75 5 (1)	168;7 6 (3)	58;30 9 (4)	136;112 13 (1)	⬚平 → 47
83;86 4 (1)					

水	冰	承	火	求	飞
shuǐ	*冰 bīng	chéng	huǒ	qiú	飛 fēi
water; liquid; river, lake	ice	undertake; indebted; &	fire	beg, request; seek	to fly; swiftly; &
125;85 4 (1)	8;15 6 (2)	5;64 8 (2)	83;86 4 (1)	1;85 7 (1)	7;183 3 (1)

八	扒	叭	趴		
bā	bā pá	bā	pā		
eight	cling; to dig up, rake; to stew; &	'bang' sound	bend over; lie prone		
-	55;64 5 (3)	58;30 5 (3)	196;157 9 (3)		
24;12 2 (1)					

引	川	训	圳	渊	
yǐn	chuān	訓 xùn	zhèn	淵 yuān	
to guide, lead; lure; cite; &	river; a plain	teach, instruct; model, example	irrigation ditch; [Shenzhen]	deep; profound	
71;57 4 (2)	4;47 3 (4)	10;149 5 (2)	49;32 6 (-)	40;85 11 (-)	

州	洲	酬	叫	纠	
zhōu	zhōu	chóu	*叫 jiào	糾 jiū	
state, prefecture	continent; shoals, islet	reward; fulfil; entertain friends	cry, call; tell; be called	entangle; rectify	
1;47 6 (4)	40;85 9 (4)	193;164 13 (3)	58;30 5 (1)	77;120 5 (2)	

形	杉	衫	彤	彩	彭
xíng	shān shā	shān	tóng	cǎi	péng
appearance, shape, form; &	China fir tree	shirt, vest	red (literary)	color; variety; acclaim; prize	(surname)
63;59 7 (2)	94;75 7 (-)	129;145 8 (2)	63;59 7 (-)	63;59 11 (1)	-
					63;59 12 (4)

彰	影	澎	膨	彬	彪
zhāng	yǐng	pēng péng	péng	bīn	biāo
apparent, evident	shadow; image, photo, movie	splash; sound of waves	[inflate, expand; swollen]	[urbane, refined]	young tiger (literary)
63;59 14 (4)	63;59 15 (1)	40;85 15 (-)	118;130 16 (3)	94;59 11 (-)	63;59 11 (-)

非	诽	啡	徘	排
fēi	誹 fēi	fēi	pái	pái pǎi
not, no, non-; wrong; evil	slander	('fi' sound); [coffee]	[hesitate, waver, linger]	line up; row, line; platoon; rehearse; raft; eject; push; pie
205;175 8 (1)	10;149 10 (4)	58;30 11 (1)	62;60 11 (4)	55;64 11 (1)

1	41
2	42
3	43
4	44
5	45
6	46
7	47
8	48
9	49
10	50
11	51
12	52
13	53
14	54
15	55
16	56
17	57
18	58
19	59
20	60
21	61
22	62
23	63
24	64
25	65
26	66
27	67
28	68
29	69
30	70
31	71
32	72
33	73
34	74
35	75
36	76
37	77
38	78
39	79
40	80

刂

刊 kān	刑 xíng	列 liè	利 lì	判 pàn	划 *劃 huà hu
print; publication	punishment; torture	arrange, line up; rank, file; list; &	profit, benefit; sharp	distinguish; to judge; &	delimit; assig scratch; &
17;18 5 (3)	17;18 6 (4)	97;18 6 (2)	149;18 7 (1)	17;18 7 (2)	101;18 6 (1

刺 cì	制 *製 zhì	则 則 zé	删 *刪 shān	剩 shèng	
thorn; prick; assassinate; &	make; draw up; control; system	rules; norm, model; then; &	delete, omit	surplus, residue	
17;18 8 (2)	17;18 8 (2)	106;18 6 (2)	17;18 7 (3)	17;18 12 (1)	

俐 lì	例 lì	侧 側 cè	测 測 cè	倒 dǎo dào	
[clever]	example; rules; precedent	side; to lean, incline	to measure; predict, infer	topple, collapse; exchange; pour; invert; go back; &	
21;9 9 (4)	21;9 8 (1)	21;9 8 (3)	40;85 9 (2)	21;9 10 (1)	

捌 bā	喇 lǎ lá lā	咧 liě liē	剩 shèng		
eight	trumpet, horn	[grin; careless]	surplus, residue		
55;64 10 (4)	58;30 12 (3)	58;30 9 (-)	17;18 12 (1)		

刘 劉 liú	剖 pōu	刻 kè	割 gē	剂 劑 jì	
(surname)	cut open; analyze	quarter (hour); engrave; &	cut, sever	prescription, dose	
84;18 6 (3)	17;18 10 (3)	17;18 8 (1)	17;18 12 (2)	160;18 8 (4)	

剃 tì	削 xiāo xuē	刹 shā chà	剑 劍 jiàn	创 創 chuàng chuāng	
shave	to peel, pare, whittle, sharpen	brake, stop; temple	sword	do for first time; wound	
17;18 9 (4)	17;18 9 (3)	17;18 8 (4)	17;18 9 (4)	17;18 6 (2)	

到 dào	副 fù	别 別 bié biè	剥 剝 bāo bō	刮 guā	剩 shèng
arrive; up to, until; thoughtful	deputy, vice-; to fit, match up	other; Don't!, to leave; &	peel off	scrape; extort; to blow; &	surplus, residue
171;18 8 (1)	17;18 11 (2)	17;18 7 (1)	17;18 10 (3)	177;18 8 (1)	17;18 12 (1

剧 劇 jù	刷 shuà shuā	刚 剛 gāng	则 則 zé	刨 *鉋 bào páo	
play, drama; acute, severe	brush	firm, solid; just, barely; just now	rules; norm, model; then; &	(carpenter's) plane; dig	
17;18 10 (2)	17;18 8 (2)	17;18 6 (1)	106;18 6 (2)	17;18 7 (4)	

亿	**忆**			
億 yì	憶 yì			
a hundred million	recollect -			
21;9 3 (1)	41;61 4 (2)			

儿	**礼**	**孔**	**轧**	**扎**
兒 ér	禮 lǐ	kǒng	軋 yà zhá gá	* 紮紥 zhā zhá zā
child, youth; son; ('r' suffix)	ceremony; etiquette; gift	hole, aperture	grind, crush; squeeze out	prick, stab; encamp; tie up
29;10 2 (1)	87;113 5 (1)	74;39 4 (2)	100;159 5 (4)	55;64 4 (2)

乱	**吼**	**乳**	**无**	**抚**	尤 → 45
亂 luàn	hǒu	rǔ	無 wú	撫 fǔ	尤 → 45
confused; riot; random; &	roar, bellow	breast; milk; give birth to; &	without; not; nothing; &	pacify; caress; nurture	
177;5 7 (1)	58;30 7 (3)	116;5 8 (4)	53;86 4 (2)	55;64 7 (4)	

北	**比**	**此**	**批**	**乖**	**乘**
běi	bǐ	cǐ	pī	guāi	chéng shèng
north -	compare; than; to gesture; &	this -	slap; criticize; batch	obedient; quick-witted	ride; multiply; make use of
39;21 5 (1)	123;81 4 (1)	102;77 6 (2)	55;64 7 (1)	4;4 8 (3)	149;4 10 (2)

死	**尼**	**匙**	**能**
sǐ	ní	chí shi	néng
die; death; rigid	Buddhist nun; ('ni' sound)	spoon -	able to; energy; capability
97;78 6 (1)	67;44 5 (4)	213;21 11 (3)	37;130 10 (1)

化	**讹**	**靴**	**龙**	龙 → 45
huà huā	訛 é	xuē	龍 lóng	
alter; -ise, -ify; melt; spend; &	error; extort; blackmail	boot -	dragon; imperial	
21;21 4 (1)	10;149 6 (4)	212;177 13 (4)	137;212 5 (2)	

兆	**挑**	**桃**	**跳**	**姚**	**飞**
zhào	tiāo tiǎo	táo	tiào	yáo	飛 fēi
omen; portend; million, mega-	choose; carry; poke; stir up	peach -	jump, leap; omit; throb	(surname) -	to fly; swiftly; &
29;10 6 (4)	55;64 9 (2)	94;75 10 (3)	196;157 13 (1)	73;38 9 (-)	7;183 3 (1)

吨	**纯**	**钝**
噸 dūn	純 chún	鈍 dùn
ton -	pure, simple; skilful	blunt; dull, stupid
58;30 7 (2)	77;120 7 (3)	147;167 9 (-)

1 41
2 **42**
3 43
4 44
5 45
6 46
7 47
8 48
9 49
10 50
11 51
12 52
13 53
14 54
15 55
16 56
17 57
18 58
19 59
20 60
21 61
22 62
23 63
24 64
25 65
26 66
27 67
28 68
29 69
30 70
31 71
32 72
33 73
34 74
35 75
36 76
37 77
38 78
39 79
40 80

十　寸　才　斗　半　羊

汁 zhī juice - 40;85 5 (4)	**计** 計 jì compute; plan; meter, gauge 10;149 4 (1)	**什** *甚 shén shí [what?]; sundry; ten 21;9 4 (1)	**叶** *葉 yè leaf; period, epoch 58;30 5 (2)	**针** 針 zhēn needle; stitch 147;167 7 (2)

寸

讨 討 tǎo discuss; incur; demand; & 10;149 5 (1)	**付** fù pay, hand over 21;9 5 (2)	**村** cūn village - 94;75 7 (1)	**衬** 襯 chèn lining; serve as contrast 129;145 8 (2)	**对** 對 duì correct, yes; regarding; versus to face; towards; deal with; & 35;41 5 (1)
肘 zhǒu elbow - 118;130 7 (-)	**射** shè shoot (gun); radiate; allude 200;41 10 (2)	**时** 時 shí time; hour; season; opportunity; present, current; now and then 103;72 7 (1)		
耐 nài endure, bear 169;126 9 (2)	**封** fēng seal up; bestow 54;41 9 (1)	**咐** fu [instruct; exhort] 58;30 8 (2)	**附** fù append; agree; near to 33;170 7 (1)	**谢** 謝 xiè thanks; politely decline; wither 10;149 12 (1)　**树** 樹 shù tree; to plant set up; uphold 94;75 9 (1)

才

材 cái materials; timber; ability 94;75 7 (2)	**财** 財 cái wealth, property 106;154 7 (3)

斗

料 liào raw materials; grain; expect 159;68 10 (2)	**科** kē area of study; section; branch 149;115 9 (1)	**斜** xié slanting, oblique 82;68 11 (2)	**抖** dǒu tremble, shake; rouse 55;64 7 (2)	**魁** kuí head, chief; outstanding 216;194 13 (-)

半

畔 pàn side, border, (river) bank 142;102 10 (3)	**伴** bàn partner; accompany 21;9 7 (3)	**拌** bàn mix - 55;64 8 (4)	**衅** 釁 xìn quarrel - 181;164 11 (4)	**胖** pàng pán fat, plump; contented 118;130 9 (2)

羊

详 詳 xiáng detailed; fully known 10;149 8 (2)	**群** qún crowd, group, herd 157;123 13 (2)	**鲜** 鮮 xiān xiǎn fresh; colorful; tasty; seafood 210;195 14 (2)	**洋** yáng ocean; foreign; Western; vast 40;85 9 (2)	**样** 樣 yàng sample; shape; appearance; & 94;75 10 (1)　**祥** xiáng good luck, auspicious 87;113 10 (2)

长 弋 戈 戋

胀 脹 zhàng	张 張 zhāng	帐 帳 賬 zhàng	账 賬 zhàng	涨 漲 zhǎng zhàng
expand, swell; bloated	open; expand; display; look	canopy, curtain; accounts	accounts, credit	rise, go up; swell
118;130 8 (3)	71;57 7 (1)	57;50 7 (3)	106;154 8 (-)	40;85 10 (2)

代 dài	试 試 shì	赋 賦 fù	腻 膩 nì
substitute for; era, generation	try, attempt; trial, test	bestow; compose poem	greasy; tired of; dirt; meticulous
21;9 5 (1)	10;149 8 (1)	106;154 12 (-)	118;130 13 (-)

伐 fá	找 zhǎo	戏 戲 xì	战 戰 zhàn
cut down (tree); attack	seek; call on; give change	to play; make fun of; a show	war, battle; tremble
21;9 6 (4)	55;64 7 (1)	35;62 6 (2)	101;62 9 (2)

戊 wù	戌 xū	成 chéng
5th; HS	EB -	to become; succeed; &
138;62 5 (-)	138;62 6 (-)	138;62 6 (1)

诫 誡 jiè	械 xiè	绒 絨 róng	贼 賊 zéi	诚 誠 chéng	城 chéng
warn, admonish	tool, weapon, instrument	soft cloth, velvet, flannel	thief; traitor; furtive; cunning	sincere -	(city) wall; city
10;149 9 (4)	94;75 11 (2)	77;120 9 (4)	106;154 10 (4)	10;149 8 (2)	49;32 9 (1)

域 yù	减 *減 jiǎn	喊 hǎn	饿 餓 è	哦 ó ò é	蛾 é
region, territory	subtract, deduct, reduce	shout, cry, call	hunger, starve	(exclamation: What?, Oh!)	moth -
49;32 11 (3)	8;15 11 (2)	58;30 12 (1)	68;184 10 (3)	58;30 10 (3)	174;142 13 (4)

浅 淺 qiǎn	栈 棧 zhàn	钱 錢 qián	线 綫 線 xiàn	残 殘 cán
shallow; simple; light (color); &	storehouse; stable; inn	money, cash, coin	thread; route; line; brink; clue	incomplete; injure; savage
40;85 8 (1)	94;75 9 (-)	147;167 10 (1)	77;120 8 (2)	97;78 9 (3)

践 踐 jiàn	贱 賤 jiàn	溅 濺 jiàn
trample; carry out	cheap; lowly; my (humble)	splash -
196;157 12 (1)	106;154 9 (3)	40;85 12 (3)

1 41
2 42
3 **43**
4 44
5 45
6 46
7 47
8 48
9 49
10 50
11 51
12 52
13 53
14 54
15 55
16 56
17 57
18 58
19 59
20 60
21 61
22 62
23 63
24 64
25 65
26 66
27 67
28 68
29 69
30 70
31 71
32 72
33 73
34 74
35 75
36 76
37 77
38 78
39 79
40 80

止

址 zhǐ
site, location
49;32 7 (2)

扯 chě
pull, to tear; chat
55;64 7 (3)

耻 *耻 chǐ
shame, disgrace
163;128 10 (4)

让 讓 ràng
cede, allow; invite; &
10;149 5 (1)

土

灶 zào
kitchen; oven, stove
83;86 7 (4)

杜 dù
prevent, shut out
94;75 7 (4)

社 shè
society; agency; &
87;113 7 (1)

牡 mǔ
male (animal)
110;93 7 (-)

吐 tǔ tù
spit; vent; vomit; disgorge
58;30 6 (2)

肚 dù dǔ
belly, abdomen; tripe
118;130 7

士

仕 shì
an official
-
21;9 5 (-)

壮 壯 zhuàng
strong, robust; boost; grand
42;33 6 (3)

生

性 xìng
quality, nature; sex
41;61 8 (2)

姓 xìng
surname, family name
73;38 8 (1)

胜 勝 shèng
victory; superb; surpass; &
118;19 9 (1)

主

注 *註 zhù
pour; pay heed; take notes; &
40;85 8 (1)

住 zhù
live, reside; stay; cease
21;9 7 (1)

往 wàng wǎng
towards; go; previous
62;60 8 (1)

拄 zhǔ
lean on (walking stick)
55;64 8 (4)

柱 zhù
pillar, column
94;75 9 (3)

驻 駐 zhù
stay; halt; be stationed
75;187 8 (3)

立

泣 qì
weep; tears
40;85 8 (4)

啦 la lā
(particle)
-
58;30 11 (1)

位 wèi
place, seat, throne
21;9 7 (1)

垃 lā
[garbage]
-
49;32 8 (2)

拉 lā lá lǎ
pull; lengthen; cut; chat; &
55;64 8 (1)

粒 lì
grain, granule
159;119 11

义

议 議 yì
opinion; discuss
10;149 5 (2)

仪 儀 yí
apparatus; gift; rite; appearance
21;9 5 (2)

蚁 蟻 yǐ
ant
-
174;142 9 (4)

坟 墳 fén grave, tomb 49;32　7　(3)	**纹** 紋 wén wrinkles; grain (of wood) 77;120　7　(3)	**蚊** wén mosquito - 174;142　10　(3)			
坑 kēng hole, pit; tunnel; entrap 49;32　7　(3)	**抗** kàng resist, defy, anti- 55;64　7　(2)	**杭** háng Hangzhou - 94;75　8　(-)	**炕** kàng to dry; kang, heated bricks 83;86　8　(4)	**航** háng boat, ship; to sail, fly 182;137　10　(2)	**吭** háng kēng throat; make a sound 58;30　7　(-)
访 訪 fǎng visit; inquire, search for 10;149　6　(1)	**坊** fáng fāng workshop, mill; lane, alley 49;32　7　(4)	**彷** páng [hesitate, waver] 62;60　7　(-)	**仿** 倣 fǎng imitate; resemble 21;9　6　(2)	**伤** 傷 shāng wound; harm, hurt; get sick of 21;9　6　(2)	
纺 紡 fǎng spin (cotton); reel 77;120　7　(2)	**防** fáng dyke; defend; guard against 33;170　6　(2)	**肪** fáng [animal fat] - 118;130　8　(4)	**妨** fáng fāng hinder, impede; harm 73;38　7　(3)		
扩 擴 kuò expand, extend 55;64　6　(2)	**矿** 礦 kuàng ore, mine 136;112　8　(2)	**旷** 曠 kuàng spacious; carefree; & 103;72　7　(4)			
沪 滬 hù Shanghai - 40;85　7　(4)	**护** 護 hù protect, guard 55;149　7　(2)	**妒** dù jealous 73;38　7　(4)	**驴** 驢 lǘ donkey 75;187　7　(3)		
沙 shā sand; granules; hoarse 40;85　7　(2)	**炒** chǎo fry, stir-fry; heat up 83;86　8　(3)	**砂** shā sand, grit 136;112　9　(4)	**妙** miào wonderful; subtle 73;38　7　(2)	**抄** chāo copy; shortcut; confiscate; & 55;64　7　(2)	**吵** chǎo chāo quarrel, make noise, disturb 58;30　7　(2)
纱 紗 shā yarn, gauze 77;120　7　(3)	**钞** 鈔 chāo banknote, paper money 147;167　9　(3)	**秒** miǎo second (of time, arc) 149;115　9　(2)	**渺** miǎo vast (lake, sea); hazy; negligible 40;85　12　(4)		

1	41
2	42
3	43
4	**44**
5	45
6	46
7	47
8	48
9	49
10	50
11	51
12	52
13	53
14	54
15	55
16	56
17	57
18	58
19	59
20	60
21	61
22	62
23	63
24	64
25	65
26	66
27	67
28	68
29	69
30	70
31	71
32	72
33	73
34	74
35	75
36	76
37	77
38	78
39	79
40	80

尤

优
優 yōu
excellent
-
21;9 6 (2)

扰
擾 rǎo
harass, disturb;
trouble
55;64 7 (2)

犹
猶 yóu
still,
yet
69;94 7 (3)

就
jiù
right away; only, just; even if;
then; precisely; concerning; &
9;43 12 (1)

龙

咙
嚨 lóng
[throat]
-
58;30 8 (3)

拢
攏 lǒng
approach; sum;
tie up; comb
55;64 8 (3)

珑
瓏 lóng
[exquisite, deft]
-
88;96 9 (4)

尢

沈
shěn
(surname)
-
40;85 7 (3)

枕
zhěn
pillow;
block
94;75 8 (3)

耽
dān
delay;
indulge in
163;128 10 (3)

也

他
tā
he, him;
other, another
21;9 5 (1)

池
chí
pond;
sunken area
40;85 6 (2)

地
dì de
earth, soil;
place; &
49;32 6 (1)

她
tā
she, her
-
73;38 6 (1)

驰
馳 chí
gallop, go fast;
far and wide
75;187 6 (4)

沐　休　林　淋　琳

mù	xiū	lín	lín lìn	lín
wash (hair),	to stop; to rest;	forest, grove;	drenched;	jade; valuables
[bathe]	Don't!	group	filter	(literary)
40;85 7 (-)	21;9 6 (1)	94;75 8 (2)	40;85 11 (3)	88;96 12 (-)

味　昧　妹　魅

wèi	mèi	mèi	mèi
taste; smell;	conceal;	younger	demon
interest	ignorant of	sister	-
58;30 8 (2)	103;72 9 (4)	73;38 8 (1)	216;194 15 (-)

沫　抹　袜

mò	mā mǒ mò	襪 wà
foam	to plaster; wipe;	socks,
-	erase; to skirt	stockings
40;85 8 (4)	55;64 8 (3)	129;145 10 (1)

株　珠　殊　蛛

zhū	zhū	shū	zhū
tree trunk;	pearl, bead,	different;	spider
a plant	(water) drop	special; very	-
94;75 10 (2)	88;96 10 (2)	97;78 10 (2)	174;142 12 (4)

冻　栋　陈　阵

凍 dòng	棟 dòng	陳 chén	陣 zhèn
freeze	supporting	exhibit, explain;	formation,
-	beam, ridgepole	old, stale	array; period
8;15 7 (2)	94;75 9 (4)	33;170 7 (3)	33;170 6 (2)

伟　纬　韩

偉 wěi	緯 wěi	韓 hán
great	latitude,	(surname)
-	weft	
21;9 6 (1)	77;120 7 (-)	203;178 12 (-)

津　律　肆

jīn	lǜ	sì
ferry; moist;	law,	reckless;
sweat; saliva	rule	unbridled; four
40;85 9 (4)	62;60 9 (2)	124;129 13 (4)

1	41
2	42
3	43
4	44
5	**45**
6	46
7	47
8	48
9	49
10	50
11	51
12	52
13	53
14	54
15	55
16	56
17	57
18	58
19	59
20	60
21	61
22	62
23	63
24	64
25	65
26	66
27	67
28	68
29	69
30	70
31	71
32	72
33	73
34	74
35	75
36	76
37	77
38	78
39	79
40	80

人 人 火 犬 丈 失 夹

人

认 認 rèn
recognize, admit; adopt
10;149 4 (1)

从 從 cóng cōng
from; to follow; secondary; &
23;60 4 (1)

队 隊 duì
squad, team
33;170 4 (2)

纵 縱 zòng
leap; vertical; indulge; release
77;120 7 (3)

巫 wū
witch; wizard
48;48 7 (4)

人

以 yǐ
using; so as to; according to; &
23;9 4 (1)

似 sì shì
similar; seem; than
21;9 6 (2)

拟 擬 nǐ
draft; intend; imitate
55;64 7 (4)

玖 jiǔ
nine
-
88;96 7 (4)

火

伙 *夥 huǒ
partner; group; provisions
21;9 6 (2)

狄 dí
(surname)
-
69;94 7 (-)

秋 qiū
fall, autumn; period, year
149;115 9 (1)

耿 gěng
honest, just; dedicated
163;128 10 (4)

揪 jiū
hold tight; seize; pull
55;64 12 (3)

锹 鍬 qiāo
spade, shovel
147;167 14

犬

伏 fú
prostrate; hide; confess; &
21;9 6 (4)

状 狀 zhuàng
form, condition; certificate; &
42;94 7 (2)

汰 tài
clean out; discard
40;85 7 (4)

驮 馱 tuó duò
carry (on back, of animals)
75;187 6 (3)

狱 獄 yù
prison, jail; lawsuit
69;94 9 (3)

袱 fú
[bundle of cloth]
129;145 11 (3)

默 mò
silent; tacit
223;203 16 (2)

献 獻 xiàn
offer, proffer; display
96;94 13 (2)

丈

仗 zhàng
hold (weapon); rely on; battle
21;9 5 (3)

杖 zhàng
cane, crutch, walking stick
94;75 7 (-)

失

秩 zhì
decade; in good order (literary)
149;115 10 (2)

铁 鐵 tiě
iron; weapons
147;167 10 (2)

跌 diē
fall, decline
196;157 12 (2)

夹

狭 狹 xiá
narrow
-
69;94 9 (4)

峡 峽 xiá
gorge, ravine
60;46 9 (3)

陕 陝 shǎn
Shaanxi
-
33;170 8 (3)

功 劝 幼 助 伪

功 gōng
merit; achieve;
effect; skill
48;19 5 (2)

劝 勸 quàn
advise; urge;
encourage
35;19 4 (2)

幼 yòu
young;
child
76;52 5 (3)

助 zhù
help,
assist
28;19 7 (1)

伪 偽僞 wěi
fake,
bogus
21;9 6 (4)

动 劲 励 锄

动 動 dòng
move, act; use;
alter; arouse
28;19 6 (1)

劲 勁 jìn jìng
strength, vigor;
mood; sturdy
28;19 7 (2)

励 勵 lì
encourage
-
28;19 7 (2)

锄 鋤 chú
hoe;
uproot
147;167 12 (4)

劫 勃 勘 勒 勤

劫 jié
disaster; rob,
raid (literary)
133;19 7 (4)

勃 bó
suddenly;
[thriving]
28;19 9 (3)

勘 kān
collate, edit;
survey
28;19 11 (4)

勒 lēi lè
tighten, rein in;
compel
212;19 11 (4)

勤 qín
diligent; duties;
frequently
28;19 13 (3)

仇 轨 执

仇 chóu
hatred;
enemy
21;9 4 (3)

轨 軌 guǐ
rail, track,
path, orbit
100;159 6 (3)

执 執 zhí
hold; manage; persist;
abide by; capture; receipt
55;32 6 (2)

决 诀 快 块 抉 缺

决 *決 jué
decide, resolve;
definitely; &
8;15 6 (1)

诀 訣 jué
farewell;
know-how
10;149 6 (-)

快 kuài
quick; soon;
sharp; happy; &
41;61 7 (1)

块 塊 kuài
clod, lump;
yuan (colloq)
49;32 7 (1)

抉 jué
pick, single out
(literary)
55;64 7 (-)

缺 quē
to lack; absent;
defect; vacancy
175;121 10 (2)

秧 殃 映

秧 yāng
seedling;
small fry; vine
149;115 10 (3)

殃 yāng
disaster; bring
misfortune
97;78 9 (4)

映 yìng
reflect;
shine
103;72 9 (2)

传

传 傳 chuán zhuàn
pass on,
transmit; &
21;9 6 (2)

砖 转

砖 磚 zhuān
brick
-
136;112 9 (3)

转 轉 zhuǎn zhuàn
revolve; change;
to forward; stroll
100;159 8 (2)

1	41
2	42
3	43
4	44
5	45
6	**46**
7	47
8	48
9	49
10	50
11	51
12	52
13	53
14	54
15	55
16	56
17	57
18	58
19	59
20	60
21	61
22	62
23	63
24	64
25	65
26	66
27	67
28	68
29	69
30	70
31	71
32	72
33	73
34	74
35	75
36	76
37	77
38	78
39	79
40	80

丁

灯	叮	钉	盯	打
燈 dēng	dīng	釘 dīng dìng	dīng	dǎ dá
lamp, light, lantern	sting; make sure	nail; sew on; press, urge	observe, gaze at	hit; make; tie up; send; fetch; buy; shoot; calculate; dozen; &
83;86 6 (1)	58;30 5 (4)	147;167 7 (3)	141;109 7 (3)	55;64 5 (1)

订	竹
訂 dìng	zhú
fix; agree on; book (seats); &	bamboo -
10;149 4 (2)	178;118 6 (2)

下

吓	虾
嚇 hè xià	蝦 xiā
intimidate; Pah! (annoyed)	shrimp -
58;30 6 (2)	174;142 9 (3)

不

环	怀	杯	坏	坯
環 huán	懷 huái	bēi	壞 huài	pī
ring, hoop; surround	bosom; cherish; yearn; pregnant	cup -	bad, evil; spoil, ruin	semi-finished product
88;96 8 (2)	41;61 7 (3)	94;75 8 (1)	49;32 7 (1)	49;32 8 (4)

干

汗	杆	秆	奸	肝	轩
hàn hán	桿 gān gǎn	稈 gǎn	*姦 jiān	gān	軒 xuān
sweat -	pole, shaft	stalk, stem	evil; traitor; crafty; illicit	liver -	balcony; ancient carria
40;85 6 (2)	94;75 7 (2)	149;115 8 (4)	73;38 6 (4)	118;130 7 (2)	100;159 7 (-

吁	许	赶
*籲 yù xū	許 xǔ	趕 gǎn
plead; groan; Oh!	allow; promise; praise; maybe	hurry; catch up; catch (bus); &
58;30 6 (4)	10;149 6 (1)	189;156 10 (2)

平

评	坪	秤	砰	呼
評 píng	píng	chèng	pēng	hū
comment on, appraise, judge	level ground	steelyard, weighing scales	bang, thump	exhale; cry out; 'whoo' sound
10;149 7 (1)	49;32 8 (-)	149;115 10 (4)	136;112 10 (-)	58;30 8 (2)

亍 丂 工 王

衍
yǎn
redundant;
spread (literary)
62;144 9 (4)

衔
衡 xián
hold (in mouth);
rank, title
62;167 11 (4)

街
jiē
street
-
62;144 12 (1)

衡
héng
scales; weigh,
measure
62;144 16 (3)

行
xíng háng
go; do, perform; capable; OK;
for now; line; (business) firm
62;144 6 (1)

朽
xiǔ
decayed,
rotten; senile
94;75 6 (3)

巧
qiǎo
skilful; cunning;
happily, luckily
48;48 5 (2)

江
jiāng
river
-
40;85 6 (1)

扛
káng gāng
to shoulder,
lift, carry
55;64 6 (2)

杠
gàng
bar, pole;
delete
94;75 7 (4)

红
红 hóng gōng
red;
bonus
77;120 6 (1)

缸
gāng
jar
-
175;121 9 (3)

虹
hóng
rainbow
-
174;142 9 (4)

汪
wāng
form puddles;
(dog's) bark
40;85 7 (4)

狂
kuáng
crazy; violent;
wild; arrogant
69;94 7 (3)

枉
wǎng
crooked; to
wrong; in vain
94;75 8 (3)

旺
wàng
flourishing;
brisk
103;72 8 (4)

班
bān
team; duty;
scheduled
88;96 10 (1)

斑
bān
spots; stripes;
speckled
88;67 12 (4)

1	41
2	42
3	43
4	44
5	45
6	46
7	**47**
8	48
9	49
10	50
11	51
12	52
13	53
14	54
15	55
16	56
17	57
18	58
19	59
20	60
21	61
22	62
23	63
24	64
25	65
26	66
27	67
28	68
29	69
30	70
31	71
32	72
33	73
34	74
35	75
36	76
37	77
38	78
39	79
40	80

瓦

瓶
píng
bottle,
vase, jug
98;98 10 (1)

甄
zhēn
examine, sift
(literary)
98;98 13 (-)

页

顷 頃 qǐng
just now; (unit
of land area)
39;181 8 (3)

顶 頂 dǐng
stand up to;
top; utmost; &
170;181 8 (2)

项 項 xiàng
item;
nape of neck
48;181 9 (2)

顿 頓 dùn
pause; arrange;
suddenly; &
170;181 10 (1)

侦 偵 zhēn
spy; scout;
detect
21;9 8 (4)

颗 顆 kē
(measure word)
-
170;181 14 (2)

颊 頰 jiá
cheeks
-
170;181 12 (4)

颇 頗 pō
quite,
rather
153;181 11 (4)

赖 賴 lài
rely; linger;
deny; shirk
192;154 13 (4)

锁 鎖 suǒ
lock,
padlock
147;167 12 (3)

烦 煩 fán
vexed; tired of;
bother, trouble
83;86 10 (1)

顺 順 shùn
obey; suitable;
along; in order
170;181 9 (2)

倾 傾 qīng
collapse; lean,
incline; pour out
21;9 10 (3)

懒 懶 lǎn
lazy;
sluggish
41;61 16 (2)

顾 顧 gù
look around;
look after; visit
170;181 10 (1)

硕 碩 shuò
huge
-
136;112 11 (-)

颐 頤 yí
cheeks; keep
fit (literary)
170;181 13 (-)

额 額 é
forehead;
specific amount
170;181 15 (3)

频 頻 pín
frequently
-
170;181 13 (4)

颠 顛 diān
summit; jolt;
topple, fall over
170;181 16 (4)

颜 顏 yán
face;
prestige; color
170;181 15 (1)

颖 穎 yǐng
tip, point; clever
(literary)
170;115 13 (4)

颤 顫 zhàn ch
shiver,
tremble
170;181 19

须 須 鬚 xū
have to, must;
beard
63;181 9 (1)

颂 頌 sòng
praise;
song, eulogy
170;181 10 (3)

颁 頒 bān
publish; to
issue, send out
170;181 10 (4)

领 領 lǐng
neck, collar; to lead, guide;
get (award); outline; &
170;181 11 (1)

预 預 yù
in advance
-
170;181 10 (1)

颈 頸 jǐng gěng
neck
-
170;181 11 (4)

顽 頑 wán
stupid; naughty;
stubborn
170;181 10 (3)

颓 頹 tuí
decadent;
ruined; dejected
170;181 13 (-)

题 題 tí
topic, subject;
inscribe
213;181 15 (1)

仟	**歼**	**纤**			
qiān	殲 jiān	纖 縴 xiān qiàn			
thousand	annihilate	tiny, slender;			
-	-	tow-rope			
21;9 5 (-)	97;78 7 (3)	77;120 6 (2)			

任	**妊**	**饪**			
rèn rén	*姙 rèn	飪 rèn			
appoint; allow;	conceive,	[cooking]			
despite; &	be pregnant	-			
21;9 6 (1)	73;38 7 (-)	68;184 7 (4)			

沃	**妖**	**袄**	**跃**		
wò	yāo	襖 ǎo	躍 yuè		
irrigate;	monster, devil;	coat,	leap,		
fertile	charming	jacket	jump		
40;85 7 (4)	73;38 7 (4)	129;145 9 (4)	196;157 11 (2)		

泛	**贬**	**眨**			
*氾 汎 fàn	貶 biǎn	zhǎ			
general, vague;	demote;	wink,			
to flood	censure	blink			
40;85 7 (2)	106;154 8 (4)	141;109 9 (4)			

讥	**机**	**饥**	**肌**	**凯**	**叽**
譏 jī	機 jī	饑 jī	jī	凱 kǎi	嘰 jī
ridicule	machine;	hunger,	muscle	triumphant	chirp,
-	opportunity; &	famine	-	-	twitter
10;149 4 (4)	94;75 6 (1)	68;184 5 (3)	118;130 6 (3)	30;16 8 (4)	58;30 5 (-)

巩	**帆**				
鞏 gǒng	fān				
consolidate;	a sail;				
stable, strong	canvas				
48;177 6 (2)	57;50 6 (4)				

观	**规**	**现**	**视**	**舰**	
觀 guān guàn	規 guī	現 xiàn	視 shì	艦 jiàn	
observe; view;	rule, law; plan;	present, now,	look at, regard,	warship	
Taoist temple	admonish	modern; appear	inspect		
35;147 6 (1)	107;147 8 (2)	88;96 8 (1)	87;147 8 (1)	182;137 10 (3)	

坝	**狈**				
壩 bà	狽 bèi				
dyke, dam,	[legendary wolf;				
embankment	dire straits]				
49;32 7 (3)	69;94 7 (4)				

1	41
2	42
3	43
4	44
5	45
6	46
7	47
8	**48**
9	49
10	50
11	51
12	52
13	53
14	54
15	55
16	56
17	57
18	58
19	59
20	60
21	61
22	62
23	63
24	64
25	65
26	66
27	67
28	68
29	69
30	70
31	71
32	72
33	73
34	74
35	75
36	76
37	77
38	78
39	79
40	80

丁

幻	刁	习	叼
huàn	diāo	習 xí	diāo
unreal; changeable	cunning	practice; be used to; habit	hold (in the mouth)
76;52 4 (3)	6;18 2 (4)	6;124 3 (1)	58;30 5 (4)

门	们	润	搁	悯	娴
門 mén	們 men	潤 rùn	擱 gē gé	憫 mǐn	嫻 嫺 xiá
gate, door; family; sect; &	(plural suffix) -	moist; lubricate; adorn; profit	put; put aside; endure	pity, sympathize	refined; ade (literary)
46;169 3 (1)	21;9 5 (1)	40;85 10 (3)	55;64 12 (2)	41;61 10 (-)	73;38 10 (-

刁

羽	翔	翻
yǔ	xiáng	fān
feather -	soar, hover	turn over; to cross; &
183;124 6 (2)	157;124 12 (4)	183;124 18 (1)

刀

切	叨	韧	初
qiē qiè	tāo dāo	韌 韌 rèn	chū
slice; eager to; accord with; &	obliged; [chatter]	tough; pliable yet strong	beginning; first, original
27;18 4 (1)	58;30 5 (4)	91;178 7 (4)	129;18 7 (1)

沏	彻	砌
qī	徹 chè	qì
infuse -	thorough; penetrate	lay (bricks); steps
40;85 7 (4)	62;60 7 (2)	136;112 9 (4)

可

河	何	柯	呵	阿	啊
hé	hé	kē	hē	ā ē	ā á ǎ a
river -	What?, Who? etc. (literary)	stalk; handle (literary)	scold; exhale; Oh!	('a' sound); pander to	(exclamation Eh?, Oh!, et
40;85 8 (1)	21;9 7 (1)	94;75 9 (-)	58;30 8 (3)	33;170 7 (2)	58;30 11 (1

司

词	伺	饲
詞 cí	sì cì	飼 sì
words, speech	to watch; await; serve	fodder; to rear (animals)
10;149 7 (1)	21;9 7 (3)	68;184 8 (3)

奶
*妳 嬭 nǎi
breast;
milk; suckle
73;38 5 (1)

仍
réng
still,
yet
21;9 4 (2)

扔
rēng
hurl;
throw away
55;64 5 (2)

吸
xī
inhale, absorb;
attract
58;30 6 (2)

圾
jī
[garbage]
-
49;32 6 (2)

级
級 jí
rank, grade;
step
77;120 6 (1)

极
極 jí
extreme,
pole, polar
94;75 7 (1)

汤
湯 tāng
hot water;
soup
40;85 6 (1)

扬
揚 yáng
raise; winnow;
publicize
55;64 6 (1)

杨
楊 yáng
poplar
-
94;75 7 (4)

场
場 chǎng cháng
site, spot,
field; &
49;32 6 (1)

肠
腸 cháng
intestines
-
118;130 7 (2)

畅
暢 chàng
smooth, fluent;
uninhibited
144;72 8 (3)

记
記 jì
recall; a mark;
note down
10;149 5 (1)

纪
紀 jì
discipline; age,
era; chronicle
77;120 6 (1)

配
pèi
mix; match up;
deserve; &
193;164 10 (2)

躬
gōng
to bend, bow;
in person
200;158 10 (4)

粥
zhōu
gruel,
porridge
71;119 12 (3)

弱
ruò
weak; inferior;
a bit less
71;57 10 (2)

冯
馮 féng
(surname)
-
8;187 5 (4)

玛
瑪 mǎ
[agate]
-
88;96 7 (-)

吗
嗎 ma má mǎ
(question
particle)
58;30 6 (1)

妈
媽 mā
mother, mum;
aunt (colloq)
73;38 6 (1)

码
碼 mǎ
numeral; wharf;
yard (3 ft)
136;112 8 (2)

蚂
螞 mǎ mà
[ant;
locust]
174;142 9 (4)

1	41
2	42
3	43
4	44
5	45
6	46
7	47
8	48
9	**49**
10	50
11	51
12	52
13	53
14	54
15	55
16	56
17	57
18	58
19	59
20	60
21	61
22	62
23	63
24	64
25	65
26	66
27	67
28	68
29	69
30	70
31	71
32	72
33	73
34	74
35	75
36	76
37	77
38	78
39	79
40	80

欠 尔 乍

欠

次	炊	软	饮	玖
cì	chuī	軟 ruǎn	飲 yǐn yìn	jiǔ
sequence; 2nd; next; inferior	to cook	soft, pliable; inferior; weak	drink	nine
8;76 6 (1)	-	-	-	-
	83;86 8 (4)	100;159 8 (2)	68;184 7 (3)	88;96 7 (4)

吹	欢	欣	砍	欺
chuī	歡 huān	xīn	kǎn	qī
blow, puff; brag; failure	pleased, happy, joyful	happy, joyful	chop, hack	deceive; bully
58;30 7 (1)	35;76 6 (1)	115;76 8 (3)	136;112 9 (2)	120;76 12 (2)

钦	欧	掀	嗽
欽 qīn	歐 ōu	xiān	sòu
respect; imperial	Europe; (surname)	lift (lid or cover)	cough -
147;76 9 (4)	120;76 8 (3)	55;64 11 (2)	58;30 14 (1)

欲	欸	款	歇	歌	歉
*慾 yù	·誒 ǎi ē é ě è	*欵 kuǎn	xiē	gē	qiàn
desire, wish; about to	(exclamation: Hey!, etc.)	funds; clause; sincere; &	stop work, take a rest	song; sing	apology; crop failure
199;76 11 (4)	120;149 11 (-)	120;76 12 (2)	120;76 13 (2)	120;76 14 (1)	120;76 14

尔

你	弥	称
*妳 nǐ	彌 瀰 mí	稱 chēng chèn
you, your	full; more; redeem	call, name; weigh; suitable
21;9 7 (1)	71;57 8 (4)	149;115 10 (2)

乍

诈	炸	咋	昨	作
詐 zhà	zhà zhá	zǎ zhā zhà	zuó	zuò zuō zuó
cheat, swindle; feign; bluff	explode; to bomb; deep-fry	Why?, How?; [boast]; bite	yesterday -	do, make, write; act as; preten regard as; get up (from bed)
10;149 7 (4)	83;86 9 (3)	58;30 8 (4)	103;72 9 (1)	21;9 7 (1)

的
de dí dì
(particle);
bull's eye
150;106 8 (1)

钓 釣 diào
to fish;
bait
147;167 8 (2)

约 約 yuē yāo
make appointment; agreement;
restrict; approx; brief; frugal; &
77;120 6 (2)

酌
zhuó
pour out (wine);
drink; consider
193;164 10 (4)

豹
bào
leopard,
panther
198;153 10 (-)

哟 喲 yo yō
(particle);
Oh!
58;30 9 (3)

均
jūn
equal, even,
balanced; all
49;32 7 (2)

韵 *韻 yùn
rhyme; melodic
tone; charming
211;180 13 (4)

胞
bāo
placenta;
siblings
118;130 9 (3)

炮
pào páo bāo
artillery; to dry;
quick-fry
83;86 9 (2)

抱
bào
cherish; adopt;
embrace; &
55;64 8 (1)

饱 飽 bǎo
full, satisfied,
eat one's fill
68;184 8 (1)

跑
pǎo
run; flee;
away
196;157 12 (1)

泡
pào pāo
bubble; soak;
dawdle; spongy
40;85 8 (3)

袍
páo
robe,
gown
129;145 10 (3)

鲍 鮑 bào
[abalone];
(surname)
210;195 13 (-)

仔
zǐ zī zǎi
young animal;
[careful]
21;9 5 (2)

籽
zī
seed
-
159;119 9 (4)

好
hǎo hào
good; be well; easy; so that;
very; to like, love; be prone to
73;38 6 (1)

野
yě
countryside;
wild; limit; &
195;166 11 (2)

舒
shū
stretch, unfold;
leisurely
23;135 12 (1)

1	41
2	42
3	43
4	44
5	45
6	46
7	47
8	48
9	49
10	**50**
11	51
12	52
13	53
14	54
15	55
16	56
17	57
18	58
19	59
20	60
21	61
22	62
23	63
24	64
25	65
26	66
27	67
28	68
29	69
30	70
31	71
32	72
33	73
34	74
35	75
36	76
37	77
38	78
39	79
40	80

▋　　攵

□攵

收 shōu — receive; collect up; cease; & — 113;66 6 (1)
改 gǎi — change, alter, rectify — 113;66 7 (1)
攻 gōng — attack; accuse; study — 48;66 7 (2)
枚 méi — (measure word) - — 94;75 8 (4)
牧 mù — to herd, tend (animals) — 110;93 8 (3)
拔 bá — root out; sele seize; & — 55;64 8 (2)

玫 méi — [rose] - — 88;96 8 (4)
政 zhèng — politics; administration — 113;66 9 (1)
救 jiù — rescue, aid — 113;66 11 (2)
败 bài — defeated; fail; defeat; spoil; & — 106;66 8 (2)

日攵

放 fàng — set free; expel; put; adjust; & — 85;66 8 (1)
效 xiào — effect; work for; imitate — 113;66 10 (2)
敦 dūn duì — sincere; ancient pot — 113;66 12 (-)
故 gù — former; to die; on purpose; & — 113;66 9 (1)
教 jiāo jiào — teach; tell; religion — 113;66 11 (1)
敷 fū — lay out; apply (lotion); suffic — 113;66 15 (

散 sàn sǎn — disperse; fall apart; dispel; & — 113;66 12 (1)
敬 jìng — respect; offer politely — 113;66 12 (2)
敞 chǎng — spacious; open; uncovered — 113;66 12 (4)
敝 bi — shabby; my, our (humble) — 113;66 11 (-)
数 shù shǔ shuò — number; a few; to count; often — 113;66 13 (1)

致 zhì — send; result in; fine, delicate; & — 171;133 10 (2)
敢 gǎn — bold; dare; be sure — 113;66 11 (1)
败 bài — defeated; fail; defeat; spoil; & — 106;154 8 (2)
敌 dí — foe; oppose — 177;66 10 (2)
敏 mǐn — nimble, agile, adroit — 113;66 11 (3)
敲 qiāo — knock, strike, hit — 218;66 14 (

□攵

做 zuò — make, do, write; be, become; & — 21;9 11 (1)
傲 ào — defy; proud, arrogant — 21;9 13 (2)
微 wēi — micro-, tiny; wane; subtle — 62;60 13 (2)
徽 huī — emblem - — 62;60 17 (4)

撤 chè — remove, withdraw — 55;64 15 (3)
撒 sā sǎ — let go; scatter; spill, drop — 55;64 15 (2)
撇 piē piě — abandon, cast off; fling; skim — 55;64 14 (4)

激 jī — violent; arouse; annoy; chill — 40;85 16 (2)
缴 jiǎo — pay, hand over; capture — 77;120 16 (4)
辙 zhé — (wheel) track, rut; rhyme — 100;159 16 (4)
嫩 nèn — tender; rookie; light (color) — 73;38 14 (3)
墩 dūn — mound; block — 49;32 15 (-)

又 反 皮 斤

汉	仅	权	叹	双	奴
漢 hàn	僅 jǐn	權 quán	嘆歎 tàn	雙 shuāng	nú
Chinese (lang); Han; man	merely; barely	rights; power, authority; &	sigh; admire; acclaim	two, twin, dual, bi-, double	slave
40;85 5 (1)	21;9 4 (2)	94;75 6 (3)	58;30 5 (3)	35;172 4 (1)	73;38 5 (3)

取	叔	叙	淑	椒	趣
qǔ	shū	*敘敍 xù	shū	jiāo	qù
take; obtain; choose; &	uncle; brother in law	chat; narrate; assess; &	virtuous (literary)	spice plant, pepper, chili	interest, liking, delight
163;29 8 (1)	35;29 8 (2)	35;29 9 (3)	40;85 11 (-)	94;75 12 (3)	189;156 15 (2)

扳	版	板	叛	饭	贩
bān	bǎn	*闆 bǎn	pàn	飯 fàn	販 fàn
pull; to turn	printing; edition, page	board, plank; hard, stiff	betray	food, meal, cooked rice	buy and sell; dealer
55;64 7 (4)	114;91 8 (2)	94;75 8 (1)	227;29 9 (4)	68;184 7 (1)	106;154 8 (4)

波	彼	坡	披	破	被
bō	bǐ	pō	pī	pò	bèi
a wave	that; the other; he, she	slope	drape over; unroll; split	destroy; split; broken; torn; &	quilt; (particle: passive verbs)
40;85 8 (3)	62;60 8 (3)	49;32 8 (2)	55;64 8 (2)	136;112 10 (1)	129;145 10 (1)

皱
皺 zhòu
crease, wrinkle
153;107 10 (3)

听	析	祈	斩	折
聽 tīng	xī	qí	斬 zhǎn	*摺 zhé zhē shé
listen; obey; allow	divide, dissect, discriminate	worship, pray, beg	chop, cut; behead	bend; fold; break; lose; rebate; be convinced; amount to; &
58;128 7 (1)	94;75 8 (2)	87;113 8 (-)	100;69 8 (4)	55;64 7 (2)

所	新	斯	断	拆	诉
suǒ	xīn	sī	斷 duàn	chāi cā	訴 sù
place; building; (particle)	new	this; thus; ('si' sound)	break off, snap; quit; decide	tear apart, dismantle	inform; accuse; complain
115;63 8 (1)	115;69 13 (1)	115;69 12 (3)	115;69 11 (2)	55;64 8 (2)	10;149 7 (1)

浙	渐	惭	撕	晰
zhè	漸 jiàn jiān	慚 cán	sī	xī
Zhejiang	gradually	ashamed	rip, tear	clear, distinct
40;85 10 (3)	40;85 11 (2)	41;61 11 (3)	55;64 15 (2)	103;72 12 (3)

1 41 / 2 42 / 3 43 / 4 44 / 5 45 / 6 46 / 7 47 / 8 48 / 9 49 / 10 50 / 11 51 / 12 52 / 13 53 / 14 54 / 15 55 / 16 56 / 17 57 / 18 58 / 19 59 / 20 60 / 21 61 / 22 62 / 23 63 / 24 64 / 25 65 / 26 66 / 27 67 / 28 68 / 29 69 / 30 70 / 31 71 / 32 72 / 33 73 / 34 74 / 35 75 / 36 76 / 37 77 / 38 78 / 39 79 / 40 80

口

加 jiā
plus; add, augment
28;19 5 (1)

如 rú
such as; as if, if; as...as...; &
73;38 6 (1)

扣 kòu
arrest; fasten; knot; deduct; &
55;64 6 (2)

和 hé hè huó huò
harmony; mild; with; sum; mix
149;30 8 (1)

知 zhī
know; inform; administer
148;111 8 (1)

咖 kā gā
('ka' sound); [coffee]
58;30 8 (1)

蜘 zhī
[spider]
-
174;142 14 (4)

中

仲 zhòng
go-between; middle (of 3)
21;9 6 (-)

冲 *沖 衝 chōng chòng
add water, rinse, flush; rush; clash; vigorous; &
8;15 6 (2)

肿 腫 zhǒng
swollen
-
118;130 8 (3)

钟 鐘 鍾 zhōng
bell, clock, o'clock; &
147;167 9 (1)

种 種 zhǒng zhòng
seed; species; type; cultivate
149;115 9 (1)

虫

浊 濁 zhuó
turbid, muddy; chaotic
40;85 9 (4)

蚀 蝕 shí
lose; erode; eclipse
68;142 9 (3)

独 獨 dú
single, alone, only
69;94 9 (2)

烛 燭 zhú
candle; watt
83;86 10 (3)

融 róng
melt, thaw; blend
174;142 16 (4)

触 觸 chù
touch
-
201;148 13

由

油 yóu
oil, grease, fat; to paint
40;85 8 (2)

抽 chōu
to extract; to smoke; whip; &
55;64 8 (1)

轴 軸 zhóu
axis, axle; spool, reel
100;159 9 (-)

袖 xiù
sleeve
-
129;145 10 (2)

铀 鈾 yóu
uranium
-
147;167 10 (4)

细 細 xì
tiny, slender; delicate; care
77;120 8 (1)

申

伸 shēn
stretch, extend
21;9 7 (2)

呻 shēn
[groan]
-
58;30 8 (4)

绅 紳 shēn
gentry
-
77;120 8 (4)

坤 kūn
feminine
-
49;32 8 (-)

神 shén
gods; magical; spirit; &
87;113 9 (1)

押 yā
detain; escort; mortgage; &
55;64 8 (3)

■◧ 巨 区 凶 西 彐

拒
jù
resist, reject,
refuse
55;64 7 (2)

柜
*櫃 guì jǔ
cupboard;
(shop) counter
94;75 8 (3)

矩
jǔ
rules; square,
rectangle
148;111 9 (3)

距
jù
distance
(from, apart)
196;157 11 (2)

呕
嘔 ǒu
vomit;
spit out
58;30 7 (4)

枢
樞 shū
axis, pivot,
hub
94;75 8 (-)

驱
驅 qū
drive (vehicle);
expel; run fast
75;187 7 (4)

躯
軀 qū
human
body
200;158 11 (-)

汹
洶 xiōng
[turbulent]
-
40;85 7 (4)

酗
xù
[get drunk]
-
193;164 11 (4)

洒
灑 sǎ
sprinkle;
spill
40;85 9 (2)

栖
棲 qī
stay;
perch (birds)
94;75 10 (-)

牺
犧 xī
animal sacrifice
(literary)
110;93 10 (2)

晒
曬 shài
to shine (sun);
sunbathe
103;72 10 (2)

酒
jiǔ
wine,
liquor
40;164 10 (1)

扫
掃 sǎo sào
clear away,
sweep
55;64 6 (2)

妇
婦 fù
woman;
wife
73;38 6 (2)

归
歸 guī
return;
converge; &
70;77 5 (3)

1	41
2	42
3	43
4	44
5	45
6	46
7	47
8	48
9	49
10	50
11	51
12	**52**
13	53
14	54
15	55
16	56
17	57
18	58
19	59
20	60
21	61
22	62
23	63
24	64
25	65
26	66
27	67
28	68
29	69
30	70
31	71
32	72
33	73
34	74
35	75
36	76
37	77
38	78
39	79
40	80

日

旧	阳
舊 jiù	陽 yáng
old, former, outdated; worn	yang, positive; sun; overt; &
103;134 5 (1)	33;170 6 (1)

白

伯	怕	泊	帕	拍	柏
bó bǎi	pà	bó pō	pà	pāi	bǎi bò bó
uncle; earl	afraid; worried; possibly	anchor, moor; lake, pool	handkerchief; turban	clap, beat time; bat, racquet; &	cypress, cedar
21;9 7 (2)	41;61 8 (1)	40;85 8 (4)	57;50 8 (-)	55;64 8 (1)	94;75 9 (3)

舶	啪
bó	pā
(sea-going) ship	'bang' sound
182;137 11 (4)	58;30 11 (-)

丑

扭	纽	钮	妞
niǔ	紐 niǔ	鈕 niǔ	niū
turn round; roll; wrench; grapple	handle, button, knob; fasten	knob, button; to tie, fasten	girl (colloq)
55;64 7 (2)	77;120 7 (4)	147;167 9 (4)	73;38 7 (-)

艮

艰	狠	恨	根	很	限
艱 jiān	hěn	hèn	gēn	hěn	xiàn
difficult	ruthless; resolute	hate; regret	root; basis; thoroughly	very	limit
-	-	-	-	-	-
35;138 8 (2)	69;94 9 (3)	41;61 9 (2)	94;75 10 (1)	62;60 9 (1)	33;170 8 (2)

银	跟	眼
銀 yín	gēn	yǎn
silver	heel; follow; with	eye; key point
-		
147;167 11 (1)	196;157 13 (1)	141;109 11 (1)

良

浪	狼	娘	粮	酿
làng	láng	孃 niáng	糧 liáng	釀 niàng niáng
wave, billow; dissolute	wolf	mother; aunt; young lady	grain, provisions	brew, ferment; lead to; wine
-	-			
40;85 10 (2)	69;94 10 (2)	73;38 10 (1)	159;119 13 (2)	193;164 14 (4)

沮	诅	姐	租	泪	相
jǔ	詛zǔ	jiě	zū	淚lèi	xiāng xiàng
dispirited; prevent	[to curse]	elder sister	rent, hire, lease	teardrop	mutual; looks; photo; &
40;85 8 (-)	10;149 7 (-)	73;38 8 (1)	149;115 10 (1)	40;85 8 (2)	94;109 9 (1)

祖	组	阻	粗
zǔ	組zǔ	zǔ	cū
ancestor; grandparent	organize; group	hinder, block, obstruct	thick, coarse, rough; careless
87;113 9 (1)	77;120 8 (1)	33;170 7 (3)	159;119 11 (2)

明	朋	阴
míng	péng	陰yīn
bright; clear; overt; next; &	friend	yin, negative; occult; shade; cloudy; moon; &
103;72 8 (1)	118;74 8 (1)	33;170 6 (1)

胡	钥	朝	朗	期
*鬍hú	鑰yuè yào	cháo zhāo	lǎng	qī jī
reckless; beard; &	key	facing; dynasty; morning; day; &	bright; loud and clear	expect; period; appointed time
118;130 9 (2)	147;167 9 (3)	203;74 12 (1)	118;74 10 (2)	118;74 12 (1)

溯	湖	瑚	蝴	糊
sù	hú	hú	hú	hú hū hù
go against flow; trace back	lake	[coral]	[butterfly]	paste, gum; plaster
40;85 13 (-)	40;85 12 (1)	88;96 13 (4)	174;142 15 (3)	159;119 15 (2)

潮	嘲	棚	绷
cháo	cháo	péng	繃bēng bèng běng
tide, upsurge; damp	to ridicule, mock	shed, shack; awning	stretch taut; rebound; crack
40;85 15 (3)	58;30 15 (4)	94;75 12 (3)	77;120 11 (4)

悄	消	俏	捎	梢	稍
qiāo qiǎo	xiāo	qiào	shāo shào	shāo	shāo
quiet; softly	vanish; dispel; leisurely	handsome; in demand	take, bring; &	tip (of twig; branch)	slightly
41;61 10 (2)	40;85 10 (1)	21;9 9 (3)	55;64 10 (4)	94;75 11 (4)	149;115 12 (2)

哨	销
shào	銷xiāo
sentry, guard; whistle; chirp	to fuse; sell; cancel; spend
58;30 10 (3)	147;167 12 (4)

1	41
2	42
3	43
4	44
5	45
6	46
7	47
8	48
9	49
10	50
11	51
12	52
13	**53**
14	54
15	55
16	56
17	57
18	58
19	59
20	60
21	61
22	62
23	63
24	64
25	65
26	66
27	67
28	68
29	69
30	70
31	71
32	72
33	73
34	74
35	75
36	76
37	77
38	78
39	79
40	80

卩 阝

卩

卯	印	即	却	卸	卵
mǎo	yìn	jí	*卻 què	xiè	luǎn
EB; mortise	print, stamp, seal; tally with	right away; approach; i.e.	but, however; retreat; refuse	unload; remove; get rid of	egg -
32;26 5 (-)	32;26 6 (2)	184;26 7 (2)	133;26 7 (2)	32;26 8 (3)	227;26 7 (3

仰	抑	柳	聊
yǎng	yì	liǔ	liáo
face up; admire; rely on	repress; restrain	willow -	merely; slightly; chat
21;9 6 (2)	55;64 7 (3)	94;75 9 (3)	163;128 11 (2)

脚	御	卿	犯	起
腳 jiǎo	*禦 yù	qīng	fàn	qǐ qí
foot, base; leg	drive (vehicle); resist; imperial	minister (archaic)	offense; attack; criminal	raise, rise; up; begin; able to
118;130 11 (1)	62;60 12 (3)	32;26 10 (-)	69;94 5 (2)	189;156 10 (1)

阝

邦	邮	邢	邪	那	耶
bāng	郵 yóu	xíng	xié	nà nèi nè nā	yē yé
nation, state	post, mail	(surname) -	evil; heretical	that; in that case	('je' sound)
34;163 6 (4)	143;163 7 (1)	34;163 6 (4)	34;163 6 (4)	34;163 6 (1)	34;128 8 (-)

邓	郎	郁	郑	邻
鄧 dèng	láng	*鬱 yù	鄭 zhèng	鄰 lín
(surname) -	man, person; darling	fragrant; lush; despondent	(surname) -	neighbor
34;163 4 (4)	34;163 8 (2)	34;163 8 (4)	34;163 8 (4)	34;163 7 (2)

郊	部	郭	都	鄙
jiāo	bù	guō	dōu dū	bǐ
suburbs, outskirts	part, section, unit; troops	outer wall (of city)	all; capital, metropolis	low, vulgar; my (humble)
34;163 8 (2)	34;163 10 (1)	34;163 10 (4)	34;163 10 (1)	34;163 13 (4)

掷	绑	椰	嘟	螂
擲 zhì zhī	綁 bǎng	yē	dū	láng
throw -	bind, tie	coconut -	toot, honk; pout	[mantis, cockroach]
55;64 11 (4)	77;120 9 (3)	94;75 12 (-)	58;30 13 (-)	174;142 14 (-)

挪	娜	哪	郎	郑	郁
nuó	nuó	na nǎ něi	láng	鄭 zhèng	*鬱 yù
move -	[fascinating; courteous]	(particle); Which?, What?	man, person; darling	(surname) -	fragrant; lush despondent
55;64 9 (4)	73;38 9 (-)	58;30 9 (1)	34;163 8 (2)	34;163 8 (4)	34;163 8 (4)

鸣 **鳴** míng — chirp; to voice; make a sound — 58;196 8 (3)	鸡 **雞 鷄** jī — chicken, cock, hen — 35;172 7 (1)

Birds (鸟)

鸣 鳴 míng — chirp; to voice; make a sound — 58;196 8 (3)

鸡 雞 鷄 jī — chicken, cock, hen — 35;172 7 (1)

鸭 鴨 yā — a duck — - — 152;196 10 (3)

鸦 鴉 yā — a crow — - — 99;196 9 (4)

鸥 鷗 ōu — gull — - — 152;196 9 (-)

鹅 鵝 é — goose — - — 152;196 12 (2)

鸽 鴿 gē — dove, pigeon — 152;196 11 (3)

鹊 鵲 què — magpie — - — 152;196 13 (4)

鹤 鶴 hè — crane (bird) — 152;196 15 (-)

鸿 鴻 hóng — swan, goose; grand — 40;196 11 (-)

鹏 鵬 péng — roc (fabled giant bird) — 152;196 13 (-)

捣 搗 dǎo — to pound, beat; harass — 55;64 10 (4)

呜 嗚 wū — hoot, toot — 58;30 7 (4)

鬼

愧 kuì — ashamed — - — 41;61 12 (3)

槐 huái — acacia, locust tree — 94;75 13 (4)

瑰 guī — marvelous (literary) — 88;96 13 (4)

魄 pò bó tuò — soul, spirit, vigor — 150;194 14 (4)

魂 hún — soul, spirit — 216;194 13 (3)

魏 wèi — (old kingdom; surname) — 216;194 18 (4)

辛

辟 *闢 pì bì — open up (land); incisive; refute — 186;160 13 (2)

辞 辭 cí — depart; decline; dismiss; & — 177;160 13 (3)

锌 鋅 xīn — zinc — - — 147;167 12 (4)

僻 pì — secluded, eccentric — 21;9 15 (4)

辨 biàn — differentiate, distinguish — 186;160 16 (4)

辩 辯 biàn — dispute, debate — 186;160 16 (3)

辫 辮 biàn — plait, braid; pigtail — 186;120 17 (4)

瓣 bàn — petal, segment, piece; valve — 186;97 19 (3)

京

凉 *涼 liáng liàng — cool, cold; disappointed — 8;15 10 (1)

谅 諒 liàng — forgive; guess, suppose — 10;149 10 (1)

惊 驚 jīng — startled, alarmed — 41;187 11 (2)

掠 lüè — plunder; sweep past — 55;64 11 (3)

琼 瓊 qióng — jade; palace (literary) — 88;96 12 (-)

晾 liàng — to air, dry in the sun — 103;72 12 (4)

鲸 鯨 jīng — whale — - — 210;195 16 (3)

1	41
2	42
3	43
4	44
5	45
6	46
7	47
8	48
9	49
10	50
11	51
12	52
13	53
14	**54**
15	55
16	56
17	57
18	58
19	59
20	60
21	61
22	62
23	63
24	64
25	65
26	66
27	67
28	68
29	69
30	70
31	71
32	72
33	73
34	74
35	75
36	76
37	77
38	78
39	79
40	80

只

识 識 shí zhì
knowledge;
know; opinion
10;149 7 (1)

积 積 jī
amass, store;
long-standing
149;115 10 (2)

帜 幟 zhì
flag,
banner (literary)
57;50 8 (3)

职 職 zhí
duty, job,
post
163;128 11 (2)

况 *况 kuàng
situation;
compare
8;15 7 (1)

祝 zhù
best wishes
-
87;113 9 ( )

支

枝 zhī
branch,
twig
94;75 8 (3)

技 jì
skill, ability,
talent
55;64 7 (1)

歧 qí
fork (in road);
diverge
102;77 8 (4)

妓 jì
prostitute
-
73;38 7 (-)

肢 zhī
limb
-
118;130 8 (4)

鼓 gǔ
drum; rouse
bellows; bul
224;207 13

殳

设 設 shè
to found,
establish; &
10;149 6 (1)

没 沒 méi mò
[not];
sink, submerge
40;85 7 (1)

役 yì
compel; battle;
service; servant
62;60 7 (4)

投 tóu
fling; leap into;
send; deliver; &
55;64 7 (2)

股 gǔ
thigh; section;
strand; a share
118;130 8 (3)

般 bān
sort, kind;
manner
182;137 10

段 duàn
section,
segment
119;79 9 (1)

殷 yīn yān
ardent; cordial;
rich; & (literary)
119;79 10 (4)

毅 yì
firm,
resolute
119;79 15 (3)

毁 huǐ
destroy;
defame
119;79 13 (3)

殿 diàn
hall, palace;
at the rear
119;79 13 (3)

殴 毆 ōu
beat,
strike
119;79 8 (4

搬 bān
move (house);
remove; &
55;64 13 (1)

缎 緞 duàn
satin
-
77;120 12 (4)

锻 鍛 duàn
forge, temper
(metals)
147;167 14 (1)

叚

假 jiǎ jià
fake; borrow;
vacation; &
21;9 11 (1)

暇 xiá
leisure
-
103;72 13 (-)

青

请 請 qǐng
please;
ask, invite
10;149 10 (1)

清 qīng
clear; settle up;
quiet; fully; &
40;85 11 (1)

情 qíng
emotion; love;
favor; situation
41;61 11 (1)

靖 jìng
tranquillity;
pacify
126;174 13 (-)

猜 cāi
guess,
suspect
69;94 11 (2)

精 jīng
splendid; sp
fine; clever;
159;119 14

蜻 qīng
[dragonfly]
-
174;142 14 (4)

晴 qíng
fine
(weather)
103;72 12 (1)

睛 jīng
eyeball
-
141;109 13 (1)

泽
澤 zé
pond, marsh; damp; luster
40;85 8 (3)

择
擇 zé zhái
pick, choose
55;64 8 (2)

释
釋 shì
explain; resolve; release
197;165 12 (2)

佳
jiā
beautiful, fine
21;9 8 (3)

挂
掛 guà
hang; to phone; worry; register
55;64 9 (1)

桂
guì
laurel, cassia; cinnamon tree
94;75 10 (4)

娃
wá
baby
-
73;38 9 (3)

哇
wā wa
cry, wail; (particle)
58;30 9 (2)

蛙
wā
frog
-
174;142 12 (3)

鞋
xié
shoe
212;177 15 (1)

准
* 準 zhǔn
allow; quasi-; definitely; &
8;15 10 (1)

淮
huái
[Huaihe river]
-
40;85 11 (4)

谁
誰 shuí shéi
Who?; anyone
10;149 10 (1)

惟
wéi
solely; thought
41;61 11 (4)

稚
zhì
young, infantile
149;115 13 (3)

榷
què
discuss
-
94;75 14 (4)

堆
duī
heap, pile
49;32 11 (2)

唯
wéi wěi
solely; [yes-man]
58;30 11 (4)

难
難 nán nàn
difficult; nasty; disaster; blame
35;172 10 (1)

雅
yǎ
proper; elegant; your (polite)
99;172 12 (4)

推
tuī
push; grind; to clip; deduce; shirk; postpone; elect; esteem
55;64 11 (1)

维
維 wéi
hold together; maintain; &
77;120 11 (2)

摊
攤 tān
spread out; booth, stall; &
55;64 13 (3)

雌
cí
female
-
208;172 14 (4)

滩
灘 tān
beach, sands; shoals, rapids
40;85 13 (3)

雄
xióng
male; mighty, grand; hero
208;172 12 (4)

雕
diāo
carve, engrave; vulture, eagle
208;172 16 (3)

浦
pǔ
river bank, river mouth
40;85 10 (-)

埔
pǔ
[Huangpu]
-
49;32 10 (4)

捕
bǔ
catch, seize, arrest
55;64 10 (2)

辅
輔 fǔ
assist
-
100;159 11 (1)

铺
鋪 pū pù
spread; pave; store, shop
147;167 12 (2)

1	41
2	42
3	43
4	44
5	45
6	46
7	47
8	48
9	49
10	50
11	51
12	52
13	53
14	54
15	**55**
16	56
17	57
18	58
19	59
20	60
21	61
22	62
23	63
24	64
25	65
26	66
27	67
28	68
29	69
30	70
31	71
32	72
33	73
34	74
35	75
36	76
37	77
38	78
39	79
40	80

占

沾 zhān
wet; moisten;
stain; touch
40;85 8 (3)

站 zhàn
station; (bus)
stop; to stand
126;117 10 (1)

粘 *黏 zhān nián
glue; sticky;
paste up
159;119 11 (2)

贴 貼 tiē
paste; nestle;
subsidize
106;154 9 (2)

帖 tiē tiě tiè
docile; fitting;
note, card
57;50 8 (4)

钻 鑽 zuān zuàn
penetrate, bore,
drill; diamond
147;167 10 (2)

各

洛 luò
(a river)
-
40;85 9 (-)

格 gé
grid; standard;
subdivision
94;75 10 (2)

略 lüè
slightly; omit;
plan; seize; &
142;102 11 (2)

胳 gē gé
[arm]
-
118;130 10 (2)

骆 駱 luò
[camel]
-
75;187 9 (3)

路 lù
road, route;
way; region; &
196;157 13 (1)

赂 賂 lù
[bribe]
-
106;154 10 (4)

铭 銘 míng
inscription;
engrave
147;167 11 (4)

㕰

沿 yán yàn
along; follow;
border, edge
40;85 8 (2)

铅 鉛 qiān
lead
(the metal)
147;167 10 (1)

船 chuán
boat,
ship
182;137 11 (1)

召

昭 zhāo
clear,
evident
103;72 9 (-)

绍 紹 shào
continue
-
77;120 8 (1)

招 zhāo
beckon; invite; recruit; incur;
provoke; confess; a trick
55;64 8 (2)

台

冶 yě
smelt
-
8;15 7 (3)

治 zhì
control; peace;
cure; study; &
40;85 8 (1)

怡 yí
happy
(literary)
41;61 8 (-)

抬 tái
raise,
lift
55;64 8 (1)

始 shǐ
beginning
-
73;38 8 (1)

胎 tāi
embryo; bir
a tire; padd
118;130 9

合

恰 qià
suitable;
exactly
41;61 9 (3)

洽 qià
harmonious;
discuss
40;85 9 (4)

哈 hā hǎ hà
exhale;
Aha!; laugh
58;30 9 (1)

拾 shí
pick up, collect;
ten
55;64 9 (1)

给 給 gěi jǐ
give; for (someone);
allow; supply; ample
77;120 9 (1)

分 令 仓 仑 它

份	扮	纷	粉	吩	盼
fèn	bàn	紛 fēn	fěn	fēn	pàn
portion, share	disguise, dress up as	in profusion; confused	dust, powder; white; pink	[command, order]	hope for; look
21;9 6 (2)	55;64 7 (2)	77;120 7 (2)	159;119 10 (2)	58;30 7 (2)	141;109 9 (2)

怜	冷	伶	龄
憐 lián	lěng	líng	齡 líng
pity, sympathy; pamper	cold, frosty; rare; deserted	actor (archaic); [clever; bereft]	age, years, duration
41;61 8 (2)	8;15 7 (1)	21;9 7 (4)	206;211 13 (2)

玲	铃	岭	吟
líng	鈴 líng	嶺 lǐng	yín
[tinkling of jade; exquisite, deft]	bell -	mountain peak, ridge, range	chant, recite; (animal's) roar
88;96 9 (4)	147;167 10 (2)	60;46 8 (4)	58;30 7 (4)

沧	枪	舱	抢
滄 cāng	槍 qiāng	艙 cāng	搶 qiǎng qiāng
deep blue (sea)	gun; spear, lance	cabin, hold (on ship)	snatch; vie for; to rush; scrape
40;85 7 (-)	94;75 8 (2)	182;137 10 (3)	55;64 7 (2)

论	沦	抡	伦	轮
論 lùn lún	淪 lún	掄 lūn lún	倫 lún	輪 lún
discuss; theory; decide; &	sink; be reduced to	brandish; choose	series; peer; (feudal) ethics	wheel; take turns
10;149 6 (1)	40;85 7 (-)	55;64 7 (4)	21;9 6 (-)	100;159 8 (2)

陀	蛇	舵	驼
tuó	shé yí	duò	駝 tuó
[(spinning) top] -	snake -	rudder, helm	camel; hump-backed
33;170 7 (-)	174;142 11 (2)	182;137 11 (4)	75;187 8 (3)

1	41
2	42
3	43
4	44
5	45
6	46
7	47
8	48
9	49
10	50
11	51
12	52
13	53
14	54
15	55
16	**56**
17	57
18	58
19	59
20	60
21	61
22	62
23	63
24	64
25	65
26	66
27	67
28	68
29	69
30	70
31	71
32	72
33	73
34	74
35	75
36	76
37	77
38	78
39	79
40	80

出巾市	拙 zhuō clumsy; my (humble) 55;64 8 (4)	礎 chǔ 础 plinth, base 136;112 10 (1)	帥 shuài 帅 commander; smart, graceful 57;50 5 (4)	沛 pèi copious - 40;85 7 (4)	肺 fèi lungs 118;130 8
赤東竞攵匕	赫 hè impressive - 190;155 14 (4)	辣 là spicy, acrid; vicious 186;160 14 (3)	兢 jīng [conscientious] - 12;10 14 (4)	敲 qiāo knock, strike, hit 218;66 14 (2)	能 néng able to; ener capability 37;130 10
亡兒关宛	忙 máng busy; hurried, hasty 41;61 6 (1)	貌 mào view; face, appearance 198;153 14 (2)	聯 lián 联 unite, join, link up 163;128 12 (1)	豌 wān [pea] - 191;151 15 (4)	
厶大夫	私 sī private; selfish; secret, illicit 149;115 7 (2)	弘 hóng great, grand; enlarge 71;57 5 (-)	馱 tuó duò 驮 carry (on back, of animals) 75;187 6 (3)	膚 fū 肤 skin; [superficial] 118;130 8 (2)	扶 fú hold on to; help 55;64 7 (2)
史女乂	駛 shǐ 驶 (of a vehicle) to go; to speed 75;187 8 (3)	妝 zhuāng 妆 adorn; apply make-up 42;38 6 (4)	汝 rǔ you (literary) 40;85 6 (-)	趙 zhào 赵 (surname) - 189;156 9 (3)	
井甘	講 jiǎng 讲 speak, discuss, tell, explain; & 10;149 6 (1)	*畊 gēng 耕 plow - 176;127 10 (3)	甜 tián sweet; (sleep) soundly 177;99 11 (2)	鉗拑 qián 钳 pincers, pliers; clamp; restrain 147;167 10 (4)	
勿勾匊	吻 wěn lips; kiss; animal's mouth 58;30 7 (3)	物 wù thing; content, substance 110;93 8 (1)	構 gòu 构 construct, compose 94;75 8 (2)	鉤 gōu 钩 hook - 147;167 9 (3)	鞠 jū to rear, bring up; nourish 212;177 17
夕多争	矽 xī silicon - 136;112 8 (-)	夥 huǒ many (literary) (see Table 1) 142;36 15 (-)	*夠 gòu 够 enough; attain; rather, quite 64;36 11 (1)	靜 jìng 静 still, calm, quiet 202;174 14 (1)	

乾
qián
male (archaic)
(see Table 1)
203;5 11 (-)

辉
辉huī
radiance;
shine
172;159 12 (2)

汇
匯 彙huì
gather, meet;
remit (money)
40;22 5 (3)

吁
*籲yù xū
plead;
groan; Oh!
58;30 6 (4)

研
yán
grind; study,
research
136;112 9 (1)

拜
bài
pay a visit;
bow to
111;64 9 (2)

鞭
biān
whip
-
212;177 18 (4)

犯
fàn
offense; attack;
criminal
69;94 5 (2)

肥
féi
fat; baggy;
fertile; fertilizer
118;130 8 (2)

把
bǎ bà
to hold; control;
a handle; &
55;64 7 (1)

服
fú
clothes; serve;
obey; &
118;74 8 (1)

报
報bào
report; reply;
newspaper
55;32 7 (1)

仁
rén
benevolence;
kernel
21;9 4 (4)

污
*汙 洿wū
dirt, filth;
smear; corrupt
40;85 6 (2)

玩
wán
play; trifle with;
enjoy; resort to
88;96 8 (1)

氓
méng máng
the common
people
43;83 8 (3)

弱
ruò
weak; inferior;
a bit less
71;57 10 (2)

疑
yí
doubt
-
39;103 14 (2)

解
jiě jiè xiè
untie; explain;
solve; dispel; &
201;148 13 (1)

钢
鋼gāng gàng
steel;
sharpen
147;167 9 (1)

枫
楓fēng
maple
-
94;75 8 (-)

飘
飄piāo
flutter;
drift on the wind
121;182 15 (2)

稣
穌sū
revive
-
210;115 13 (-)

掰
bāi
break (with the
fingers)
111;64 12 (4)

耗
hào
use up; dawdle;
bad news
176;127 10 (3)

托
*託tuō
entrust; pretext;
support; &
55;64 6 (2)

豁
huō huò
crack; forsake;
open; exempt
199;150 17 (4)

1	41
2	42
3	43
4	44
5	45
6	46
7	47
8	48
9	49
10	50
11	51
12	52
13	53
14	54
15	55
16	56
17	**57**
18	58
19	59
20	60
21	61
22	62
23	63
24	64
25	65
26	66
27	67
28	68
29	69
30	70
31	71
32	72
33	73
34	74
35	75
36	76
37	77
38	78
39	79
40	80

之 zhī
(particle, object pronoun)
1;4 3 (1)

广 廣 guǎng
wide, broad; spread; many
44;53 3 (1)

户 hù
door; family; bank account
86;63 4 (1)

良 liáng
good; very
184;138 7 (2)

义 義 yì
justice; meaning; &
25;123 3 (1)

以 yǐ
using; so as according t[
23;9 4 (1)

主 zhǔ
master, host, lord; manage; &
88;3 5 (1)

永 yǒng
eternal, forever
1;85 5 (1)

心 xīn
heart; core; feelings
81;61 4 (1)

必 bì
necessarily; certainly
1;61 5 (1)

书 書 shū
write; letter, book, document
3;73 4 (1)

启 →
启 →
疖 →
问 →
亩 →
亩 →

斗 *鬥 dòu dǒu
fight; dovetail; dipper; &
82;68 4 (2)

头 頭 tóu tou
head; top; first, chief; end; &
52;181 5 (1)

术 *術 shù zhú
art, technique, skill; method
94;75 5 (1)

求 qiú
beg, request; seek
1;85 7 (1)

为 為 wéi wèi
do, act, act as; become; be equal to; for the sake of
1;86 4 (1)

尤 yóu
especially; blame, fault
53;43 4 (1)

龙 龍 lóng
dragon; imperial
137;212 5 (2)

发 發 髮 fā fà
emit; become; develop; hair; &
35;105 5 (1)

戈 gē
lance, spear, (an old weapon)
101;62 4 (4)

成 chéng
to become; succeed; &
138;62 6 (1)

我 wǒ
I, me, my, we, our
101;62 7 (

白 bái
white; blank, in vain; gratis; &
150;106 5 (1)

自 zì
self; oneself; from; certainly
180;132 6 (1)

血 xuè xiě
blood
-
181;143 6 (2)

身 shēn
body, torso; life; oneself
200;158 7 (1)

向 *嚮 xiàng
facing; towards; direction; &
4;30 6 (1)

囪 cōng
[chimney]
-
4;31 7 (3)

乌 烏 wū
crow; black, dark
4;86 4 (4)

鸟 鳥 niǎo
bird
-
152;196 5 (2)

岛 島 dǎo
island
-
60;46 7 (2)

舟 zhōu
boat (literary)
182;137 6 (4)

盘 盤 pán
dish, tray; coil; examine; build
182;108 11 (2)

兜 dōu
pocket; bag, wrap; solicit
29;10 11 (

皂 zào
soap; black
150;106 7 (2)

泉 quán
spring, fountain
150;85 9 (4)

皇 huáng
emperor, sovereign
150;106 9 (2)

息 xī
breath; cease; news; grow; &
180;61 10 (1)

臭 chòu xiù
stink; disgusting
180;132 10 (2)

鼻 bí
nose
-
226;209 14

卑 bēi
low, inferior, modest
12;24 8 (4)

鬼 guǐ
ghost; stealthy; sinister; &
216;194 9 (2)

粤 yuè
Guangdong
-
4;119 12 (4)

奥 ào
profound; hard to understand
52;37 12 (3)

长 長 cháng zhǎng
long; long-term; steadily; forte grow; senior, chief; get, acqui[
4;168 4 (1)

弟	**兑**	**总**	**单**	**兽**	**曾**
dì	duì	總 zǒng	單 dān	獸 shòu	céng zēng
younger brother	to exchange; to dilute	chief; anyway; always; sum up	single, alone; list; (bed) sheet	beast -	formerly; great (grandchild)
24;57 7 (1)	24;10 7 (3)	81;120 9 (1)	24;30 8 (1)	24;94 11 (3)	103;73 12 (2)
丫	**米**	**半**	**炎**	**脊**	
yā	mǐ	bàn	yán	jǐ jí	
fork (in tree), bifurcation	rice; meter (length)	half, semi-; partly	hot; blazing; inflammation	backbone, spine; ridge	
24;2 3 (-)	159;119 6 (1)	3;24 5 (1)	83;86 8 (4)	118;130 10 (4)	
兰	**羊**	**并**	**关**	**养**	
蘭 lán	yáng	併並 bing	關 guān	養 yǎng	
orchid -	sheep; goat	actually; also; merge; equally	shut; switch off; involve; &	maintain; raise, nurture; &	
24;140 5 (3)	157;123 6 (1)	24;9 6 (2)	24;169 6 (1)	24;184 9 (2)	
益	**首**	**兼**	**兹**	**慈**	
yì	shǒu	jiān	*兹 zī	cí	
benefit; profit; increasingly	head; chief, first; indict	concurrent; both; double	this; now; year (literary)	kind, loving, merciful	
146;108 10 (2)	24;185 9 (1)	24;12 10 (3)	24;140 9 (-)	81;61 13 (4)	
前	**煎**	**剪**	**普**	**奠**	**尊**
qián	jiān	jiǎn	pǔ	diàn	zūn
front, in front of, forward; former	fry, boil, simmer	scissors; clip, trim; wipe out	universal -	settle (a place); funeral offerings	senior; esteem, respect
24;18 9 (1)	80;86 13 (3)	27;18 11 (2)	103;72 12 (2)	52;37 12 (3)	54;41 12 (2)
盖	**姜**	**羡**	**羞**	**差**	
蓋 gài	薑 jiāng	xiàn	xiū	chà chā chāi cī	
lid, cover; affix; surpass; build	ginger -	envy, admire	shy; ashamed	differ; err; wrong; difference; lacking; errand	
157;140 11 (2)	157;140 9 (4)	157;123 12 (2)	157;123 10 (4)	157;48 9 (1)	
养	**美**	**善**	**着**		
養 yǎng	měi	shàn	zháo zhāo zhuó zhe		
maintain; raise, nurture; &	beautiful; America	good; expert; apt to; friendly	touch; catch (cold); burn; to wear; use, apply; -ing; &		
24;184 9 (2)	157;123 9 (2)	157;30 12 (2)	157;109 11 (1)		

1	41
2	42
3	43
4	44
5	45
6	46
7	47
8	48
9	49
10	50
11	51
12	52
13	53
14	54
15	55
16	56
17	57
18	**58**
19	59
20	60
21	61
22	62
23	63
24	64
25	65
26	66
27	67
28	68
29	69
30	70
31	71
32	72
33	73
34	74
35	75
36	76
37	77
38	78
39	79
40	80

小 业 尚 ⺌

小

少
shǎo shào
few; lacking;
Stop!; young; &
79;42 4 (1)

尘
塵 chén
dust, dirt; this
(mortal) world
79;32 6 (3)

尖
jiān
tip, pinnacle;
sharp, pointed
79;42 6 (2)

劣
liè
inferior,
poor quality
79;19 6 (3)

雀
què qiǎo
sparrow
-
79;172 11 (4)

省
shěng xǐng
save; omit; province;
visit; aware; introspection
79;109 9 (1)

业

尚
shàng
esteem,
respect; yet
79;42 8 (3)

肖
xiào xiāo
resemble
-
79;130 7 (4)

当
當 噹 dāng dàng
act as; when, whilst; ought;
regard as; equal to; proper; &
79;102 6 (1)

类
類 lèi
kind, type;
similar to
159;181 9 (2)

粪
糞 fèn
dung,
excrement
159;119 12 (3)

米
mǐ
rice;
meter (length)
159;119 6 (1)

光
guāng
light; glory; scenery; bare;
smooth; depleted; alone
172;10 6 (2)

业

尝
嘗 cháng
to taste, test;
ever, already
139;30 9 (2)

学
學 xué
study, learn;
knowledge; &
74;39 8 (1)

觉
覺 jué jiào
feel; conscious;
realize; sleep
107;147 9 (1)

党
黨 dǎng
political party;
club, gang
139;203 10 (2)

堂
táng
hall, court;
cousin
139;32 11 (1)

掌
zhǎng
palm (of hand);
control
139;64 12 (1)

常
cháng
often; constant;
normal
139;50 11 (1)

裳
cháng shang
a skirt
(ancient)
139;145 14 (4)

赏
賞 shǎng
bestow; rew
appreciate
139;154 12

⺌

兴
興 xīng xìng
start; prosper;
excitement
24;134 6 (1)

誉
譽 yù
reputation;
praise
185;149 13 (4)

举
舉 jǔ
raise; praise; deed; cite;
entire; behavior; choose; start
227;134 9 (1)

学
學 xué
study, learn;
knowledge; &
74;39 8 (1)

觉
覺 jué jiào
feel; conscious;
realize; sleep
107;147 9 (1)

一 入 八

个	介	伞	企	众	仓
個 gè gě	jiè	傘 sǎn	qǐ	眾 衆 zhòng	倉 cāng
(measure word); item; individual	between; take seriously	umbrella -	expect, await; stand on tiptoe	numerous; a crowd	warehouse, granary
23;9 3 (1)	23;9 4 (1)	23;9 6 (2)	23;9 6 (2)	23;109 6 (2)	23;9 4 (3)

全	金	余	舍
quán	jīn	*餘 yú	*捨 shě shè
completely; whole, all	gold; metal; money	remainder, surplus; after	abandon; house, shed; &
23;11 6 (1)	209;167 8 (2)	23;9 7 (2)	23;135 8 (1)

今	令	合	会
jīn	lìng lǐng	hé gě	會 huì kuài
now, present; today; modern	command; your (resp); &	join; add up to; shut; to suit; &	meet; meeting; union, society; going to; know how to; &
23;9 4 (1)	23;9 5 (2)	23;30 6 (1)	23;73 6 (1)

念	含	贪	俞	命
*唸 niàn	hán	貪 tān	yú	mìng
study; recite; think of, yearn	contain; hold in mouth	corrupt; greedy; covet	(surname) -	life; command; destiny; assign
81;61 8 (1)	58;30 7 (2)	106;154 8 (4)	23;9 9 (-)	23;30 8 (2)

食	盒	拿	愈	禽
shí sì	hé	ná	*瘉 癒 yù	qín
eat; food, meal; edible; eclipse	box, case, casket	grasp; using; treat as; &	get well; better; more and more	birds -
217;184 9 (1)	146;108 11 (2)	111;64 10 (1)	81;61 13 (3)	23;114 12 (4)

分	公
fēn fèn	gōng
small unit; part; divide; duty; &	public; official; general; impartial; metric units; male (animal)
24;18 4 (1)	24;12 4 (1)

岔	贫	盆	翁
chà	貧 pín	pén	wēng
branch off, turn off	poor, destitute; talkative	basin, pot, tub	old man, father, father in law
60;46 7 (4)	106;154 8 (3)	146;108 9 (2)	183;124 10 (3)

父	谷	斧	爷	爸	爹
fù	*穀 gǔ	fǔ	爺 yé	bà	diē
father -	valley; grain, cereal	axe -	father; uncle, grandpa (polite)	father -	father, dad (colloq)
108;88 4 (1)	199;150 7 (3)	108;69 8 (4)	108;88 6 (2)	108;88 8 (1)	108;88 10 (3)

1	41
2	42
3	43
4	44
5	45
6	46
7	47
8	48
9	49
10	50
11	51
12	52
13	53
14	54
15	55
16	56
17	57
18	58
19	**59**
20	60
21	61
22	62
23	63
24	64
25	65
26	66
27	67
28	68
29	69
30	70
31	71
32	72
33	73
34	74
35	75
36	76
37	77
38	78
39	79
40	80

■
一

一

二	三	云	元	示	亏
èr	sān	*雲 yún	yuán	shì	虧 kuī
two	three	cloud	first; chief;	show;	deficit; unfa
-	-	-	unit; yuan	notify	thanks to; &
11;7 2 (1)	2;1 3 (1)	11;7 4 (1)	11;10 4 (1)	132;113 5 (1)	11;141 3 (

灭	丽	画	豆	买
滅 miè	麗 lì	畫 huà	dòu	買 mǎi
snuff out;	beautiful	picture; (of	beans,	buy
wipe out; drown	-	Ch char) stroke	pulses	-
83;85 5 (2)	2;198 7 (2)	38;102 8 (1)	191;151 7 (2)	5;154 6 (1)

丁	不	平	下
dīng zhēng	bù bú	píng	xià xia
4th; HS; man,	no, not, un-;	flat, even, level;	below, down; descend; unload;
population	can't	calm; average	next; inferior; send; decide; &
2;1 2 (3)	95;1 4 (1)	2;51 5 (1)	16;1 3 (1)

开	牙	无	于	干
開 kāi kai	yá	無 wú	*於 yú	*乾 幹 gān gàn
open; start;	tooth;	without; not;	in, at, to,	dry; futile; adopt (child);
operate; &	ivory	nothing; &	from, than	main part, trunk; do, work; figh
51;169 4 (1)	99;92 4 (2)	53;86 4 (2)	11;7 3 (2)	11;51 3 (1)

万	歹	瓦	丐	天
*萬 wàn mò	dǎi	wǎ wà	gài	tiān
ten thousand;	bad,	(roof) tile;	beg; beggar	sky, Heaven; God; day; seaso
many; utterly	evil	earthenware	(literary)	weather; nature, natural
2;1 3 (1)	97;78 4 (4)	98;98 4 (3)	2;1 4 (-)	90;37 4 (1)

石	百	死	至	严
shí dàn	bǎi	sǐ	zhì	嚴 yán
stone, rock;	a hundred;	die; death;	until, up to;	tight;
inscription	numerous	rigid	arrive at	strict, severe
136;112 5 (2)	150;106 6 (1)	97;78 6 (1)	171;133 6 (2)	168;30 7 (2)

丙	页	面	耍	夏	
bǐng	頁 yè	*麵 麪 miàn	shuǎ	xià	雪 →
3rd;	page	face; surface;	to play	summer	酉 →
HS	-	extent; flour; &	-	-	丁 →
2;1 5 (3)	170;181 6 (1)	2;176 9 (1)	169;126 9 (3)	65;35 10 (1)	吾 →

两	而	雨	再	更	天 →
兩 liǎng	ér	yǔ	zài	gèng gēng	甚 →
two, a couple;	and; due to;	rain	again; further;	even more;	巫 →
both; a few; &	but; (from …) to	-	more; before; &	to change	五
2;11 7 (1)	169;126 6 (1)	204;173 8 (1)	2;13 6 (1)	2;73 7 (1)	

一 罒 禾 不

千 qiān
thousand; numerous
12;24 3 (1)

升 *昇 shēng
rise, raise; promote; liter
4;24 4 (2)

禾 hé
grain, cereal; rice
149;115 5 (4)

币 幣 bì
money
-
57;50 4 (2)

乏 fá
deficiency; exhausted
4;4 4 (2)

壬 rén
9th; HS
49;33 4 (-)

系 *係 繫 xì
fasten; system; department; &
77;120 7 (1)

舌 shé
tongue
-
177;135 6 (2)

乎 hū
(suffix; particle)
2;4 5 (2)

手 shǒu
hand; by hand; hold; person
111;64 4 (1)

毛 máo
fur, hair, wool; sc
gross (profit); 1/1
112;82 4 (1)

乖 guāi
obedient; quick-witted
4;4 8 (3)

乘 chéng shèng
ride; multiply; make use of
149;4 10 (2)

秉 bǐng
grasp; control (literary)
149;115 8 (4)

垂 chuí
droop; hang down
4;32 8 (3)

重 chóng zhòng
repeat; heavy; to stress; &
4;166 9 (1)

熏 xūn xùn
smoke
-
80;86 14 (4)

乔 喬 qiáo
tall; disguise
90;30 6 (4)

丢 diū
lose; throw away
133;1 6 (1)

悉 xī
know; all, entire
197;61 11 (2)

番 fān
a time, a turn
197;102 12 (3)

舌 → 61

乐 樂 yuè lè
music; enjoy; happy
4;75 5 (1)

氏 shì
family name; surname; née
122;83 4 (3)

丘 qiū
mound, grave
4;1 5 (3)

我 wǒ
I, me, my, we, our
101;62 7 (1)

么 麼 me
[what; such as] (suffix)
4;200 3 (1)

妥 tuǒ
arranged; appropriate
116;38 7 (3)

采 *採 cǎi cài
pick, pluck, select; &
197;165 8 (2)

受 shòu
receive, accept; endure
116;29 8 (2)

爱 愛 ài
love; be fond of; cherish; apt to
116;61 10 (1)

爵 jué
nobility; wine cup
116;87 17 (-)

秃 tū+G24
bald; blunt; unsatisfactory
149;115 7 (4)

季 jì
season, quarterly
149;39 8 (2)

秀 xiù
beautiful; excellent
149;115 7 (2)

委 wěi wēi
appoint; indirect; &
149;38 8 (2)

香 xiāng
fragrant; appetizing; heartily; perfume, incense; popular
215;186 9 (1)

否 fǒu pǐ
deny; not; evil; censure
95;30 7 (2)

歪 wāi
crooked, askew; devious
95;77 9 (2)

甭 béng
don't; needn't
-
95;101 9 (3)

1	41
2	42
3	43
4	44
5	45
6	46
7	47
8	48
9	49
10	50
11	51
12	52
13	53
14	54
15	55
16	56
17	57
18	58
19	59
20	**60**
21	61
22	62
23	63
24	64
25	65
26	66
27	67
28	68
29	69
30	70
31	71
32	72
33	73
34	74
35	75
36	76
37	77
38	78
39	79
40	80

乞 qǐ
beg
-
20;5 3 (4)

每 měi
each, every;
habitually
20;80 7 (1)

舞 wǔ
dance
-
20;136 14 (1)

复 *復複覆 fù
duplicate, repeat; complex;
resume; reply; revenge
20;60 9 (1)

气 氣 qì
air, gas, breath;
odor; enrage; &
109;84 4 (1)

氛 fēn
atmosphere,
vapor
109;84 8 (3)

氧 yǎng
oxygen
-
109;84 10 (3)

氮 dàn
nitrogen
-
109;84 12 (4)

氢 氫 qīng
hydrogen
-
109;84 9 (4)

与 與 yǔ yù
and; with; to
help; give; &
2;134 3

午 wǔ
noon;
EB
20;24 4 (1)

矢 shǐ
arrow;
vow
148;111 5 (-)

年 nián
year; annual;
age; New Year
20;51 6 (1)

乍 zhà
suddenly;
at first; extend
20;4 5 (-)

行 xíng háng
go; do, perform; capable; OK;
for now; line; (business) firm
62;144 6 (1)

冤 yuān
injustice; bad
luck; hatred
18;14 10 (3)

罕 hǎn
rare
-
18;122 7 (4)

写 寫 xiě xiè
write;
draw; depict
18;40 5 (1)

买 買 mǎi
buy
-
5;154 6 (1)

军 軍 jūn
army,
troops
18;159 6 (2)

冥 míng
dark; deep;
stupid; Hades
18;14 10 (-)

冠 guàn guān
precede; crown,
hat; champion
18;14 9 (2)

尔 爾 ěr
you; like that,
that (literary)
79;89 5 (3)

色 sè shǎi
color; scene;
looks; lust; &
27;139 6 (1)

免 miǎn
avoid; exempt;
dismiss
27;10 7 (2)

兔 tù
rabbit,
hare
27;10 8 (2)

危 wēi
danger;
near death
27;26 6 (1)

负 負 fù
to shoulder; suffer; rely on
minus; owe; fail; be defeated
27;154 6 (1)

争 爭 zhēng
compete (for),
argue (about)
27;87 6 (2)

急 jí
quick; urgent;
hurry; annoyed
81;61 9 (1)

龟 龜 guī jūn
tortoise,
turtle
27;213 7 (4)

鱼 魚 yú
fish
-
210;195 8 (1)

角 jiǎo jué
angle, corner; 1/10 yuan; horn;
role; actor; contend
201;148 7 (1)

象 *像 xiàng
elephant;
be like; shape
27;152 11 (2)

鲁 魯 lǔ
stupid;
rude
210;195 12 (4)

1	41
2	42
3	43
4	44
5	45
6	46
7	47
8	48
9	49
10	50
11	51
12	52
13	53
14	54
15	55
16	56
17	57
18	58
19	59
20	60
21	**61**
22	62
23	63
24	64
25	65
26	66
27	67
28	68
29	69
30	70
31	71
32	72
33	73
34	74
35	75
36	76
37	77
38	78
39	79
40	80

多 duō
many; more; over-; &
64;36 6 (1)

名 míng
name; renown; famous
64;30 6 (1)

冬 dōng
winter; drum sound
65;15 5 (1)

条 條 tiáo
twig; clause; slip of paper
65;75 7 (1)

备 備 bèi
prepare, equip; fully
65;9 8 (1)

务 務 wù
affair, business; work at
65;19 5 (1)

各 gè
each, every
65;30 6 (1)

灸 jiǔ
moxibustion (Ch. medicine)
83;86 7 (3)

圣 聖 shèng
sacred; sage; Majesty
35;128 5 (3)

桑 sāng
mulberry tree
94;75 10 (4)

叠 *疊 疉 dié
pile up; repeat
35;29 13 (2)

予 yǔ yú
grant, bestow
31;6 4 (3)

矛 máo
spear, lance
155;110 5 (2)

柔 róu
soft, pliable; gentle
155;75 9 (3)

勇 yǒng
brave
-
31;19 9 (2)

承 chéng
undertake; indebted; &
5;64 8 (2)

子 zǐ zi
child; son; egg; seed; person; thing; EB
74;39 3 (1)

矣 yǐ
(particle, archaic)
37;111 7 (-)

允 yǔn
allow; equitable
37;10 4 (2)

台 *臺 檯 颱 tái
platform, stage; support; desk; (TV) station; Taiwan
37;30 5 (2)

怠 dài
idle, lazy
81;61 9 (4)

垒 壘 lěi
rampart, fort; build
49;32 9 (4)

叁 sān
three
-
37;28 8 (4)

参 參 cān cēn shēn
join in; consult; refer; ginseng
37;28 8 (1)

乒 pīng
gunshot sound; [ping-pong]
4;4 6 (2)

乓 pāng
banging sound; [ping-pong]
4;3 6 (2)

兵 bīng
soldier; army; military; arms
24;12 7 (2)

岳 yuè
high mountain; wife's parents
60;46 8 (4)

亠 亡 去 亦

六	亡	之	方	立	亢
liù	wáng	zhī	fāng	lì	kàng
six	die; lose;	(particle,	direction; place;	to stand; to set	proud, haugh
-	flee; subjugate	object pronoun)	square; &	up; at once; &	excessively
9;12 4 (1)	43;8 3 (3)	1;4 3 (1)	85;70 4 (1)	126;117 5 (1)	9;8 4 (4)

文	交
wén	jiāo
writing; culture;	exchange; meet; join; befriend;
rite; civilian; &	to hand over; mutual; &
84;67 4 (1)	9;8 6 (1)

衣	玄	亥	市	亦	夜
yī	xuán	hài	shì	yì	yè
garment,	black, dark;	EB	market;	also, too	night
clothes, cover	profound	-	city	(literary)	-
161;145 6 (1)	9;95 5 (-)	9;8 6 (-)	9;50 5 (1)	162;8 6 (4)	9;36 8 (1)

亩	言	卒	率	裔
畝 mǔ	yán	zú	shuài lǜ	yì
mu (unit of land	word; speech;	soldier; servant;	to lead; frank;	posterity; far-off
area, 1/6 acre)	say, talk	finish; die	rate, ratio; &	land (literary)
9;102 7 (2)	185;149 7 (1)	9;24 8 (-)	9;95 11 (2)	161;145 13 (-)

离	衷	衰	裹	襄	片
離 lí	zhōng	shuāi	guǒ	xiāng	piàn piān
depart; apart;	sincere,	grow weak,	wrap;	assist	sheet, slice;
distant from	heartfelt	decline	bind up	(literary)	fragment; film
9;172 10 (1)	9;145 10 (3)	9;145 10 (3)	9;145 14 (3)	9;145 17 (-)	114;91 4 (1

忘	妄	盲	赢
wàng wáng	wàng	máng	贏 yíng
forget	absurd;	blind,	win (game);
-	presumptuous	blindly	profit
43;61 7 (1)	43;38 6 (4)	43;109 8 (3)	43;154 17 (1)

充	弃	畜	育
chōng	*棄 qì	xù chù	yù yō
full, ample;	discard,	raise (animals);	give birth to;
act as	abandon	livestock	raise, rear
9;10 6 (2)	9;55 7 (2)	142;102 10 (4)	118;130 8 (1)

恋	弯	变	蛮
戀 liàn	彎 wān	變 biàn	蠻 mán
love,	bend, curve;	change,	fierce,
romance	curved	transform	rugged
162;61 10 (2)	162;57 9 (2)	162;149 8 (1)	162;142 12 (4)

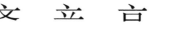
齐 齋
齊 qí 齋 zhāi
alike; together; | to fast, abstain;
neat; ready; & | a room; &
160;210 6 (1) | 84;210 10 (-)

产 辛 亲 帝 旁 商
産 chǎn | xīn | 親 qīn qìng | dì | páng | shāng
give birth to; | hardship; bitter, | parent, relative; | God; | side; | merchant;
produce | acrid; 8th; HS | dear to; kiss; & | emperor | besides, other | trade; discuss
126;100 6 (1) | 186;160 7 (1) | 126;147 9 (1) | 9;50 9 (2) | 85;70 10 (1) | 9;30 11 (1)

竞 音 章 竟 意 童
競 jìng | yīn | zhāng | jìng | yì | tóng
compete | sound, tone; | chapter; rules; | finish; finally; | idea; a desire; | child; virgin;
- | news | badge, seal | surprisingly; & | opinion; expect | bare (hills)
126;117 10 (2) | 211;180 9 (1) | 211;117 11 (1) | 211;117 11 (2) | 211;61 13 (1) | 126;117 12 (2)

彦
彦 yàn
a good man
(literary)
63;59 9 (-)

亨 享 烹 京 哀 高
hēng | xiǎng | pēng | jīng | āi | gāo
successful, | enjoy | boil, cook, | capital (city); | grief, sorrow; | tall, high; loud;
go smoothly | - | quick-fry | Beijing | to pity | expensive
9;8 7 (-) | 9;8 8 (2) | 80;86 11 (4) | 9;8 8 (2) | 9;30 9 (3) | 218;189 10 (1)

亭 亮 毫 豪 膏
tíng | liàng | háo | háo | gāo gào
pavilion, | bright; shine; | hair; milli-; | hero; bold, | fat, grease, oil;
kiosk, stall | enlighten; & | (not) at all; & | wilful; despot | lubricate; &
9;8 9 (3) | 9;8 9 (1) | 112;82 11 (2) | 9;152 14 (3) | 218;130 14 (3)

1	41
2	42
3	43
4	44
5	45
6	46
7	47
8	48
9	49
10	50
11	51
12	52
13	53
14	54
15	55
16	56
17	57
18	58
19	59
20	60
21	61
22	**62**
23	63
24	64
25	65
26	66
27	67
28	68
29	69
30	70
31	71
32	72
33	73
34	74
35	75
36	76
37	77
38	78
39	79
40	80

宀 宀 宁 宁 宁

宀

宁 níng nìng	宇 yǔ	字 zì	它 *牠 tā	宅 zhái	农 農 nóng
tranquil; Nanjing; prefer	house; eaves; (outer) space	word, (written) character; &	it	residence	agriculture; peasant
45;40 5 (3)	45;40 6 (3)	45;39 6 (1)	45;40 5 (1)	45;40 6 (3)	18;161 6 (

宋 sòng	牢 láo	安 ān	定 dìng	宝 寶 bǎo	家 *傢 jiā
Song (dynasty)	prison; secure, durable	peace; calm, safe; install; &	decide; calm; book (seats); &	precious; your (polite)	household; specialist; &
45;40 7 (3)	45;93 7 (3)	45;40 6 (1)	45;40 8 (1)	45;40 8 (2)	45;40 10 (

宜 yí	官 guān	宙 zhòu	审 審 shěn
appropriate; should	an official; organ (of body)	(universal) time; cosmos	examine, try (case); careful
45;40 8 (1)	45;40 8 (2)	45;40 8 (3)	45;40 8 (3)

宀

穴 xué	灾 災 zāi	实 實 shí
hole; cave; lair; grave	disaster	solid, real; seed, fruit
128;116 5 (4)	45;86 7 (2)	45;40 8 (1)

宛 wǎn	宿 sù xiǔ xiù	寂 jì	寝 寢 qǐn
winding, tortuous	stay overnight	still, quiet; lonely	sleep; bedroom; mausoleum
45;40 8 (-)	45;40 11 (1)	45;40 11 (3)	45;40 13 (-)

宀 宁 宁

守 shǒu	宏 hóng	宠 寵 chǒng	寇 kòu
keep watch, guard; nearby	great, vast, grand	dote on; pamper	bandit; invader
45;40 6 (2)	45;40 7 (3)	45;40 8 (-)	45;40 11 (4)

宀 官 宫

宰	宪	案	害	寄	宵
zǎi	憲 xiàn	àn	hài	jì	xiāo
to rule, govern; to butcher	law, statute; constitution	table; proposal; (legal) case; &	harm; murder; get (illness); &	send, mail; entrust; rely on	night -
45;40 10 (4)	45;61 9 (3)	45;75 10 (2)	45;40 10 (2)	45;40 11 (1)	45;40 10 (3)
宽	寞	寒	塞	寨	赛
寬 kuān	mò	hán	sāi sài sè	zhài	賽 sài
broad; lenient; relaxed; well off	lonely, deserted	cold; shiver; poor, needy	stopper; jam in; strategic place	stockade, camp	contest, game; to rival, surpass
45;40 10 (2)	45;40 13 (3)	45;40 12 (1)	45;32 13 (3)	45;40 14 (4)	45;154 14 (1)
完	宗	宣	富	寅	寡
wán	zōng	xuān	fù	yín	guǎ
whole, intact; finish; use up	ancestor; clan; purpose; model	proclaim; drain off	rich, wealthy	EB -	few; rare; insipid; widow
45;40 7 (1)	45;40 8 (3)	45;40 9 (2)	45;40 12 (1)	45;40 11 (-)	45;40 14 (3)
室	宫	宴	寓	宾	
shì	宮 gōng	yàn	yù	賓 bīn	
a room -	palace, temple; womb	banquet; at ease; entertain	reside, abode; moral (of story)	guest -	
45;40 9 (1)	45;40 9 (3)	45;40 10 (1)	45;40 12 (3)	45;154 10 (2)	
客	密	蜜	察		
kè	mì	mì	chá		
guest, visitor, customer; &	closely; dense; precise; secret	honey; sweet, candied	examine, inspect		
45;40 9 (1)	45;40 11 (2)	45;142 14 (2)	45;40 14 (2)		
空	究	突	帘	穷	窄
kōng kòng	jiū	tū	* 簾 lián	窮 qióng	zhǎi
sky, air; in vain; empty, vacant	investigate; after all	abrupt; rush at; protruding	screen, curtain	poor; limit; extremely	narrow; petty; hard up
128;116 8 (1)	128;116 7 (1)	128;116 9 (2)	128;50 8 (3)	128;116 7 (2)	128;116 10 (2)
穿	容	窜	窃	窑	
chuān	róng	竄 cuàn	竊 qiè	窯 yáo	
penetrate; wear, put on	contain; permit; tolerate; looks	flee; amend	steal; furtive, secretly	kiln; cave; pit	
128;116 9 (1)	45;40 10 (1)	128;116 12 (3)	128;116 9 (4)	128;116 11 (3)	
窝	窗	窿	窟	交	
窩 wō	chuāng	lóng	kū	jiāo	
nest, lair, pit; to bend; &	window -	[hole; deficit]	hole, cave; den	exchange; meet; join; befriend; to hand over; mutual; &	
128;116 12 (4)	128;116 12 (1)	128;116 16 (3)	128;116 13 (3)	9;8 6 (1)	

1	41
2	42
3	43
4	44
5	45
6	46
7	47
8	48
9	49
10	50
11	51
12	52
13	53
14	54
15	55
16	56
17	57
18	58
19	59
20	60
21	61
22	62
23	**63**
24	64
25	65
26	66
27	67
28	68
29	69
30	70
31	71
32	72
33	73
34	74
35	75
36	76
37	77
38	78
39	79
40	80

艹

芯
xìn xīn
core;
pith
50;140 7 (-)

芦
蘆 lú lǔ
reed
50;140 7 (4)

芳
fāng
fragrant;
good name
50;140 7 (4)

芒
máng wáng
awn
(beard of barley)
50;140 6 (4)

芝
zhī
[sesame;
iris]
50;140 6 (4)

茂
mào
luxuriant;
splendid
50;140 8 (4)

菩
pú
[Bodhi tree,
Buddha]
50;140 11 (-)

蒂
dì
base
(of a fruit)
50;140 12 (4)

荒
huāng
neglect; famine;
desolate; &
50;140 9 (3)

蓄
xù
store up;
grow (beard)
50;140 13 (4)

蓉
róng
[hibiscus];
Chengdu
50;140 13 (-)

萱
xuān
[tawny
daylily]
50;140 12

苦
kǔ
bitter; pain,
suffering
50;140 8 (1)

著
zhù
outstanding;
book; write
50;140 11 (2)

萧
蕭 xiāo
desolate
-
50;140 11 (-)

菁
jīng
lush;
essence
50;140 11 (-)

荔
lì
[lychee]
-
50;140 9 (4)

茅
máo
cogon grass
-
50;140 8 (3)

茎
莖 jīng
stem, stalk
(of plant)
50;140 8 (4)

苹
蘋 píng
[apple]
-
50;140 8 (1)

葬
zàng
bury
-
50;140 12 (4)

蕾
lěi
bud
-
50;140 16 (4)

萬
wàn
ten thousand
-
50;140 12 (-)

萝
蘿 luó
vine, ivy;
[radish]
50;140 11 (2)

薯
shǔ
cassava,
yam, potato
50;140 16 (4)

蔑
*蠛 miè
nothing; disdain
(literary)
50;140 14 (3)

菜
cài
vegetable; food;
(meal) course
50;140 11 (1)

萎
wēi wěi
decline, wane,
wither
50;140 11 (-)

蕃
fán fān
luxuriant;
foreigner; &
50;140 15 (-)

薰
xūn
fragrance
(literary)
50;140 17 (-)

董
dǒng
director,
trustee
50;140 12 (4)

芬
fēn
fragrant
-
50;140 7 (4)

茶
chá
tea
-
50;140 9 (1)

苍
蒼 cāng
green; blue;
gray, ashen
50;140 7 (3)

惹
rě
provoke, incite,
stir up
81;61 12 (2)

葱
蔥 cōng
onion;
green
50;140 12 (4)

蓝
藍 lán la
blue,
indigo
50;140 13 (1)

蕉
jiāo
broad-leaf plant;
[banana]
50;140 15 (1)

蒸
zhēng
evaporate;
to steam (food)
50;140 13 (3)

葵
kuí
sunflower;
mallow
50;140 12 (4)

蔡
cài
(surname)
-
50;140 14 (-)

劳
劳 láo
toil; fatigue;
good deed; &
134;19 7 (1)

荣
榮 róng
thrive;
honor
134;75 9 (2)

营
營 yíng
operate; seek;
barracks; &
134;86 11 (2)

萤
螢 yíng
firefly
-
134;142 11 (-)

莺
鶯 yīng
oriole,
warbler
134;196 10 (-)

蒙
*濛矇 mēng méng měng
cheat; guess; unconscious;
cover; ignorant; misty; Mongolia
134;140 13 (3)

草
cǎo
grass, straw;
rough, careless
50;140 9 (1)

莫
mò
no, not;
Don't!
50;140 10 (4)

葛
gé gě
kudzu vine,
creeping plant
50;140 12 (3)

墓
mù
tomb,
grave
50;32 13 (3)

幕
mù
screen, curtain;
act (of play)
50;50 13 (3)

募
mù
solicit, enlist;
raise (funds)
50;19 12 (-)

慕
mù
admire;
yearn for
50;61 14 (2)

暮
mù
dusk, evening;
late on
50;72 14 (4)

共
gòng
collectively,
together; share
93;12 6 (1)

昔
xī
the past,
former
93;72 8 (-)

恭
gōng
respectful,
reverent
93;61 10 (4)

巷
xiàng hàng
lane,
alley
93;49 9 (3)

黄
黃 huáng
yellow
-
93;201 11 (1)

带
帶 dài
belt, zone; to
lead; carry; &
57;50 9 (1)

革
gé
leather, hide; to
change; expel
212;177 9 (2)

某
mǒu
a certain
(thing, person)
135;75 9 (2)

燕
yàn yān
swallow
(bird)
93;86 16 (3)

曹
cáo
people (of some
kind) (literary)
103;73 11 (4)

1	41
2	42
3	43
4	44
5	45
6	46
7	47
8	48
9	49
10	50
11	51
12	52
13	53
14	54
15	55
16	56
17	57
18	58
19	59
20	60
21	61
22	62
23	63
24	**64**
25	65
26	66
27	67
28	68
29	69
30	70
31	71
32	72
33	73
34	74
35	75
36	76
37	77
38	78
39	79
40	80

艹

芯	苏	花	荷	蔼	蒋
xìn xīn	蘇 嚇 sū	huā	hé hè	藹 ǎi	蔣 jiǎng
core; pith	revive; ('su' sound)	flower; flowery; expend; &	lotus; burden; to shoulder	friendly	(surname) -
50;140 7 (-)	50;140 7 (4)	50;140 7 (1)	50;140 10 (4)	50;140 14 (4)	50;140 12

茫	范	荡	莎	萍
máng	*範 fàn	蕩 盪 dàng	suō	píng
vast, vague; perplexed	example, model; scope	flush away; a pool; swing; &	[nutgrass] -	duckweed -
50;140 9 (4)	50;118 8 (2)	50;140 9 (4)	50;140 10 (-)	50;140 11 (4)

菠	落	薄
bō	luò là lào	báo bó bò
[spinach; pineapple]	fall; drop; omit; lag behind; &	flimsy; meager; unkind; &
50;140 11 (3)	50;140 12 (2)	50;140 16 (2)

获	茄	菇	菲	莉	藉
獲 穫 huò	qié jiā	gū	fēi fěi	lì	jí
get, obtain, reap; capture	eggplant, aubergine	mushroom -	luxuriant, rich; unworthy, poor	[jasmine]	[cluttered] (see Table 1
50;94 10 (2)	50;140 8 (4)	50;140 11 (4)	50;140 11 (-)	50;140 10 (-)	50;140 17

萨	荫	蕴	药	苑
薩 sà	蔭 yìn yīn	蘊 yùn	藥 yào	yuàn
('sa' sound); (surname)	shaded; chilly	contain; stored up (literary)	medicine; chemicals	garden; cultural center (literary)
50;140 11 (4)	50;140 9 (-)	50;140 15 (4)	50;140 9 (1)	50;140 8 (-)

萌	薛	藤
méng	xuē	téng
sprout, bud, germinate	(surname) -	rattan cane; vine, creeper
50;140 11 (4)	50;140 16 (-)	50;140 18 (4)

葫	蒜	蔬	薪	蔽
hú	suàn	shū	xīn	bì
[gourd] -	garlic -	vegetables -	salary; firewood	shelter, conceal
50;140 12 (4)	50;140 13 (4)	50;140 15 (2)	50;140 16 (4)	50;140 14 (4)

艾	芙	英	芽	节

艾 ài yì
artemisia plant
50;140 5 (4)

芙 fú
[lotus, hibiscus]
50;140 7 (-)

英 yīng
hero; English
50;140 8 (1)

芽 yá
bud, shoot, sprout
50;140 7 (3)

节 節 jié jiē
segment; node, joint; festival; agenda; economize; &
50;118 5 (1)

艺 藝 yì
skill; art
50;140 4 (1)

苹 蘋 píng
[apple]
-
50;140 8 (1)

茂 mào
luxuriant; splendid
50;140 8 (4)

莱 萊 lái
('le' sound); [radish]
50;140 10 (-)

茧 繭 jiǎn
cocoon; callus
50;120 9 (4)

芭 bā
('ba' sound); (a herb)
50;140 7 (4)

苗 miáo
seedling; small fry; vaccine
50;140 8 (3)

萬 wàn
ten thousand (see Table 1)
50;140 12 (-)

若 ruò
as if; like; seem
50;140 8 (3)

荐 薦 jiàn
recommend
-
50;140 9 (3)

芹 qín
[celery]
-
50;140 7 (4)

蔗 zhè
sugar cane
-
50;140 14 (4)

蘑 mó
mushroom
-
50;140 19 (4)

藏 cáng zàng
conceal; store; scriptures
50;140 17 (2)

菊 jú
chrysanthemum
-
50;140 11 (4)

萄 táo
grape
-
50;140 11 (3)

葡 pú
[grape]
-
50;140 12 (3)

莲 蓮 lián
lotus
-
50;140 10 (4)

蓬 péng
disheveled; fluffy
50;140 13 (3)

菌 jùn jūn
mushroom; fungus; bacteria
50;140 11 (2)

1	41
2	42
3	43
4	44
5	45
6	46
7	47
8	48
9	49
10	50
11	51
12	52
13	53
14	54
15	55
16	56
17	57
18	58
19	59
20	60
21	61
22	62
23	63
24	64
25	**65**
26	66
27	67
28	68
29	69
30	70
31	71
32	72
33	73
34	74
35	75
36	76
37	77
38	78
39	79
40	80

竿 gān	笑 xiào	笔 筆bǐ	笨 bèn	策 cè	第 dì
rod, pole, cane	laugh, smile; ridicule	write; pen; (of Ch char) stroke	stupid, dull; clumsy	plan, scheme; urge, spur on	number (as in 'No.
178;118 9 (4)	178;118 10 (1)	178;118 10 (1)	178;118 11 (2)	178;118 12 (2)	178;118 1

笋 筍sūn	笃 篤dǔ	笆 bā	笛 dí		
bamboo shoot	sincere; serious (illness)	basket; bamboo fence	flute, whistle		
178;118 10 (4)	178;118 9 (-)	178;118 10 (4)	178;118 11 (4)		

符 fú	筷 kuài	*築 zhù zhú	筛 篩shāi	筋 jīn	箱 xiāng
accord with; symbol	chopsticks -	build; Guiyang	sift, sieve	muscle, tendon	box, case, trunk
178;118 11 (2)	178;118 13 (2)	178;118 12 (2)	178;118 12 (4)	178;118 12 (3)	178;118 1

簸 bǒ bò	籍 jí	簿 bù			
winnow; winnowing fan	register, record; domicile	book, register			
178;118 19 (4)	178;118 20 (3)	178;118 19 (-)			

等 děng	管 guǎn	答 dá dā	签 簽籤qiān	箭 jiàn	篱 籬lí
etc.; grade; await; equal	tube, pipe, flute; attend to; &	respond, answer	sign, autograph; label, sticker	arrow -	hedge, fence
178;118 12 (1)	178;118 14 (2)	178;118 12 (1)	178;118 13 (2)	178;118 15 (2)	178;118 1

筝 箏zhēng	算 suàn	箩 籮luó	篮 籃lán		
zheng (zither); [kite]	count, reckon; count as; &	bamboo basket	basket -		
178;118 12 (4)	178;118 14 (1)	178;118 14 (4)	178;118 16 (1)		

筹 籌chóu	笼 籠lóng lǒng	篇 piān	筒 tǒng	简 簡jiǎn	筐 kuāng
plan, prepare; counter, token	cage, basket; envelope; trunk	piece of paper; (written) article	cylinder, tube	abbreviated; simple; letter	basket -
178;118 13 (4)	178;118 11 (3)	178;118 15 (1)	178;118 12 (3)	178;118 13 (1)	178;118 1

览 覽lǎn	监 監jiān jiàn	鉴 鑒鑑jiàn			
see, to view; read	supervise; prison	mirror, reflect; inspect; warn			
107;147 9 (1)	146;108 10 (3)	209;167 13 (3)			

贤	**肾**	**紧**		
賢 xián	腎 shèn	緊 jǐn		
able and virtuous	kidney -	tight; taut; strict; urgent		
106;154 8 (4)	118;130 8 (4)	77;120 10 (1)		

癸	**凳**	**登**		
guǐ	dèng	dēng		
HS 10th;	bench, stool	register; publish; ascend; step on; get on or off (vehicle); &		
154;105 9 (-)	154;16 14 (3)	154;105 12 (2)		

占	**贞**	**点**	**卢**	**卡**
*佔 zhàn zhān	貞 zhēn	點 diǎn	盧 lú	kǎ qiǎ
seize, occupy; comprise; &	pure; loyal; chaste	a little; o'clock; dot, point; &	(surname) -	get stuck; checkpoint
16;25 5 (1)	16;154 6 (4)	80;203 9 (1)	16;108 5 (4)	16;25 5 (1)

卓	**桌**	**与**	**上**
zhuō	zhuō	與 yǔ yù yú	shàng shang shǎng
tall, erect; eminent	table -	and; with; to; help; give; &	above, on, up; ascend; go to; previous; first; put in position; &
16;24 8 (4)	94;75 10 (1)	2;134 3 (2)	16;1 3 (1)

唐 → 33

步	**齿**	**肯**
bù	齒 chǐ	kěn
step, pace; walk; situation	tooth -	willing; consent
102;77 7 (1)	206;211 8 (3)	102;130 8 (2)

岂	**岁**	**崇**	**嵩**	**出**
豈 qǐ	歲 suì	chóng	sōng	chū
(particle, literary)	year, years old	lofty, dignified; esteem	high, lofty (mountain)	exit; go out; to issue, produce, vent; exceed; occur; expenditure
60;151 6 (4)	60;77 6 (1)	60;46 11 (2)	60;46 13 (-)	61;17 5 (1)

岩	**炭**	**岸**	**崖**	**岗**
*巖 yán	tàn	àn	yá	崗 gǎng
rock; cliff	charcoal -	shore, coast, river bank	cliff, precipice	mound; sentry
60;46 8 (3)	60;86 9 (4)	60;46 8 (2)	60;46 11 (3)	60;46 7 (3)

崔	**崭**	**嵌**	**崩**	**巍**
cuī	嶄 zhǎn	qiàn	bēng	wēi
(surname)	high; [brand new]	inlay, embed	collapse, burst	lofty, towering (mountain)
60;46 11 (4)	60;46 11 (3)	60;46 12 (4)	60;46 11 (4)	60;46 20 (-)

1	41
2	42
3	43
4	44
5	45
6	46
7	47
8	48
9	49
10	50
11	51
12	52
13	53
14	54
15	55
16	56
17	57
18	58
19	59
20	60
21	61
22	62
23	63
24	64
25	65
26	**66**
27	67
28	68
29	69
30	70
31	71
32	72
33	73
34	74
35	75
36	76
37	77
38	78
39	79
40	80

十 土 士 生

十

古 gǔ
ancient;
old fashioned
12;30 5 (2)

支 zhī
branch; erect,
prop up; pay; &
12;65 4 (1)

克 kè
able to; subdue;
gram; digest; &
12;10 7 (1)

丧 喪 sāng sàng
mourning;
lose
12;30 8 (3)

南 nán
south
-
12;24 9 (1)

市 shì
market;
city
9;50 5 (1)

直 *直 zhí
straight; direct;
frank; upright; &
12;24 8 (1)

真 *眞 zhēn
true, genuine;
really; clearly
12;12 10 (1)

衷 zhōng
sincere,
heartfelt
9;145 10 (3)

辜 gū
guilt;
crime
186;160 12 (3)

卖 賣 mài
sell; betray;
show off; strive
12;154 8 (1)

索 suǒ
rope, cable
search; ask
77;120 10

妻 qī
wife
-
73;38 8 (2)

惠 huì
favor,
kindness
81;61 12 (4)

囊 náng
bag,
pocket
12;30 22 (4)

土

赤 chì
red; bare;
loyal
190;155 7 (3)

寺 sì
temple
-
49;41 6 (4)

去 qù qu
go, depart; away;
discard; last (year)
133;28 5 (1)

击 擊 jī
strike, hit,
attack
38;64 5 (2)

走 zǒu
walk, go;
depart; leak out
189;156 7 (1)

幸 *倖 xìng
good fortune;
luckily; rejoice
49;51 8 (1)

袁 yuán
(surname)
-
49;145 10 (4)

卖 賣 mài
sell; betray;
show off; strive
12;154 8 (1)

老 →

士

吉 jí
lucky,
auspicious
49;30 6 (4)

志 *誌 zhì
intention; recall;
annals; sign
49;61 7 (1)

声 聲 shēng
sound, voice;
tone; fame
49;128 7 (1)

壳 殼 ké qiào
shell, husk,
crust, casing
49;79 7 (3)

壶 壺 hú
pot, kettle,
flask
49;33 10 (2)

壹 yī
one
-
49;33 12 (4)

喜 xǐ
happy event;
happy; liking for
49;30 12 (1)

嘉 jiā
good, fine;
praise
49;30 14 (4)

生

告 gào
notify; accuse;
request
58;30 7 (1)

先 xiān
first; ahead;
early; deceased
29;10 6 (1)

靠 kào
lean on; rely on;
keep to; near
205;175 15 (2)

麦 麥 mài wheat; cereals 188;199 7 (2)	素 sù basic; habitual; vegetable; & 89;120 10 (2)	表 *錶 biǎo list, form, chart; to show; gauge, (wrist) watch; surface; cousin; & 89;145 8 (1)
责 責 zé duty; require; reprove; punish 89;154 8 (1)	青 qīng green; blue 202;174 8 (1)	毒 dú poison, drugs; malicious 89;80 9 (3)

共 gòng collectively, together; share 93;12 6 (1)	恭 gōng respectful, reverent 93;61 10 (4)	巷 xiàng hàng lane, alley 93;49 9 (3)	昔 xī the past, former 93;72 8 (-)	黃 黄 huáng yellow - 93;201 11 (1)
杰 *傑 jié hero; outstanding 94;75 8 (4)	李 lǐ plum - 94;75 7 (2)	杏 xìng apricot - 94;75 7 (4)	查 chá zhā investigate, check, look up 94;75 9 (1)	森 sēn forested; dark, gloomy 94;75 12 (2)
奋 奮 fèn raise; rouse; zealous 52;37 8 (2)	夺 奪 duó by force; seize; strive 52;37 6 (2)	奇 qí jī weird; surprise; odd (number) 52;37 8 (2)	夸 *誇 kuā praise; brag; exaggerate 52;37 6 (3)	奈 nài [in vain; do (to someone)] 52;37 8 (3)

太 tài excessive, too, over-; utmost 52;37 4 (1)	态 態 tài form; attitude; condition, state 81;61 8 (1)	牵 牽 qiān lead (by the hand); involve 52;93 9 (2)	奔 bēn bèn rush, run, flee; head for 52;37 8 (3)	套 tào cover, sheath; knot; coax; & 52;37 10 (2)	奢 shē extravagant, excessive 52;37 11 (4)
奉 fèng serve; proffer; obey; revere; & 130;37 8 (4)	泰 tài peaceful, calm; extreme, -most 130;85 10 (4)	秦 qín Qin (dynasty); Shaanxi 130;115 10 (4)	奏 zòu play music; achieve; & 130;37 9 (4)	春 chūn springtime; vitality 130;72 9 (1)	蠢 chūn stupid; wriggle 130;142 21 (3)
拳 quán fist; boxing 158;64 10 (3)	眷 juàn family, dependant 158;109 11 (-)	卷 *捲 juǎn juàn roll up; roll (of); book, dossier 158;26 8 (2)	券 quàn xuàn ticket, certificate; arch 158;18 8 (4)	养 養 yǎng maintain; raise, nurture; & 24;184 9 (2)	

1	41
2	42
3	43
4	44
5	45
6	46
7	47
8	48
9	49
10	50
11	51
12	52
13	53
14	54
15	55
16	56
17	57
18	58
19	59
20	60
21	61
22	62
23	63
24	64
25	65
26	66
27	**67**
28	68
29	69
30	70
31	71
32	72
33	73
34	74
35	75
36	76
37	77
38	78
39	79
40	80

口

足 zú
foot; leg; ample
196;157 7 (1)

另 lìng
separate, other
58;30 5 (2)

兄 xiōng
elder brother
58;10 5 (2)

只 *隻 祇 zhǐ zhī
only, merely; one (of a pair)
58;30 5 (1)

吊 *弔 diào
suspend, hoist; condole; revoke
58;30 6 (2)

号 號 hào háo
number; date; sign; horn; &
58;141 5 (1)

吴 *吳 wú
(old kingdom); (surname)
58;30 7 (3)

呆 dāi ái
dull, stupid; stay
58;30 7 (2)

呈 chéng
to present, show, offer
58;30 7 (4)

吕 呂 lǚ
(surname) -
58;30 6 (4)

员 員 yuán
person, -er; member
58;30 7 (1)

虽 雖 suī
although; even if
58;172 9 (1)

品 pǐn
grade, quality; goods; to savor
58;30 9 (1)

吕吕

咒 zhòu
a charm, spell; curse
30;30 8 (-)

哭 kū
cry, weep
96;30 10 (1)

骂 罵 mà
curse, rebuke
75;122 9 (2)

器 qì
utensil; talent; organ (of body)
58;30 16 (1)

嚣 囂 xiāo
clamor
58;30 18 (-)

四

罚 罰 fá
punish -
145;122 9 (3)

罪 zuì
crime; guilt, blame; suffering
145;122 13 (3)

罗 *羅 囉 luó luō
net; sift; collect; display; &
145;122 8 (4)

罢 罷 bà
stop; dismiss
145;122 10 (3)

署 shǔ
office; arrange; to sign; proxy
145;122 13 (3)

罩 zhào
cover; (lamp) shade
145;122 13 (3)

置 *置 zhì
put, place, install; buy
145;122 13 (2)

蜀 shǔ
Sichuan
145;142 13 (-)

田

果 guǒ
fruit; result; sure enough; &
94;75 8 (1)

男 nán
man, male; son
142;102 7 (1)

界 jiè
boundary; scope; world
142;102 9 (1)

畏 wèi
fear; respect
142;102 9 (4)

思 sī
think, thought
142;61 9 (1)

里 *裏 裡 lǐ
in, inside; mile, 1/2 km
195;166 7

胃 wèi
stomach -
142;130 9 (2)

累 lèi lěi léi
toil; tired; pile up; implicate; &
142;120 11 (1)

愚 yú
foolish, stupid; to dupe
81;61 13 (3)

贯 貫 guàn
pierce; link up; birthplace
106;154 8 (2)

黑 hēi
black; dark; shady, sinister
223;203 12 (1)

墨 mò
black; ink; writing; lear
223;32 15

旦	早	旱	是	易	星
dàn	zǎo	hàn	shì	yì	xīng
day; dawn	early; morning; before; long ago	drought; (dry) land	is, are; indeed; yes, correct	easy; amiable; exchange	star, planet; particle
103;72 5 (3)	103;72 6 (1)	103;72 7 (3)	213;72 9 (1)	103;72 8 (1)	103;72 9 (1)
显	晃	昌	晕	晨	冒
顯 xiǎn	huàng huǎng	chāng	暈 yūn yùn	chén	mào
obvious; to display; &	sway; dazzle; (pass) in a flash	prosperous, thriving	dizzy; to faint	morning -	emit; take risk; bold; fraud
103;181 9 (2)	103;72 10 (3)	103;72 8 (4)	103;72 10 (3)	103;72 11 (1)	104;13 9 (1)
景	暴	暑	量	曼	
jǐng	bào	shǔ	liáng liàng	màn	
scenery; revere; situation	violent; cruel; stand out	hot weather	measure; capacity	prolonged; graceful	
103;72 12 (2)	103;72 15 (3)	103;72 12 (2)	103;166 12 (2)	103;73 11 (-)	
昆	昂	晶	最		
kūn	áng	jīng	zuì		
elder brother	high, soaring; hold (head) high	brilliant; crystal	most, utmost		
103;72 8 (3)	103;72 8 (4)	103;72 12 (4)	103;73 12 (1)		

要	栗	票	贾	覆
yào yāo	lì	piào	賈 gǔ	fù
want, ask for; if; need, must; &	chestnut; tremble	ticket, note, bill; ballot; hostage	merchant; to do business	cover; capsize (see Table 1)
166;146 9 (1)	166;75 10 (4)	166;113 11 (1)	166;154 10 (-)	166;146 18 (4)

雪	雷	需	雨		
xuě	léi	xū	yǔ		
snow; avenge, set right	thunder -	need, require; requirement	rain -		
204;173 11 (1)	204;173 13 (2)	204;173 14 (1)	204;173 8 (1)		
零	雾	霉	震	雹	
líng	霧 wù	méi	zhèn	báo	
zero; tiny bit; fall (leaves)	fog, mist	mold, mildew	shake, quake; shocked	hail, hailstone	
204;173 13 (1)	204;173 13 (2)	204;173 15 (3)	204;173 15 (3)	204;173 13 (4)	
霍	霖	霜	露	霸	霞
huò	lín	shuāng	lù lòu	bà	xiá
quickly, suddenly	downpour, heavy rain	frost -	reveal; dew; syrup	tyrant, overload; dominate	rosy clouds, at dawn or sunset
204;173 16 (4)	204;173 16 (-)	204;173 17 (3)	204;173 21 (2)	204;173 21 (4)	204;173 17 (4)

1	41
2	42
3	43
4	44
5	45
6	46
7	47
8	48
9	49
10	50
11	51
12	52
13	53
14	54
15	55
16	56
17	57
18	58
19	59
20	60
21	61
22	62
23	63
24	64
25	65
26	66
27	67
28	**68**
29	69
30	70
31	71
32	72
33	73
34	74
35	75
36	76
37	77
38	78
39	79
40	80

中 虫	忠	贵	患		
	zhōng	貴 guì	huàn		
	loyal,	expensive,	afflicted;		
	devoted	precious	hardship; worry		
	105;61 8 (3)	105;154 9 (1)	81;61 11 (3)		

米 火 灬 匕	粪	类	炎	脊	旨
	糞 fèn	類 lèi	yán	jǐ jí	zhǐ
	dung,	kind, type;	hot; blazing;	backbone;	aim, intentic
	excrement	similar to	inflammation	spine; ridge	decree
	159;119 12 (3)	159;181 9 (2)	83;86 8 (4)	118;130 10 (4)	39;72 6 (4

九 车 龙 戈	杂	轰	聋	袭	尧
	雜 zá	轟 hōng	聾 lóng	襲 xí	堯 yáo
	miscellaneous;	bang, boom;	deaf	raid;	(a legendar
	to mix, blend	bombard	-	follow suit	chieftain)
	94;172 6 (1)	100;159 8 (4)	137;128 11 (4)	137;145 11 (3)	29;32 6 (-)

廿 业 卅	革	燕	凿	带	
	gé	yàn yān	鑿 záo zuò	帶 dài	
	leather, hide; to	swallow	chisel; mortise;	belt, zone; to	
	change; expel	(bird)	make a hole	lead; carry; &	
	212;177 9 (2)	93;86 16 (3)	140;167 12 (3)	57;50 9 (1)	

甚 甘 弗	其	甚	基	某	费
	qí	shèn shén	jī	mǒu	費 fèi
	he, she, it; that;	very; more;	foundation,	a certain	fees; consur
	his, her, its; &	[what?]	base, basis	(thing, person)	use up; was
	24;12 8 (1)	2;99 9 (3)	49;32 11 (1)	135;75 9 (2)	106;154 9

久 勿 乍	灸	忽	怎		
	jiǔ	hū	zěn		
	moxibustion	neglect, ignore;	How?, Why?		
	(Ch. medicine)	suddenly	-		
	83;86 7 (3)	81;61 8 (1)	81;61 9 (1)		

乂 臼	杀	希	鼠	舅	
	殺 shā	xī	shǔ	jiù	
	kill; fight;	hope;	rat;	uncle;	
	reduce; very	rare	mouse	brother in law	
	25;79 6 (2)	25;50 7 (1)	225;208 13 (4)	179;134 13 (3)	

巛 珏 羽 非	巢	瑟	翠	翼	斐
	cháo	sè	cuì	yì	fēi
	nest	se	green; jade;	wing	[striking]
	-	(Chinese zither)	kingfisher	-	('fi' sound)
	78;47 11 (-)	88;96 13 (-)	183;124 14 (4)	183;124 17 (4)	205;67 12

丮 尹				
灵	寻	肃	隶	君
靈 líng	尋 xún xín	蕭 sù	隸 lì	jūn
clever; effective; spirit; fairy, elf	seek -	solemn; respectful	subordinate, servant, slave	monarch; gentleman; Mr.
70;173 7 (2)	70;41 6 (2)	124;129 8 (2)	124;171 8 (3)	58;30 7 (4)

尾彐可子				
买	蛋	录	哥	孟
買 mǎi	dàn	錄 lù	gē	mèng
buy	egg; oval	record; employ	older brother	first -
5;154 6 (1)	156;142 11 (1)	70;167 8 (1)	58;30 10 (1)	74;39 8 (3)

刀乃及己				
召	忍	孕	盈	忌
zhào	rěn	yùn	yíng	ji
call, summon	endure; hardheartedly	pregnant -	full of; surplus	jealousy; fear; abstain from
27;30 5 (2)	81;61 7 (2)	74;39 5 (4)	146;108 9 (4)	72;61 7 (4)

王工				
吾	弄	汞	贡	无
wú	nòng lòng	gǒng	貢 gòng	無 wú
I, we, my, our (literary)	handle; get; do; play with; alley	mercury -	contribute; pay tribute	without; not; nothing; &
58;30 7 (-)	88;55 7 (2)	48;85 7 (4)	48;154 7 (2)	53;86 4 (2)

亚				
吞	蚕	晋	恶	严
tūn	蠶 cán	晉 jìn	惡 è ě wù	嚴 yán
swallow, gulp; to annex	silkworm -	promote; advance; enter	evil; fierce; nauseous; hate	tight; strict, severe
90;30 7 (3)	90;142 10 (3)	168;72 10 (4)	168;61 10 (3)	168;30 7 (2)

几云而				
贝	见	朵	至	耍
貝 bèi	見 jiàn	duǒ	zhì	shuǎ
sea shell -	see; meet; visit; evident; opinion	(measure word) -	until, up to; arrive at	to play -
106;154 4 (4)	107;147 4 (1)	30;75 6 (2)	171;133 6 (2)	169;126 9 (3)

目壬氏				
导	异	鼎	丢	昏
導 dǎo	*異 yì	dǐng	diū	hūn
direct, guide; transmit	different; strange	cauldron; tripod, tripartite	lose; throw away	dusk; confused; dim; to faint
72;41 6 (1)	72;55 6 (2)	141;206 12 (-)	133;1 6 (1)	122;72 8 (2)

耳,冊 里				
聂	骨	贯	黑	墨
聶 niè	骨 gǔ gú gū	貫 guàn	hēi	mò
(surname) -	bone; skeleton, framework	pierce; link up; birthplace	black; dark; shady, sinister	black; ink; writing; learning
163;128 10 (4)	214;188 9 (2)	106;154 8 (2)	223;203 12 (1)	223;32 15 (2)

1	41
2	42
3	43
4	44
5	45
6	46
7	47
8	48
9	49
10	50
11	51
12	52
13	53
14	54
15	55
16	56
17	57
18	58
19	59
20	60
21	61
22	62
23	63
24	64
25	65
26	66
27	67
28	68
29	**69**
30	70
31	71
32	72
33	73
34	74
35	75
36	76
37	77
38	78
39	79
40	80

丿

兵
pīng
gunshot sound;
[ping-pong]
4;4 6 (2)

丶

乓
pāng
banging sound;
[ping-pong]
4;3 6 (2)

头 頭 tóu tou
head; top; first,
chief; end; &
52;181 5 (1)

买 買 mǎi
buy
-
5;154 6 (1)

实 實 shí
solid, real;
seed, fruit
45;40 8 (1)

卖 賣 mài
sell; betray;
show off; strive
12;154 8 (1)

太
tài
excessive, too,
over-; utmost
52;37 4 (1)

底
dǐ
bottom, base;
end; rough copy
44;53 8 (2)

凡
fán
common,
ordinary; every
30;16 3 (2)

舟
zhōu
boat
(literary)
182;137 6 (4)

为 為 wéi wèi
do, act, act as; become;
be equal to; for the sake of
1;86 4 (1)

丿

少
shǎo shào
few; lacking;
Stop!; young; &
79;42 4 (1)

步
bù
step, pace;
walk; situation
102;77 7 (1)

参 參 cān cēn shēn
join in; consult,
refer; ginseng
37;28 8 (1)

口少 →

丨

个 個 gè gē
(measure word);
item; individual
23;9 3 (1)

爪
zhǎo zhuǎ
claw,
talon
116;87 4 (4)

丫
yā
fork (in tree),
bifurcation
24;2 3 (-)

乙

乞
qǐ
beg
-
20;5 3 (4)

艺 藝 yì
skill;
art
50;140 4 (1)

无 無 wú
without; not;
nothing; &
53;86 4 (2)

匕

它 *牠 tā
it
-
45;40 5 (1)

尼
ní
Buddhist nun;
('ni' sound)
67;44 5 (4)

死
sǐ
die; death;
rigid
97;78 6 (1)

毙 斃 bì
die;
kill
123;66 10 (4)

七

皂
zào
soap;
black
150;106 7 (2)

龙 龍 lóng
dragon;
imperial
137;212 5 (2)

宠 寵 chǒng
dote on,
pamper
45;40 8 (-)

笼 籠 lóng lǒng
cage, basket;
envelope; trunk
178;118 11 (3)

■ 冫 十 寸

冬 dōng	寒 hán	棗 zǎo 枣	盡 儘 jìn jǐn 尽
winter; drum sound 65;15 5 (1)	cold; shiver; poor, needy 45;40 12 (1)	date (palm), jujube 167;75 8 (4)	used up; entire; utmost; & 117;108 6 (2)

辛 xīn	卒 zú	宰 zǎi	幸 *倖 xìng	毕 畢 bì	华 華 huá huà
hardship; bitter, acrid; 8th; HS 186;160 7 (1)	soldier; servant; finish; die 9;24 8 (-)	to rule, govern; to butcher 45;40 10 (4)	good fortune; luckily; rejoice 49;51 8 (1)	finish, complete 123;102 6 (2)	splendid; China; your (polite); & 12;140 6 (3)

率 shuài lǜ	辜 gū	翠 cuì	哗 嘩 譁 huā huá
to lead; frank; rate, ratio; & 9;95 11 (2)	guilt; crime 186;160 12 (3)	green; jade; kingfisher 183;124 14 (4)	clamor, noise 58;30 9 (3)

早 zǎo	旱 hàn	罩 zhào	单 單 dān	卑 bēi	早 → 74
early; morning; before; long ago 103;72 6 (1)	drought; (dry) land 103;72 7 (3)	cover, (lamp) shade 145;122 13 (3)	single, alone; list; (bed) sheet 24;30 8 (1)	low, inferior; modest 12;24 8 (4)	

卓 zhuō	草 cǎo	章 zhāng	干 *乾 幹 gān gàn
tall, erect; eminent 16;24 8 (4)	grass, straw; rough, careless 50;140 9 (1)	chapter; rules; badge, seal 211;117 11 (1)	dry; futile; adopt (child); main part, trunk; do, work; fight 11;51 3 (1)

辱 rǔ	寻 尋 xún xín	尊 zūn	夺 奪 duó	导 導 dǎo
disgrace; to insult 187;161 10 (3)	seek - 70;41 6 (2)	senior; esteem, respect 54;41 12 (2)	by force; seize; strive 52;37 6 (2)	direct, guide; transmit 72;41 6 (1)

守 shǒu	等 děng	筹 籌 chóu	寺 sì	寿 壽 shòu
keep watch, guard; nearby 45;40 6 (2)	etc.; grade; await; equal 178;118 12 (1)	plan, prepare; counter, token 178;118 13 (4)	temple - 49;41 6 (4)	longevity; age; birthday; funeral 54;33 7 (3)

1	41
2	42
3	43
4	44
5	45
6	46
7	47
8	48
9	49
10	50
11	51
12	52
13	53
14	54
15	55
16	56
17	57
18	58
19	59
20	60
21	61
22	62
23	63
24	64
25	65
26	66
27	67
28	68
29	69
30	**70**
31	71
32	72
33	73
34	74
35	75
36	76
37	77
38	78
39	79
40	80

八　又　人

八

六 liù
six
-
9;12 4 (1)

穴 xué
hole; cave; lair; grave
128;116 5 (4)

兴 (興) xīng xìng
start; prosper; excitement
24;134 6 (1)

共 gòng
collectively, together; share
93;12 6 (1)

只 *隻 祇 zhǐ zhī
only, merely; one (of a pair)
58;30 5 (1)

兵 bīng
soldier; army; military; arms
24;12 7 (2)

宾 (賓) bīn
guest
-
45;154 10 (2)

冥 míng
dark; deep; stupid; Hades
18;14 10 (-)

其 qí
he, she, it; that; his, her, its; &
24;12 8 (1)

典 diǎn
reference book; ceremony; &
24;12 8 (1)

具 jù
tool, utensil; possess
24;12 8 (2)

真 *眞 zhēn
true, genuine; really; clearly
12;12 10 (1)

寅 yín
EB
-
45;40 11 (-)

黄 (黃) huáng
yellow
-
93;201 11 (1)

粪 (糞) fèn
dung, excrement
159;119 12 (3)

冀 jì
look forward to (literary)
24;12 16 (4)

翼 yì
wing
-
183;124 17 (4)

舆 (輿) yú
public; territory
24;159 14 (4)

员 →

又

父 fù
father
-
108;88 4 (1)

义 (義) yì
justice; meaning; &
25;123 3 (1)

文 wén
writing; culture; rite; civilian; &
84;67 4 (1)

艾 ài yì
artemisia plant
50;140 5 (4)

交 jiāo
exchange; meet; join; befriend to hand over; mutual; &
9;8 6 (1)

斐 fěi
[striking]; ('fi' sound)
205;67 12 (-)

岗 (崗) gǎng
mound; sentry
60;46 7 (3)

风 (風) fēng
wind; scenery; habits; news
121;182 4 (1)

冈 (岡) gāng
ridge (of hill)
19;46 4 (4)

人

贝 (貝) bèi
sea shell
-
106;154 4 (4)

闪 (閃) shǎn
flash; lightning; dodge; sprain
46;169 5 (2)

肉 ròu
meat, flesh; pulp
19;130 6 (1)

质 (質) zhi
quality, nature; simple; query
22;154 8 (2)

内 nèi
inside, inner; one's wife
19;11 4 (1)

哭 →
哭 →
冗 →
员 →

亥 hài
EB
-
9;8 6 (-)

窝 (窩) wō
nest, lair, pit; to bend; &
128;116 12 (4)

介	乔	齐	界	养	鼻
jiè	喬 qiáo	齊 qí	jiè	養 yǎng	bí
between; take seriously	tall; disguise	alike; together; neat; ready; &	boundary; scope; world	maintain; raise, nurture; &	nose -
23;9 4 (1)	90;30 6 (4)	160;210 6 (1)	142;102 9 (1)	24;184 9 (2)	226;209 14 (2)
肃	萧				咠 → 77
肅 sù	蕭 xiāo				
solemn; respectful	desolate -				
124;129 8 (2)	50;140 11 (-)				

允	先	充	元	光
yǔn	xiān	chōng	yuán	guāng
allow; equitable	first; ahead; early; deceased	full, ample; act as	first; chief; unit; yuan	light; glory; scenery; bare; smooth; depleted; alone
37;10 4 (2)	29;10 6 (1)	9;10 6 (2)	11;10 4 (1)	172;10 6 (2)
兄	见	尧	完	宪	无
xiōng	見 jiàn	堯 yáo	wán	憲 xiàn	無 wú
elder brother	see; meet; visit; evident; opinion	(a legendary chieftain)	whole, intact; finish; use up	law, statute; constitution	without; not; nothing; &
58;10 5 (2)	107;147 4 (1)	29;32 6 (-)	45;40 7 (1)	45;61 9 (3)	53;86 4 (2)
兑	克	党	竞	竟	觅 → 77
duì	kè	黨 dǎng	競 jìng	jìng	
to exchange; to dilute	able to; subdue; gram; digest; &	political party; club, gang	compete -	finish; finally; surprisingly; &	
24;10 7 (3)	12;10 7 (1)	139;203 10 (2)	126;117 10 (2)	211;117 11 (2)	
晃	兜	免	兔	冤	
huàng huǎng	dōu	miǎn	tù	yuān	
sway; dazzle; (pass) in a flash	pocket; bag; wrap; solicit; &	avoid; exempt; dismiss	rabbit, hare	injustice; bad luck; hatred	
103;72 10 (3)	29;10 11 (4)	27;10 7 (2)	27;10 8 (2)	18;14 10 (3)	
荒	鬼	冠	寇		
huāng	guǐ	guàn guān	kòu		
neglect; famine; desolate; &	ghost; stealthy; sinister; &	precede; crown, hat; champion	bandit; invader		
50;140 9 (3)	216;194 9 (2)	18;14 9 (2)	45;40 11 (4)		

秃	壳	凭	咒	凳	亮
tū	殼 ké qiào	憑 píng	zhòu	dèng	liàng
bald; blunt; unsatisfactory	shell, husk, crust, casing	lean on, rely on; evidence; &	a charm, spell, curse	bench, stool	bright; shine; enlighten; &
149;115 7 (4)	49;79 7 (3)	30;61 8 (3)	30;30 8 (-)	154;16 14 (3)	9;8 9 (1)

1	41
2	42
3	43
4	44
5	45
6	46
7	47
8	48
9	49
10	50
11	51
12	52
13	53
14	54
15	55
16	56
17	57
18	58
19	59
20	60
21	61
22	62
23	63
24	64
25	65
26	66
27	67
28	68
29	69
30	70
31	**71**
32	72
33	73
34	74
35	75
36	76
37	77
38	78
39	79
40	80

小 示 小 灬

小

尔
爾 ěr
you; like that, that (literary)
79;89 5 (3)

示
shì
show; notify
132;113 5 (1)

京
jīng
capital (city); Beijing
9;8 8 (2)

景
jǐng
scenery; revere; situation
103;72 12 (2)

乐
樂 yuè lè
music; enjoy; happy
4;75 5 (1)

荒
huāng
neglect; fam desolate; &
50;140 9 (

示

奈
nài
[in vain; do (to someone)]
52;37 8 (3)

崇
chóng
lofty, dignified; esteem
60;46 11 (2)

票
piào
ticket, note, bill; ballot; hostage
166;113 11 (1)

禁
jìn jīn
prohibit; endure, bear
132;113 13 (2)

祭
jì
mourn; worship; sacrifice
132;113 11 (-)

察
chá
examine, inspect
45;40 14 (2)

蔡
cài
(surname)
-
50;140 14 (-)

小

恭
gōng
respectful, reverent
93;61 10 (4)

慕
mù
admire; yearn for
50;61 14 (2)

灬

杰
*傑 jié
hero; outstanding
94;75 8 (4)

点
點 diǎn
a little; o'clock; dot, point; &
80;203 9 (1)

烹
pēng
boil, cook, quick-fry
80;86 11 (4)

煮
zhǔ
to cook, boil
80;86 12 (2)

黑
hēi
black; dark; shady, sinister
223;203 12 (1)

熏
xūn xùn
smoke
-
80;86 14 (

煎
jiān
fry, boil, simmer
80;86 13 (3)

燕
yàn yān
swallow (bird)
93;86 16 (3)

蒸
zhēng
evaporate; to steam (food)
50;140 13 (3)

蕉
jiāo
broad-leaf plant; [banana]
50;140 15 (1)

薰
xūn
fragrance (literary)
50;140 17 (-)

蔗
zhè
sugar cane
-
50;140 14

焦
jiāo
burnt, scorched; anxious
208;86 12 (3)

烈
liè
intense, fiery; self-sacrificing
80;86 10 (2)

然
rán
correct; but; so; this; -ly
80;86 12 (1)

热
熱 rè
heat, thermo-; fever; craze
80;86 10 (1)

熟
shú shóu
ripe; cooked, processed; familiar; skilled; deeply
80;86 15 (1)

熬
āo áo
endure; to boil, stew
80;86 14 (3)

煞
shà shā
demon; very; stop; reduce
80;86 13 (-)

熊
xióng
a bear
-
80;86 14 (2)

熙
xī
bright; happy; thriving
80;86 14 (-)

照
zhào
shine; reflect; photo; license; according to; towards; &
80;86 13 (1)

心

志	忠	忌	忍	忽	怎
*誌 zhì	zhōng	jì	rěn	hū	zěn
intention; recall; annals; sign	loyal, devoted	jealousy; fear; abstain from	endure; hardheartedly	neglect, ignore; suddenly	How?, Why? -
49;61 7 (1)	105;61 8 (3)	72;61 7 (4)	81;61 7 (2)	81;61 8 (1)	81;61 9 (1)

思	恳	患	惠	恶
sī	懇 kěn	huàn	huì	惡 噁 è ě wù
think, thought	sincerely; beseech	afflicted; hardship; worry	favor, kindness	evil; fierce; nauseous; hate
142;61 9 (1)	184;61 10 (2)	81;61 11 (3)	81;61 12 (4)	168;61 10 (3)

忘	恋	总	息	意	慈
wàng wǎng	戀 liàn	總 zǒng	xī	yì	cí
forget -	love, romance	chief; anyway; always; sum up	breath; cease; news; grow; &	idea; a desire; opinion; expect	kind, loving, merciful
43;61 7 (1)	162;61 10 (2)	81;120 9 (1)	180;61 10 (1)	211;61 13 (1)	81;61 13 (4)

态	急	惫	惹	葱	慧
態 tài	jí	憊 bèi	rě	蔥 cōng	huì
form; attitude; condition, state	quick; urgent; hurry; annoyed	exhausted, tired out	provoke, incite, stir up	onion; green	intelligent, wise
81;61 8 (1)	81;61 9 (1)	81;61 12 (4)	81;61 12 (2)	50;140 12 (4)	81;61 15 (3)

念	愈	怠	悉	愚	悬
*唸 niàn	*瘉 癒 yù	dài	xī	yú	懸 xuán
study; recite; think of, yearn	get well; better; more and more	idle, lazy	know; all, entire	foolish, stupid; to dupe	hang; pending; far apart; &
81;61 8 (1)	81;61 13 (3)	81;61 9 (4)	197;61 11 (2)	81;61 13 (3)	81;61 11 (3)

您	悠	惩	悲	恐	怨
nín	yōu	懲 chéng	bēi	kǒng	yuàn
you (polite)	leisurely; long lasting; distant	punish -	sad, sorrow, compassion	fear; terrify	resent; blame; complain
81;61 11 (1)	81;61 11 (2)	81;61 12 (4)	205;61 12 (2)	81;61 10 (2)	81;61 9 (3)

怒	恕	想	愁	慰	憋
nù	shù	xiǎng	chóu	wèi	biē
anger, fury; raging	forgive, excuse	think; want to; miss, long for	worry -	to console; be relieved	stifle, hold back
81;61 9 (2)	81;61 10 (-)	81;61 13 (1)	81;61 13 (2)	81;61 15 (2)	81;61 15 (4)

感	惑	思	恩	瑟
gàn	huò	sī	ēn	sè
feel, touch; be moved, grateful	mislead; be puzzled	think, thought	favor, kindness	se (Chinese zither)
81;61 13 (1)	81;61 12 (4)	142;61 9 (1)	81;61 10 (4)	88;96 13 (-)

1	41
2	42
3	43
4	44
5	45
6	46
7	47
8	48
9	49
10	50
11	51
12	52
13	53
14	54
15	55
16	56
17	57
18	58
19	59
20	60
21	61
22	62
23	63
24	64
25	65
26	66
27	67
28	68
29	69
30	70
31	71
32	**72**
33	73
34	74
35	75
36	76
37	77
38	78
39	79
40	80

二 èr
two
-
11;7 2 (1)

三 sān
three
-
2;1 3 (1)

蘭 兰 lán
orchid
-
24;140 5 (3)

叢 从 cóng
crowd, group, clump; thicket
2;29 5 (3)

絲 丝 sī
silk; thread; tiny amount
2;120 5 (2)

旦 dàn
day; dawn
103;72 5 (3)

魚 鱼 yú
fish
-
210;195 8 (1)

叁 sān
three
-
37;28 8 (4)

些 xiē
few; some; a bit
11;7 8 (1)

查 chá zhā
investigate, check, look up
94;75 9 (1)

宣 xuān
proclaim; drain off
45;40 9 (2)

畫 昼 zhòu
daytime
-
117;72 9 (4)

萱 xuān
[tawny daylily]
50;140 12 (-)

立 lì
to stand; to set up; at once; &
126;117 5 (1)

豆 dòu
beans, pulses
191;151 7 (2)

豎 竖 shù
vertical, upright
126;151 9 (4)

壹 yī
one
-
49;33 12 (4)

登 dēng
register; publish; ascend; step on; get on or off (vehicle
154;105 12 (2)

簽 籤 qiān
sign, autograph; label, sticker
178;118 13 (2)

鑒 鑑 鉴 jiàn
mirror, reflect; inspect; warn
209;167 13 (3)

應 应 yīng yìng
should; agree; respond; cope
44;61 7 (1)

坯 pī
semi-finished product
49;32 8 (4)

坦 tǎn
level, smooth; calm; candid
49;32 8 (3)

擔 担 dān dàn
undertake; burden
55;64 8 (2)

渣 zhā
shards; dregs, sediment
40;85 12 (3)

與 与 yǔ yù yú
and; with; to; help; give; &
2;134 3 (2)

寫 写 xiě xiè
write; draw; depict
18;40 5 (1)

烏 乌 wū
crow; black, dark
4;86 4 (4)

鳥 鸟 niǎo
bird
-
152;196 5 (2)

鶯 莺 yīng
oriole, warbler
134;196 10 (-)

鷹 鹰 yīng
eagle, hawk
152;196 18

馬 马 mǎ
horse
-
75;187 3 (1)

篤 笃 dǔ
sincere; serious (illness)
178;118 9 (-)

罵 骂 mà
curse, rebuke
75;122 9 (2)

駕 驾 jià
to harness; drive (vehicle)
75;187 8 (1)

或 huò
or; either; perhaps
101;62 8 (1)

吗 →

呜 →

止
zhǐ
stop, halt;
until; limited to
102;77 4 (2)

上
shàng shang shǎng
above, on, up; ascend; go to;
previous; first; put in position; &
16;1 3 (1)

土
tǔ
soil, ground;
local, native; &
49;32 3 (2)

士
shì
person; knight;
scholar; &
49;33 3 (2)

生
shēng
give birth; grow; life; livelihood;
raw, unripe, un-; student; &
4;100 5 (1)

工
gōng
to work, worker;
industry; skill
48;48 3 (1)

巫
wū
witch,
wizard
48;48 7 (4)

王
wáng
king
-
88;96 4 (2)

玉
yù
jade;
your (polite)
131;96 5 (2)

正
zhèng zhēng
correct, straight, upright, proper;
exactly; main, chief; January; &
102;77 5 (1)

五
wǔ
five
-
2;7 4 (1)

互
hù
mutual
-
2;7 4 (1)

且
qiě
as well as;
for a while
2;1 5 (1)

丑
*醜 chǒu
ugly;
disgraceful; EB
2;1 4 (3)

卫
衛 wèi
protect,
defend, guard
32;144 3 (2)

丘
qiū
mound,
grave
4;1 5 (3)

壬
rén
9th;
HS
49;33 4 (-)

垂
chuí
droop;
hang down
4;32 8 (3)

重
chóng zhòng
repeat; heavy;
to stress; &
4;166 9 (1)

业
業 yè
business;
already
140;75 5 (1)

亚
亞 yà
inferior;
Asia
168;7 6 (3)

壶
壺 hú
pot, kettle,
flask
49;33 10 (2)

显
顯 xiǎn
obvious;
to display; &
103;181 9 (2)

鉴
鑒 鑑 jiàn
mirror, reflect;
inspect; warn
209;167 13 (3)

宜
yí
appropriate;
should
45;40 8 (1)

直
*直 zhí
straight; direct;
frank; upright; &
12;24 8 (1)

置
*置 zhì
put, place,
install; buy
145;122 13 (2)

叠
*疊 疊 dié
pile up;
repeat
35;29 13 (2)

罕 ➙ 75
罕 ➙ 75
罕 ➙ 75
罘 ➙ 75
皿 ➙ 80

1	41
2	42
3	43
4	44
5	45
6	46
7	47
8	48
9	49
10	50
11	51
12	52
13	53
14	54
15	55
16	56
17	57
18	58
19	59
20	60
21	61
22	62
23	63
24	64
25	65
26	66
27	67
28	68
29	69
30	70
31	71
32	72
33	**73**
34	74
35	75
36	76
37	77
38	78
39	79
40	80

丁	宁 (寧) níng nìng	亭 tíng	予 yǔ yú		
	tranquil; Nanjing; prefer	pavilion, kiosk, stall	grant, bestow		
	45;40　5　(3)	9;8　9　(3)	31;6　4　(3)		

干	竿 gān	旱 hàn	宇 yǔ	岸 àn	南 nán
	rod, pole, cane	drought; (dry) land	house; eaves; (outer) space	shore, coast, river bank	south
	178;118　9　(4)	103;72　7　(3)	45;40　6　(3)	60;46　8　(2)	12;24　9　(1)

火	灸 jiǔ	灵 (靈) líng	焚 fén	烫 (燙) tàng	炎 yán
	moxibustion (Ch. medicine)	clever; effective; spirit; fairy, elf	burn -	scald, burn; to iron, perm	hot; blazing; inflammation
	83;86　7　(3)	70;173　7　(2)	83;86　12　(-)	83;86　10　(2)	83;86　8　(4)
	灭 (滅) miè	炭 tàn	氮 dàn	灾 (災) zāi	灰 huī
	snuff out; wipe out; drown	charcoal -	nitrogen -	disaster -	ash, dust, gray; disheartened
	83;85　5　(2)	60;86　9　(4)	109;84　12　(4)	45;86　7　(2)	14;86　6　(2)

大	尖 jiān	类 (類) lèi	契 qì	奖 (獎) jiǎng	奥 ào	奠 diàn
	tip, pinnacle; sharp, pointed	kind, type; similar to	contract; agree; carve (literary)	praise, reward, encourage	profound; hard to understand	settle (a pla funeral offe
	79;42　6　(2)	159;181　9　(2)	52;37　9　(-)	52;37　9　(2)	52;37　12　(3)	52;37　12
	头 (頭) tóu tou	买 (買) mǎi	实 (實) shí	卖 (賣) mài	矣 yǐ	
	head; top; first; chief; end; &	buy -	solid, real; seed, fruit	sell; betray; show off; strive	(particle, archaic)	
	52;181　5　(1)	5;154　6　(1)	45;40　8　(1)	12;154　8　(1)	37;111　7　(-)	

天	吴 (*吳) wú	笑 xiào	癸 guǐ	奏 zòu	葵 kuí
	(old kingdom); (surname)	laugh, smile; ridicule	HS 10th;	play music; achieve; &	sunflower; mallow
	58;30　7　(3)	178;118　10　(1)	154;105　9　(-)	130;37　9　(4)	50;140　12　(4)

丰	奉 fèng	举 (舉) jǔ			
	serve; proffer; obey; revere; &	raise; praise; deed; cite; entire; behavior; choose; start			
	130;37　8　(4)	227;134　9　(1)			

□ 廾 木

弄 nòng lòng handle; get; do; play with; alley 88;55 7 (2)	**弊** bì malpractice; disadvantage 51;55 14 (4)	**异** *異 yì different; strange 72;55 6 (2)
算 suàn count, reckon; count as; & 178;118 14 (1)	**奔** bēn bèn rush, run, flee; head for 52;37 8 (3)	**葬** zàng bury - 50;140 12 (4)
并 併並 bìng actually; also; merge; equally 24;9 6 (2)	**弃** *棄 qì discard, abandon 9;55 7 (2)	**鼻** bí nose - 226;209 14 (2)

宋 sòng — Song (dynasty) — 45;40 7 (3)
杀 殺 shā — kill; fight; reduce; very — 25;79 6 (2)
条 條 tiáo — twig; clause; slip of paper — 65;75 7 (1)
杂 雜 zá — miscellaneous; to mix, blend — 94;172 6 (1)
朵 duǒ — (measure word) — - — 30;75 6 (2)
某 mǒu — a certain (thing, person) — 135;75 9 (2)

呆 dāi ái — dull, stupid; stay — 58;30 7 (2)
果 guǒ — fruit; result; sure enough; & — 94;75 8 (1)
栗 lì — chestnut; tremble — 166;75 10 (4)
桌 zhuō — table — - — 94;75 10 (1)
巢 cháo — nest — - — 78;47 11 (-)

亲 親 qīn qìng — parent, relative; dear to; kiss; & — 126;147 9 (1)
案 àn — table; proposal; (legal) case; & — 45;75 10 (2)
寨 zhài — stockade, camp — 45;40 14 (4)
茶 chá — tea — - — 50;140 9 (1)
荣 榮 róng — thrive; honor — 134;75 9 (2)
菜 cài — vegetable; food; (meal) course — 50;140 11 (1)

采 *採 cǎi cài — pick, pluck, select; & — 197;165 8 (2)
柔 róu — soft, pliable; gentle — 155;75 9 (3)
桑 sāng — mulberry tree — 94;75 10 (4)
秦 qín — Qin (dynasty); Shaanxi — 130;115 10 (4)
笨 bèn — stupid, dull; clumsy — 178;118 11 (2)

染 rǎn — dye; pollute; catch (disease) — 94;75 9 (2)
柒 qī — seven — - — 94;75 9 (4)
渠 qú — ditch, channel — 94;85 11 (2)
梁 *樑 liáng — bridge; ridge; roof beam — 94;75 11 (2)
粱 liáng — millet (literary) — 159;119 13 (3)

集 jí — gather, collect; market — 208;172 12 (1)
桨 槳 jiǎng — oar, paddle — 94;75 10 (4)
柴 chái — firewood — - — 94;75 10 (2)
梨 lí — pear — - — 94;75 11 (2)
架 jià — erect; prop up; shelf, rack; & — 94;75 9 (2)

1 41 / 2 42 / 3 43 / 4 44 / 5 45 / 6 46 / 7 47 / 8 48 / 9 49 / 10 50 / 11 51 / 12 52 / 13 53 / 14 54 / 15 55 / 16 56 / 17 57 / 18 58 / 19 59 / 20 60 / 21 61 / 22 62 / 23 63 / 24 64 / 25 65 / 26 66 / 27 67 / 28 68 / 29 69 / 30 70 / 31 71 / 32 72 / 33 73 / 34 **74** / 35 75 / 36 76 / 37 77 / 38 78 / 39 79 / 40 80

■ 土 牛 车

土

圣
聖 shèng
sacred; sage;
Majesty
35;128 5 (3)

至
zhì
until, up to;
arrive at
171;133 6 (2)

垄
壟 lǒng
ridge
(in paddy field)
137;32 8 (3)

基
jī
foundation,
base, basis
49;32 11 (1)

垦
墾 kěn
cultivate;
reclaim (land)
184;32 9 (4)

里
*裏 裡 li lǐ
in, inside;
mile, 1/2 km; &
195;166 7 (1)

在
zài
exist; be -ing;
at; depends; &
14;32 6 (1)

堂
táng
hall, court;
cousin
139;32 11 (1)

童
tóng
child; virgin;
bare (hills)
126;117 12 (2)

室
shì
a room
-
45;40 9 (1)

塞
sāi sài sè
stopper; jam in;
strategic place
45;32 13 (3)

墓
mù
tomb,
grave
50;32 13 (3)

垒
壘 lěi
rampart, fc
build
49;32 9 (

至
zhì
until, up to;
arrive at
171;133 6 (2)

量
liáng liàng
measure;
capacity
103;166 12 (2)

墨
mò
black; ink;
writing; learning
223;32 15 (2)

崖
yá
cliff,
precipice
60;46 11 (3)

尘
塵 chén
dust, dirt; this
(mortal) world
79;32 6 (3)

坐
zuò
sit; ride on;
recoil; &
49;32 7 (1)

坚
堅 jiān
strong; resolute;
stronghold
49;32 7 (1)

堡
bǎo
fortress
-
49;32 12 (4)

垫
墊 diàn
cushion; to pay
(for now); &
49;32 9 (3)

型
xíng
mold, mod
type, temp
49;32 9 (

坠
墜 zhuì
fall; sag,
weighed down
49;32 7 (-)

堕
墮 duò
sink,
fall
49;32 11 (4)

壁
bì
wall
-
49;32 16 (2)

塑
sù
model,
mold
49;32 13 (2)

牛

牢
láo
prison; secure,
durable
45;93 7 (3)

牵
牽 qiān
lead (by the
hand); involve
52;93 9 (2)

犁
*犂 lí
plow
-
110;93 11 (4)

车

军
軍 jūn
army,
troops
18;159 6 (2)

晕
暈 yūn yùn
dizzy;
to faint
103;72 10 (3)

辈
輩 bèi
people; lifetime,
generation
205;159 12 (3)

空 kōng kòng sky, air; in vain; empty, vacant 128;116 8 (1)	**茎** 莖 jīng stem, stalk (of plant) 50;140 8 (4)	**氢** 氫 qīng hydrogen - 109;84 9 (4)	**左** zuǒ left (hand); different; wrong 14;48 5 (1)	**差** chà chā chāi cī differ; err; wrong; difference; lacking; errand 157;48 9 (1)	
主 zhǔ master, host, lord; manage; & 88;3 5 (1)	**全** quán completely; whole, all 23;11 6 (1)	**呈** chéng to present, show, offer 58;30 7 (4)	**皇** huáng emperor, sovereign 150;106 9 (2)	**望** wàng hope; gaze; visit; repute; & 88;74 11 (1)	**宝** 寶 bǎo precious; your (polite) 45;40 8 (2)
歪 wāi crooked, askew; devious 95;77 9 (2)	**整** zhěng entire; orderly; repair; punish 192;66 16 (1)				
定 dìng decide; calm; book (seats); & 45;40 8 (1)	**是** shì is, are; indeed; yes, correct 213;72 9 (1)	**走** zǒu walk, go; depart; leak out 189;156 7 (1)	**楚** chǔ clear, distinct; pain 156;75 13 (1)	**足** zú foot; leg; ample 196;157 7 (1)	
币 幣 bì money - 57;50 4 (2)	**市** shì market; city 9;50 5 (1)	**吊** * 弔 diào suspend, hoist; condole; revoke 58;30 6 (2)	**帝** dì God; emperor 9;50 9 (2)	**帘** * 簾 lián screen, curtain 128;50 8 (3)	**布** * 佈 bù cloth; spread; deploy; declare 14;50 5 (1)
带 帶 dài belt, zone; to lead; carry; & 57;50 9 (1)	**常** cháng often; constant; normal 139;50 11 (1)	**蒂** dì base (of a fruit) 50;140 12 (4)	**幕** mù screen, curtain; act (of play) 50;50 13 (3)	**帮** 幫 bāng help, assist; gang; & 57;50 9 (1)	**希** xī hope; rare 25;50 7 (1)
击 擊 jí strike, hit, attack 38;64 5 (2)	**出** chū exit; go out; to issue, produce, vent; exceed; occur; expenditure 61;17 5 (1)				
岔 chà branch off, turn off 60;46 7 (4)	**岳** yuè high mountain; wife's parents 60;46 8 (4)	**密** mì closely; dense; precise; secret 45;40 11 (2)	**岛** 島 dǎo island - 60;46 7 (2)	**窟** kū hole, cave; den 128;116 13 (3)	

1	41
2	42
3	43
4	44
5	45
6	46
7	47
8	48
9	49
10	50
11	51
12	52
13	53
14	54
15	55
16	56
17	57
18	58
19	59
20	60
21	61
22	62
23	63
24	64
25	65
26	66
27	67
28	68
29	69
30	70
31	71
32	72
33	73
34	74
35	**75**
36	76
37	77
38	78
39	79
40	80

又

支 zhī
branch; erect, prop up; pay; &
12;65 4 (1)

变 變 biàn
change, transform
162;149 8 (1)

受 shòu
receive, accept; endure
116;29 8 (2)

曼 màn
prolonged; graceful
103;73 11 (-)

凤 鳳 fèng
phoenix
-
30;196 4 (4)

皮 pí
skin, leather; outer layer; &
153;107 5 (2)

友 yǒu
friend
-
14;29 4 (1)

发 發 髮 fā fà
emit; become; develop; hair; &
35;105 5 (1)

爱 愛 ài
love; be fond of; cherish; apt to
116;61 10 (1)

夂

麦 麥 mài
wheat; cereals
188;199 7 (2)

夏 xià
summer
-
65;35 10 (1)

复 *復 複 覆 fù
duplicate, repeat; complex; resume; reply; revenge
20;60 9 (1)

女

安 ān
peace; calm, safe; install; &
45;40 6 (1)

妥 tuǒ
arranged; appropriate
116;38 7 (3)

委 wěi wēi
appoint; indirect; &
149;38 8 (2)

耍 shuǎ
to play
-
169;126 9 (3)

要 yào yāo
want, ask for; if; need, must; &
166;146 9 (1)

妄 wàng
absurd; presumptuous
43;38 6 (4)

宴 yàn
banquet; at ease; entertain
45;40 10 (1)

妻 qī
wife
-
73;38 8 (2)

姜 薑 jiāng
ginger
157;140 9 (4)

萎 wēi wěi
decline, wane, wither
50;140 11 (-)

姿 zī
looks; posture; gesture
73;38 9 (3)

婆 pó
old woman; mother in law
73;38 11 (3)

娶 qǔ
marry (a woman)
73;38 11 (3)

婴 嬰 yīng
baby, infant
73;38 11 (3)

夕

岁 歲 suì
year, years old
60;77 6 (1)

多 duō
many; more; over-; &
64;36 6 (1)

梦 夢 mèng
dream
-
64;36 11 (2)

爹 diē
father, dad (colloq)
108;88 10 (3)

萝 蘿 luó
vine, ivy; [radish]
50;140 11 (2)

箩 籮 luó
bamboo basket
178;118 14 (4)

罗 *羅 囉 luó luō
net; sift; collect; display; &
145;122 8 (4)

另	男	务	劣	穷	劳
lìng	nán	務 wù	liè	窮 qióng	勞 láo
separate, other	man, male; son	affair, business; work at	inferior, poor quality	poor; limit; extremely	toil; fatigue; good deed; &
58;30 5 (2)	142;102 7 (1)	65;19 5 (1)	79;19 6 (3)	128;116 7 (2)	134;19 7 (1)

努	势	舅	勇	雾	募
nǔ	勢 shì	jiù	yǒng	霧 wù	mù
exert oneself; bulge	power; gesture; appearance; &	uncle; brother in law	brave –	fog, mist	solicit, enlist, raise (funds)
28;19 7 (1)	28;19 8 (2)	179;134 13 (3)	31;19 9 (2)	204;173 13 (2)	50;19 12 (-)

分	芬	券	氛
fēn fèn	fēn	quàn xuàn	fēn
small unit; part; divide; duty; &	fragrant –	ticket, certificate; arch	atmosphere, vapor
24;18 4 (1)	50;140 7 (4)	158;18 8 (4)	109;84 8 (3)

劈	剪	寡
pī pǐ	jiǎn	guǎ
split; strike; right up against	scissors; clip; trim; wipe out	few; rare; insipid; widow
27;18 15 (4)	27;18 11 (2)	45;40 14 (3)

令	零	琴
lìng lǐng	líng	qín
command; your (resp); &	zero; tiny bit; fall (leaves)	zither; stringed instrument
23;9 5 (2)	204;173 13 (1)	88;96 12 (3)

字	学	李	季	孕
zì	學 xué	lǐ	jì	yùn
word, (written) character; &	study, learn; knowledge; &	plum –	season, quarterly	pregnant –
45;39 6 (1)	74;39 8 (1)	94;75 7 (2)	149;39 8 (2)	74;39 5 (4)

拿	掌	拳	挚	攀	擎
ná	zhǎng	quán	摯 zhì	pān	qíng
grasp; using; treat as; &	palm (of hand); control	fist; boxing	sincere (literary)	climb; implicate	lift up, hold up, raise
111;64 10 (1)	139;64 12 (1)	158;64 10 (3)	111;64 10 (4)	111;64 19 (3)	111;64 16 (-)

笔	毫	髦	尾
筆 bǐ	háo	máo	wěi
write; pen; (of Ch char) stroke	hair; milli-; (not) at all; &	[fashionable] –	tail, end
178;118 10 (1)	112;82 11 (2)	220;190 14 (4)	67;44 7 (2)

1 41
2 42
3 43
4 44
5 45
6 46
7 47
8 48
9 49
10 50
11 51
12 52
13 53
14 54
15 55
16 56
17 57
18 58
19 59
20 60
21 61
22 62
23 63
24 64
25 65
26 66
27 67
28 68
29 69
30 70
31 71
32 72
33 73
34 74
35 75
36 **76**
37 77
38 78
39 79
40 80

水

泉	汞	浆	尿	聚
quán	gǒng	漿 jiāng jiàng	niào suī	jù
spring, fountain	mercury	thick liquid, syrup; starch	urine; urinate	assemble, get together
150;85 9 (4)	48;85 7 (4)	125;85 10 (3)	67;44 7 (4)	163;128 14 (3)

氺

求	录	隶	泰	暴	黎
qiú	錄 lù	隸 lì	tài	bào	lí
beg, request; seek	record; employ	subordinate, servant, slave	peaceful, calm; extreme, -most	violent; cruel; stand out	multitude (literary)
1;85 7 (1)	70;167 8 (1)	124;171 8 (3)	130;85 10 (4)	103;72 15 (3)	149;202 1

糸

紫	繁	紧	絮
zǐ	fán	緊 jǐn	xù
purple	numerous; propagate	tight; taut; strict; urgent	cotton wadding; garrulous
77;120 12 (2)	77;120 17 (2)	77;120 10 (1)	77;120 12 (4)

系	累	索	素
*係繫 xì	lèi lěi léi	suǒ	sù
fasten; system; department; &	toil; tired; pile up; implicate; &	rope, cable; search; ask for	basic; habitual; vegetable; &
77;120 7 (1)	142;120 11 (1)	77;120 10 (3)	89;120 10 (2)

氏

畏	丧	长
wèi	喪 sāng sàng	長 cháng zhǎng
fear; respect	mourning; lose	long; long-term; steadily; forte; grow; senior, chief; get, acquire
142;102 9 (4)	12;30 8 (3)	4;168 4 (1)

衣

衣	农	哀	袁	衰	衷
yī	農 nóng	āi	yuán	shuāi	zhōng
garment, clothes, cover	agriculture; peasant	grief, sorrow; to pity	(surname)	grow weak, decline	sincere, heartfelt
161;145 6 (1)	18;161 6 (1)	9;30 9 (3)	49;145 10 (4)	9;145 10 (3)	9;145 10

裹	囊	襄	表
guǒ	náng	xiāng	*錶 biǎo
wrap; bind up	bag, pocket	assist (literary)	list, form, chart; to show; gauge; (wrist) watch; surface; cousin; &
9;145 14 (3)	12;30 22 (4)	9;145 17 (-)	89;145 8 (1)

衣

裳	袭	袋	裂	装
cháng shang	襲 xí	dài	liè	裝 zhuāng
a skirt (ancient)	raid; follow suit	bag, sack, pocket	crack, split, rip	pretend; act out; dress up; ou to pack, load; install
139;145 14 (4)	137;145 11 (3)	161;145 11 (2)	161;145 12 (3)	161;145 12 (1)

1	41
2	42
3	43
4	44
5	45
6	46
7	47
8	48
9	49
10	50
11	51
12	52
13	53
14	54
15	55
16	56
17	57
18	58
19	59
20	60
21	61
22	62
23	63
24	64
25	65
26	66
27	67
28	68
29	69
30	70
31	71
32	72
33	73
34	74
35	75
36	76
37	**77**
38	78
39	79
40	80

幺
yāo
one (on dice; when speaking)
76;52 3 (-)

玄
xuán
black, dark; profound
9;95 5 (-)

么 麼 me
[what; such as] (suffix)
4;200 3 (1)

公
gōng
public; official; general; impartial; metric units; male (animal)
24;12 4 (1)

罢 罷 bà
stop; dismiss
145;122 10 (3)

套
tào
cover, sheath; knot; coax; &
52;37 10 (2)

县 縣 県 xiàn
county, district
37;120 7 (2)

丢
diū
lose; throw away
133;1 6 (2)

去
qù qu
go, depart; away; discard; last (year)
133;28 5 (1)

宏
hóng
great, vast, grand
45;40 7 (3)

瓜
guā
melon, gourd
151;97 5 (2)

云 *雲 yún
cloud
-
11;7 4 (1)

尝 嘗 cháng
to taste, test; ever, already
139;30 9 (2)

会 會 huì kuài
meet; meeting; union, society; going to; know how to; &
23;73 6 (1)

览 覽 lǎn
see, to view; read
107;147 9 (1)

宽 寬 kuān
broad; lenient; relaxed; well off
45;40 10 (2)

觅 覓 mì
seek
-
116;147 8 (-)

觉 覺 jué jiào
feel; conscious; realize; sleep
107;147 9 (1)

贞 貞 zhēn
pure; loyal; chaste
16;154 6 (4)

页 頁 yè
page
-
170;181 6 (1)

贡 貢 gòng
contribute; pay tribute
48;154 7 (2)

责 責 zé
duty; require; reprove; punish
89;154 8 (1)

负 負 fù
to shoulder; suffer; rely on minus; owe; fail; be defeated
27;154 6 (1)

员 員 yuán
person, -er; member
58;30 7 (1)

贵 貴 guì
expensive, precious
105;154 9 (1)

贯 貫 guàn
pierce; link up; birthplace
106;154 8 (2)

贾 賈 gǔ
merchant; to do business
166;154 10 (-)

费 費 fèi
fees; consume; use up; waste
106;154 9 (2)

贤 賢 xián
able and virtuous
106;154 8 (4)

货 貨 huò
commodity, goods; money
106;154 8 (2)

贷 貸 dài
lend; borrow; evasive; forgive
106;154 9 (4)

贸 貿 mào
trade, commerce
106;154 9 (2)

贺 賀 hè
congratulate; greetings
106;154 9 (2)

资 資 zī
money; provide; subsidize; aptitude; qualifications
106;154 10 (2)

贪 貪 tān
corrupt; greedy; covet
106;154 8 (4)

贫 貧 pín
poor, destitute; talkative
106;154 8 (3)

赏 賞 shǎng
bestow; reward; appreciate
139;154 12 (3)

赛 賽 sài
contest, game; to rival, surpass
45;154 14 (1)

赞 贊 讚 zàn
to praise, favor, support
106;154 16 (2)

质 質 zhì
quality, nature; simple; query
22;154 8 (2)

□

占
*佔 zhàn zhān
seize, occupy;
comprise; &
16;25 5 (1)

古 gǔ
ancient;
old fashioned
12;30 5 (2)

杏
xìng
apricot
-
94;75 7 (4)

吉
jí
lucky,
auspicious
49;30 6 (4)

告
gào
notify; accuse;
request
58;30 7 (1)

呂
呂 lǚ
(surname)
-
58;30 6 (4)

吾
wú
I, we, my, our
(literary)
58;30 7 (-)

吞
tūn
swallow, gulp;
to annex
90;30 7 (3)

否
fǒu pǐ
deny; not;
evil; censure
95;30 7 (2)

召
zhào
call,
summon
27;30 5 (2)

舌
shé
tongue
-
177;135 6

各
gè
each,
every
65;30 6 (1)

台
*臺檯颱 tái
platform, stage; support;
desk; (TV) station; Taiwan
37;30 5 (2)

售
shòu
sell
-
208;30 11 (3)

咨
諮 zī
consult
-
58;149 9 (4)

哲
zhé
wise;
philosopher
58;30 10 (2)

唇
*脣 chún
lips
-
187;30 10 (3)

言
yán
word; speech;
say, talk
185;149 7 (1)

害
hài
harm; murder;
get (illness); &
45;40 10 (2)

容
róng
contain; permit,
tolerate; looks
45;40 10 (1)

宮
宮 gōng
palace, temple;
womb
45;40 9 (3)

客
kè
guest, visitor,
customer; &
45;40 9 (1)

喜
xǐ
happy ever
happy; likin
49;30 12

苦
kǔ
bitter; pain,
suffering
50;140 8 (1)

菩
pú
[Bodhi tree,
Buddha]
50;140 11 (-)

蓉
róng
[hibiscus];
Chengdu
50;140 13 (-)

營
營 yíng
operate; seek;
barracks; &
134;86 11 (2)

答
dá dā
respond,
answer
178;118 12 (1)

合
hé gě
join; add up to;
shut; to suit; &
23;30 6 (1)

含
hán
contain;
hold in mouth
58;30 7 (2)

舍
*捨 shě shè
abandon;
house, shed; &
23;135 8 (1)

谷
*穀 gǔ
valley;
grain, cereal
199;150 7 (3)

兽
獸 shòu
beast
-
24;94 11 (3)

善
shàn
good; expe
apt to; frien
157;30 12

誉
譽 yù
reputation;
praise
185;149 13 (4)

誓
shì
oath,
vow
185;149 14 (4)

譬
pì
example,
analogy
185;149 20 (3)

警
jǐng
warn; vigilant;
police
185;149 19 (2)

石　口

石
shí dàn
stone, rock;
inscription
136;112 5 (2)

右
yòu
right (hand)
-
14;30 5 (1)

名
míng
name;
renown; famous
64;30 6 (1)

君
jūn
monarch;
gentleman; Mr.
58;30 7 (4)

后
*後 hòu
back, behind,
after; empress
22;30 6 (1)

启
啓 qǐ
open, begin;
enlighten
86;30 7 (2)

岩
*巖 yán
rock;
cliff
60;46 8 (3)

碧
bì
green; blue
(literary)
136;112 14 (4)

可
kě
approve; indeed;
can, may; &
58;30 5 (1)

司
sī
attend to;
department
6;30 5 (2)

句
jù
sentence,
line of verse
26;30 5 (1)

奇
qí jī
weird; surprise;
odd (number)
52;37 8 (2)

寄
jì
send, mail;
entrust; rely on
45;40 11 (1)

哥
gē
older
brother
58;30 10 (1)

向
*嚮 xiàng
facing; towards;
direction; &
4;30 6 (1)

同
tóng tòng
same, equal;
together, with
19;30 6 (1)

周
*週 zhōu
circuit; week;
thoughtful; &
19;30 8 (1)

问
問 wèn
ask; ask after;
interrogate
46;30 6 (1)

尚
shàng
esteem,
respect; yet
79;42 8 (3)

商
shāng
merchant;
trade; discuss
9;30 11 (1)

高
gāo
tall, high; loud;
expensive
218;189 10 (1)

嵩
sōng
high, lofty
(mountain)
60;46 13 (-)

筒
tǒng
cylinder,
tube
178;118 12 (3)

阁
閣 gé
pavilion;
Excellency; &
46;169 9 (4)

官
guān
an official;
organ (of body)
45;40 8 (2)

管
guǎn
tube, pipe, flute;
attend to; &
178;118 14 (2)

1	41
2	42
3	43
4	44
5	45
6	46
7	47
8	48
9	49
10	50
11	51
12	52
13	53
14	54
15	55
16	56
17	57
18	58
19	59
20	60
21	61
22	62
23	63
24	64
25	65
26	66
27	67
28	68
29	69
30	70
31	71
32	72
33	73
34	74
35	75
36	76
37	77
38	**78**
39	79
40	80

曰　目　且

曰

白	百	旨	昏	香
bái	bǎi	zhǐ	hūn	xiāng
white; blank, in vain; gratis; &	a hundred; numerous	aim, intention; decree	dusk; confused; dim; to faint	fragrant; appetizing; heartily; perfume, incense; popular
150;106 5 (1)	150;106 6 (1)	39;72 6 (4)	122;72 8 (2)	215;186 9 (1)

昔	音	者	春	奢
xī	yīn	zhě	chūn	shē
the past, former	sound, tone; news	person, -er, -ist; this	springtime; vitality	extravagant, excessive
93;72 8 (-)	211;180 9 (1)	92;125 8 (1)	130;72 9 (1)	52;37 11 (4)

普	曾	著	薯	暮	曹
pǔ	céng zēng	zhù	shǔ	mù	cáo
universal -	formerly; great (grandchild)	outstanding; book; write	cassava, yam, potato	dusk, evening; late on	people (of s kind) (litera
103;72 12 (2)	103;73 12 (2)	50;140 11 (2)	50;140 16 (4)	50;72 14 (4)	103;73 11

晋	昌	暑	署	鲁	馨
晉 jìn	chāng	shǔ	shǔ	魯 lǔ	xīn
promote; advance; enter	prosperous, thriving	hot weather	office; arrange; to sign; proxy	stupid; rude	fragrance (literary)
168;72 10 (4)	103;72 8 (4)	103;72 12 (2)	145;122 13 (3)	210;195 12 (4)	215;186 20

皆	暂	替	智	间	简
jiē	暫 zàn	tì	zhì	間 jiān jiàn	簡 jiǎn
all, every (literary)	temporary; brief	substitute; on behalf of	wisdom, wit	between; room; to separate; &	abbreviated simple; lette
123;106 9 (4)	103;72 12 (2)	103;73 12 (2)	103;72 12 (3)	46;169 7 (1)	178;118 13

目

首	卷	盲	冒	省
shǒu	juàn	máng	mào	shěng xǐng
head; chief, first; indict	family, dependant	blind, blindly	emit; take risk; bold; fraud	save; omit; province; visit; aware; introspection
24;185 9 (1)	158;109 11 (-)	43;109 8 (3)	104;13 9 (1)	79;109 9 (1)

督	瞥	看	眉	着
dū	piē	kàn kān	méi	zhaó zhāo zhuó zhe
supervise -	glimpse; dart a look at	watch; look at; look after; &	eyebrow -	touch; catch (cold); burn; to wear; use, apply; -ing; &
141;109 13 (3)	141;109 16 (4)	141;109 9 (1)	141;109 9 (3)	157;109 11 (1)

且

宜	叠	查	直	置
yí	*疊 畳 dié	chá zhā	*直 zhí	*置 zhì
appropriate; should	pile up; repeat	investigate, check, look up	straight; direct; frank; upright; &	put, place, install; buy
45;40 8 (1)	35;29 13 (2)	94;75 9 (1)	12;24 8 (1)	145;122 13 (2)

繭 **jiǎn**
cocoon; callus
50;140 9 (4)

蠶 **cán**
silkworm
-
90;142 10 (3)

蠻 **mán**
fierce; rugged
162;142 12 (4)

蛋 **dàn**
egg; oval
156;142 11 (1)

螢 **yíng**
firefly
134;120 11 (-)

雖 **suī**
although; even if
58;172 9 (1)

蜜 **mì**
honey; sweet, candied
45;142 14 (2)

蟹 **xiè**
crab
-
174;142 19 (-)

肯 **kěn**
willing; consent
102;130 8 (2)

育 **yù yō**
give birth to; raise, rear
118;130 8 (1)

青 **qīng**
green; blue
202;174 8 (1)

骨 **gǔ gú gū**
bone; skeleton, framework
214;188 9 (2)

胃 **wèi**
stomach
-
142;130 9 (2)

有 **yǒu yòu**
have, possess; there is / are; &
14;74 6 (1)

肖 **xiào xiāo**
resemble
-
79;130 7 (4)

脊 **jǐ jí**
backbone, spine; ridge
118;130 10 (4)

宵 **xiāo**
night
-
45;40 10 (3)

膏 **gāo gào**
fat, grease, oil; lubricate; &
218;130 14 (3)

菁 **jīng**
lush; essence
50;140 11 (-)

肩 **jiān**
shoulder
-
86;130 8 (2)

腎 **shèn**
kidney
-
118;130 8 (4)

臂 **bì bei**
arm (of the body)
118;130 17 (4)

背 **bèi bēi**
the back; turn one's back on; by rote; to shoulder; &
118;130 9 (2)

倉 **cāng**
warehouse, granary
23;9 4 (3)

蒼 **cāng**
green; blue; gray, ashen
50;140 7 (3)

*捲 **juǎn juàn**
roll up; roll (of); book, dossier
158;26 8 (2)

危 **wēi**
danger; near death
27;26 6 (1)

巷 **xiàng hàng**
lane, alley
93;49 9 (3)

雹 **báo**
hail, hailstone
204;173 13 (4)

色 **sè shǎi**
color; scene; looks; lust; &
27;139 6 (1)

芭 **bā**
('ba' sound); (a herb)
50;140 7 (4)

笆 **bā**
basket; bamboo fence
178;118 10 (4)

爸 **bà**
father
-
108;88 8 (1)

1	41
2	42
3	43
4	44
5	45
6	46
7	47
8	48
9	49
10	50
11	51
12	52
13	53
14	54
15	55
16	56
17	57
18	58
19	59
20	60
21	61
22	62
23	63
24	64
25	65
26	66
27	67
28	68
29	69
30	70
31	71
32	72
33	73
34	74
35	75
36	76
37	77
38	78
39	**79**
40	80

耳

聋 聾 lóng
deaf
-
137;128 11 (4)

耸 聳 sǒng
towering;
startle
163;128 10 (4)

闻 聞 wén
hear; smell;
news; fame
46;128 9 (1)

母

毒 dú
poison, drugs;
malicious
89;80 9 (3)

每 měi
each, every;
habitually
20;80 7 (1)

霉 méi
mold,
mildew
204;173 15 (3)

田

亩 畝 mǔ
mu (unit of land
area, 1/6 acre)
9;102 7 (2)

苗 miáo
seedling; small
fry; vaccine
50;140 8 (3)

备 備 bèi
prepare, equip;
fully
65;9 8 (1)

奋 奮 fèn
raise; rouse;
zealous
52;37 8 (2)

宙 zhòu
(universal) time;
cosmos
45;40 8 (3)

笛 dí
flute,
whistle
178;118 1·

番 fān
a time,
a turn
197;102 12 (3)

畜 xù chù
raise (animals);
livestock
142;102 10 (4)

富 fù
rich,
wealthy
45;40 12 (1)

留 liú
remain; detain;
keep; accept; &
142;102 10 (1)

雷 léi
thunder
-
204;173 13 (2)

蕃 fán fān
luxuriant;
foreigner; &
50;140 15 (-)

蓄 xù
store up;
grow (beard)
50;140 13 (4)

皿

孟 mèng
first
-
74;39 8 (3)

盈 yíng
full of;
surplus
146;108 9 (4)

盏 盞 zhǎn
small cup
-
146;108 10 (3)

盘 盤 pán
dish, tray; coil;
examine; build
182;108 11 (2)

盛 chéng shèng
contain; to dish
out; thriving; &
146;108 11 (3)

盆 pén
basin,
pot, tub
146;108 9 (2)

盒 hé
box, case,
casket
146;108 11 (2)

益 yì
benefit; profit;
increasingly
146;108 10 (2)

盖 蓋 gài
lid, cover; affix;
surpass; build
157;140 11 (2)

盗 dào
steal, rob;
thief
146;108 11 (2)

盟 méng míng
league,
alliance; oath
146;108 13 (3)

监 監 jiān jiàn
supervise;
prison
146;108 10 (3)

盐 鹽 yán
salt
-
146;108 10 (2)

篮 籃 lán
basket
-
178;118 16 (1)

蓝 藍 lán la
blue,
indigo
50;140 13·

■

究
jiū
investigate;
after all
128;116 7 (1)

芳
fāng
fragrant;
good name
50;140 7 (4)

旁
páng
side;
besides, other
85;70 10 (1)

参 cān cēn shēn
join in; consult;
refer; ginseng
37;28 8 (1)

窄
zhǎi
narrow; petty;
hard up
128;116 10 (2)

宅
zhái
residence
-
45;40 6 (3)

秦
qín
Qin (dynasty);
Shaanxi
130;115 10 (4)

聚
jù
assemble,
get together
163;128 14 (3)

瑟
sè
se
(Chinese zither)
88;96 13 (-)

鼻
bí
nose
-
226;209 14 (2)

斋 齋 zhāi
to fast, abstain;
a room; &
84;210 10 (-)

需
xū
need, require;
requirement
204;173 14 (1)

瓷
cí
porcelain
-
98;98 10 (3)

毙 斃 bì
die;
kill
123;66 10 (4)

穿
chuān
penetrate;
wear, put on
128;116 9 (1)

酱 醬 jiàng
sauce, paste;
soy sauce
193;164 13 (2)

器
qì
utensil; talent;
organ (of body)
58;30 16 (1)

嚣 囂 xiāo
clamor
-
58;30 18 (-)

豁
huō huò
crack; forsake;
open; exempt
199;150 17 (4)

亨
hēng
successful,
go smoothly
9;8 7 (-)

矛
máo
spear,
lance
155;110 5 (2)

茅
máo
cogon grass
-
50;140 8 (3)

岂 豈 qǐ
(particle,
literary)
60;151 6 (4)

弯 彎 wān
bend, curve;
curved
162;57 9 (2)

气 氣 qì
air, gas, breath;
odor; enrage; &
109;84 4 (1)

秀
xiù
beautiful;
excellent
149;115 7 (2)

爷 爺 yé
father; uncle,
grandpa (polite)
108;88 6 (2)

节 節 jié jiē
segment; node, joint; festival;
agenda; economize; &
50;118 5 (1)

笋 筍 sǔn
bamboo
shoot
178;118 10 (4)

雪
xuě
snow; avenge,
set right
204;173 11 (1)

当 當 噹 dāng dàng
act as; when, whilst; ought;
regard as; equal to; proper; &
79;102 6 (1)

琴
qín
zither; stringed
instrument
88;96 12 (3)

黎
lí
multitude
(literary)
149;202 15 (3)

鉴 鑒 鑑 jiàn
mirror, reflect;
inspect; warn
209;167 13 (3)

餐
cān
eat; food;
meal
217;184 16 (2)

1	41
2	42
3	43
4	44
5	45
6	46
7	47
8	48
9	49
10	50
11	51
12	52
13	53
14	54
15	55
16	56
17	57
18	58
19	59
20	60
21	61
22	62
23	63
24	64
25	65
26	66
27	67
28	68
29	69
30	70
31	71
32	72
33	73
34	74
35	75
36	76
37	77
38	78
39	79
40	**80**

APPENDIX: Traditional Characters

This appendix contains all the traditional character equivalents of the characters in the main pages 1–80 (but not repeating those which are unchanged on simplification). The appendix uses the same method as the main book (except there is no thumbnail index) and has its own finder chart, opposite.

If a particular traditional character you are looking for is not in the appendix, this means that it is identical to the simplified character. Thus it is to be found on the main pages. Indeed, in the case of some traditional characters, you might prefer to try looking in the main pages 1–80 first: either for simple characters (which are often unchanged) or where you can try guessing what the simplified character will be like. (For example, any character with the traditional radical 訁 on the left hand side is likely to simplify to something with the modern radical 讠.)

For each traditional character the information given is in the following sequence: the simplified form(s); pronunciation(s); traditional radical (the numbers referring to Table 4 at the back of the book); stroke-count; and the page number where the simplified character appears (so you can look it up in the main part of the book).

If two traditional characters simplify to the same simplified character, then as a rule the simplified character will inherit both meanings and both pronunciations. (Typically the pronunciations will be the same anyway, or will differ only in tone.)

Variants and older versions of some characters are still around, and some are given in the appendix. There are also variants of character components such as: 咼 (咼), 令 (令), and 寽 (寽).

You will also sometimes see older forms of some of the traditional radicals. For example: 忄(忄), ⁺⁺ (⁺⁺) and 辶 (辶).

For the appendix, I have applied the historical conventions for stroke-count often used by dictionaries for traditional characters: these sometimes differ from the actual number of strokes used to write the characters. Note the stroke-counts for the following components:

Radical:	阝	⁺⁺	辶	辵
Stroke-count for simplified characters:	2	3	2	2
Stroke-count for traditional characters:	3	4	3	3

Watch out also for: 乏 巨 垂 瓦 及 鬼

Even for simplified characters, stroke-counts can be tricky: be careful with characters containing the following components, for example: 世 甘 冊 乗

A1	彡 丿 刂 忄 火
A2	氵
A3	亻 彳 忄 扌 土 人
A4	扌
A5	犭 孑 弓 巾 屮 阝 阝
A6	木 禾 釆 米 爿 牛 夫
A7	丁 工 王 矢 缶 方 衤 礻
A8	糸
A9	金
A10	口 日 目 貝 田
A11	耳 歹 石 足 酉 車 卓 幸 孝 虫
A12	月 舟 身 自 血 臣 臣 區 食
A13	言
A14	馬 魚 莫 骨 豐
A15	other ◧

A16	◱
A17	◪ ◩
A18	▬ ◻ ▯ ▣ ▮ ⊞ ◼

A19	丶 丿 卜 上 刂 乚 七 屯 也
A20	十 寸 少 弋 戈 主 交 方 亥 京
A21	羊 并 人 夾 犬 力 丸 央
A22	丁 干 几 長 王 氏 刀 己 司 勺 包 句
A23	欠 攵 反 斤 殳 辛 馬 鳥 隹
A24	占 由 甫 見 且 丑 弓 頁
A25	卩 阝 艮 鬼 風 冊 區 各 令
A26	other ◧

A27	八 丷 八 半 人 一 覀 宀 勹 夂
A28	亠 宀 穴 十 士 大 止 山
A29	廿 竹 羽 炏
A30	口 品 四 目 目 田 西 雪 畫 髟
A31	other ⬒

A32	八 儿 彡 一 巛 心
A33	火 犬 木 巾 山 十 寸 扌 牛 土
A34	糸 水 民 衣 又 攵 女 力 手
A35	口 日 田 月 皿 虫 車 貝 見
A36	other ⬓

A1

凍 冻 dòng
15 10 [45]

馮 冯 féng
187 12 [3]

氷 冰 bīng
85 5 [3]

須 须 xū
181 12 [1]

順 顺 shùn
181 12 [48]

鬥 斗 dòu
191 10 [1]

恆
恒 héng
61 9 [2]

慚
惭 cán
61 14 [2]

懶
懒 lǎn
61 19 [2]

悽
凄 qī
61 11 [3]

憤
愤 fèn
61 16 [2]

憐
怜 lián
61 15 [2]

憶
忆 yì
61 16 [2]

懷
怀 huái
61 19 [2]

惱
恼 nǎo
61 12 [2]

慘
惨 cǎn
61 14 [2]

懼
惧 jù
61 21 [2]

慣
惯 guàn
61 14 [2]

憫
悯 mǐn
61 15 [49]

煉
炼 liàn
86 13 [3]

燒
烧 shāo
86 16 [3]

煩
烦 fán
86 13 [3]

煙
烟 yān
86 13 [3]

燭
烛 zhú
86 17 [3]

煥
焕 huàn
86 13 [3]

燦
灿 càn
86 17 [3]

爍
烁 shuò
86 19 [3]

燈
灯 dēng
86 16 [3]

爛
烂 làn

爐
炉 lú

氾
泛 fàn
85 5 [48]

決
决 jué
15 7 [46]

汙
污 wū
85 6 [7]

污
污 wū
85 6 [7]

沖
冲 chōng
15 7 [52]

洩
泄 xiè
85 9 [7]

淵
渊 yuān
85 12 [7]

鴻
鸿 hóng
196 17 [54]

測
测 cè
85 12 [42]

漸
渐 jiàn jiān
85 14 [51]

瀰
弥 mí
85 20 [14]

漲
涨 zhǎng zhàng
85 14 [7]

滌
涤 dí
85 14 [6]

濺
溅 jiàn
85 18 [43]

澱
淀 diàn
85 16 [5]

灘
滩 tān
85 22 [7]

澀
涩 sè
85 17 [6]

淚
泪 lèi
85 11 [7]

滬
沪 hù
85 14 [5]

瀝
沥 lì
85 19 [7]

濾
滤 lù
85 18 [7]

洶
汹 xiōng
85 9 [52]

汛
泛 fàn
85 6 [48]

潤
润 rùn
85 15 [7]

減
减 jiǎn
0 12 [43]

滅
灭 miè
85 13 [60]

涼	滾	濟	濱	瀉
凉 liáng liàng	滚 gǔn	济 jǐ jì	滨 bīn	泻 xiè
15 11 [54]	85 14 [5]	85 17 [5]	85 17 [5]	85 18 [6]
滬	淚	澳		
沪 hù	泪 lèi	澳 ào		
85 14 [5]	85 11 [7]	85 16 [5]		
淒	澆	濤	潰	湊	淺
凄 qī	浇 jiāo	涛 tāo	溃 kuì	凑 còu	浅 qiǎn
15 11 [3]	85 15 [5]	85 17 [7]	85 15 [5]	15 12 [3]	85 11 [5]
滿	漢	溝	濃		
满 mǎn	汉 hàn	沟 gōu	浓 nóng		
85 14 [5]	85 14 [7]	85 13 [7]	85 16 [5]		
濛	瀟	滯			
蒙 méng	潇 xiāo	滞 zhì			
85 17 [64]	85 20 [5]	85 14 [6]			
況	渦	湯	濕	澤	濁
况 kuàng	涡 wō	汤 tāng	湿 shī	泽 zé	浊 zhuó
15 8 [3]	85 12 [6]	85 12 [49]	85 17 [6]	85 16 [55]	85 16 [7]
溼	湧	淨			
湿 shī	涌 yǒng	净 jìng			
85 13 [6]	85 12 [6]	15 11 [6]			
渾	沒	漁	滲	淪	滄
浑 hún	没 méi mò	渔 yú	渗 shèn	沦 lún	沧 cāng
85 12 [6]	85 7 [6]	85 14 [6]	85 14 [6]	85 11 [56]	85 13 [56]
澇	澀	潔	潛	濫	
涝 lào	涩 sè	洁 jié	潜 qián	滥 làn	
85 15 [5]	85 17 [6]	85 15 [5]	85 15 [5]	85 17 [6]	
潑	灑	灣			
泼 pō	洒 sǎ	湾 wān			
85 15 [41]	85 22 [7]	85 25 [5]			

█▌ 亻

亻⟋

俠	倆	偽
侠 xiá	俩 liǎ liǎng	伪 wěi
9 9 [9]	9 10 [9]	9 11 [9]

亻⟌

傾	們	條	倣	側	儲
倾 qīng	们 men	条 tiáo	仿 fǎng	侧 cè	储 chǔ
9 13 [48]	9 10 [9]	75 11 [61]	9 10 [8]	9 11 [9]	9 17 [9]

亻⟏

佔	偵	傢	億	偽
占 zhàn zhān	侦 zhēn	家 jiā	亿 yì	伪 wěi
9 7 [66]	9 11 [8]	9 12 [63]	9 15 [42]	9 11 [9]

倖	債	儘	偉	傳
幸 xing	债 zhài	尽 jǐn	伟 wěi	传 chuán zhuàn
9 10 [67]	9 13 [8]	9 16 [36]	9 11 [45]	9 13 [46]

併	儀	償	僕	僅	備
并 bìng	仪 yí	偿 cháng	仆 pú	仅 jǐn	备 bèi
9 8 [74]	9 15 [8]	9 17 [8]	9 14 [9]	9 13 [51]	9 12 [61]

侶	優	價	僑	係	偽
侣 lǚ	优 yōu	价 jià jie	侨 qiáo	系 xì	伪 wěi
9 9 [8]	9 17 [45]	9 15 [9]	9 14 [8]	9 9 [60]	9 14 [9]

傷	倫	儉	傑
伤 shāng	伦 lún	俭 jiǎn	杰 jié
9 10 [8]	9 10 [9]	9 15 [8]	9 12 [67]

亻⟎

佈	備	傭
布 bù	备 bèi	佣 yòng yōng
9 7 [32]	9 12 [61]	9 13 [9]

亻⟐

個
个 gè gě
9 10 [59]

佛	復	後	從	徑
佛 fú	复 fù	后 hòu	从 cóng cōng	径 jìng
60 8 [9]	60 12 [76]	60 9 [78]	60 11 [30]	60 10 [10]

術	銜	衝	衛	徵	徹
术 shù zhú	衔 xián	冲 chòng	卫 wèi	征 zhēng	彻 chè
144 11 [41]	167 14 [10]	144 15 [52]	144 15 [39]	60 15 [10]	60 14 [10]

協
协 xié
24 8 [10]

頃
顷 qǐng
181 11 [48]

塊	壞	壇	墳	潭	壜
块 kuài	坏 huài	坛 tán	坟 fén	坛 tán	坛 tán
32 13 [10]	32 19 [47]	32 16 [10]	32 15 [44]	32 19 [10]	32 9 [10]

壩	場
坝 bà	场 chǎng cháng
32 24 [48]	32 12 [49]

夾	來
夹 jiā jiá gā	来 lái lai
37 7 [38]	9 8 [38]

扣　扣　扣　扣　扣

扣

拑
钳 qián
64 8 [21]

挾
挟 xié
64 10 [13]

揀
拣 jiǎn
64 12 [13]

扣

掛
挂 guà
64 11 [55]

攤
摊 tān
64 22 [55]

擲
掷 zhì zhī
64 18 [54]

擬
拟 nǐ
64 17 [13]

攏
拢 lǒng
64 19 [45]

扣

據
据 jù jū
64 16 [13]

擴
扩 kuò
64 18 [13]

扣

擱
搁 gē gé
64 17 [49]

攔
拦 lán
64 20 [11]

扣

摳
抠 kōu
64 14 [13]

搗 搗 dǎo 64 13 [11]	擁 拥 yōng 64 16 [13]	擠 挤 jǐ 64 17 [11]	擰 拧 níng nǐng nìng 64 17 [11]
撓 挠 náo 64 15 [11]	摟 搂 lōu lǒu 64 14 [11]	攜 携 xié 64 21 [12]	
撲 扑 pū 64 15 [13]	捲 卷 juǎn 64 11 [67]	擋 挡 dǎng dàng 64 16 [11]	

拐 拐 guǎi 64 8 [12]	損 损 sǔn 64 13 [12]	揚 扬 yáng 64 12 [49]	擾 扰 rǎo 64 18 [45]	擇 择 zé zhái 64 16 [12]	擺 摆 bǎi 64 18 [12]

攝 摄 shè 64 21 [12]	掃 扫 sǎo sào 64 11 [52]	採 采 cǎi 64 11 [74]	掙 挣 zhèng zhēng 64 11 [12]

撫 抚 fǔ 64 15 [13]	揮 挥 huī 64 12 [12]	搖 摇 yáo 64 13 [12]	換 换 huàn 64 12 [12]	擔 担 dān dàn 64 16 [12]	攙 搀 chān 64 20 [12]

捨 舍 shě shè 64 11 [78]	掄 抡 lūn lún 64 11 [12]	撿 捡 jiǎn 64 16 [12]	搶 抢 qiāng qiǎng 64 13 [56]

拚 拼 pīn 64 8 [11]	摻 掺 chān 64 14 [12]

撚 捻 niǎn 64 15 [12]	撵 撵 niǎn 64 18 [12]	撈 捞 lāo 64 15 [11]	撥 拨 bō 64 15 [41]

攢 攒 zǎn cuán 64 22 [12]	攪 搅 jiǎo 64 23 [11]	攬 揽 lǎn 64 24 [12]

犭 犭 子 弓 巾 山

犭

狹	狽	猶	獲	獨	獵
狭 xiá	狈 bèi	犹 yóu	获 huò	独 dú	猎 liè
94 10 [46]	94 10 [14]	94 12 [14]	94 17 [65]	94 16 [14]	94 18 [14]

獅	獄	豬	貓
狮 shī	狱 yù	猪 zhū	猫 māo máo
94 13 [14]	94 14 [46]	152 15 [14]	153 16 [14]

子

孫	預
孙 sūn	预 yù
39 10 [41]	181 13 [48]

弓

張	彈	強
张 zhāng	弹 tán dàn	强 qiáng qiǎng jiàng
57 11 [43]	57 15 [14]	57 11 [14]

彌	彊
弥 mí	强 qiáng qiǎng jiàng
57 17 [50]	57 16 [14]

巾

帳	幟
帐 zhàng	帜 zhì
50 11 [14]	50 15 [55]

山

峽	嶼
峡 xiá	屿 yǔ
46 10 [14]	46 17 [14]

妳
你 奶 nǐ nǎi
38 8 [9]

媽
妈 mā
38 13 [22]

嫻
娴 xián
38 15 [22]

嫺
娴 xián
38 15 [22]

姙
妊 rèn
38 9 [22]

嬸
婶 shěn
38 18 [22]

孃
娘 niáng
38 20 [22]

娛
娱 yú
38 10 [22]

婦
妇 fù
38 11 [22]

孋
奶 nǎi
38 17 [22]

嬌
娇 jiāo
38 15 [22]

陣
阵 zhèn
170 10 [22]

陳
陈 chén
170 11 [22]

陝
陕 shǎn
170 10 [46]

隙
隙 xì
170 11 [22]

陸
陆 liù lù
170 11 [22]

隊
队 duì
170 12 [22]

陽
阳 yáng
170 12 [22]

階
阶 jiē
170 12 [22]

際
际 jì
170 14 [22]

隱
隐 yǐn
170 17 [22]

險
险 xiǎn
170 16 [22]

陰
阴 yīn
170 11 [22]

隂
阴 yīn
170 12 [22]

隨
随 suí
170 16 [22]

木

棟	栅
栋 dòng	栅 zhà shān
75 12 [45]	75 9 [17]

樹	橢
树 shù	椭 tuǒ
75 16 [17]	75 16 [17]

樓	棲	檯	檸	椿	棧
楼 lóu	栖 qī	台 tái	柠 níng	桩 zhuāng	栈 zhàn
75 15 [16]	75 12 [17]	75 18 [78]	75 18 [16]	75 15 [17]	75 12 [43]

樣	檔	樸	權	橫	構
样 yàng	档 dàng	朴 pǔ	权 quán	横 héng hèng	构 gòu
75 15 [16]	75 17 [16]	75 16 [17]	75 22 [17]	75 16 [16]	75 14 [17]

桿	楊	楞	標	極	橘
杆 gān gǎn	杨 yáng	棱 léng	标 biāo	极 jí	桔 jú
75 11 [47]	75 13 [17]	75 13 [16]	75 15 [16]	75 13 [17]	75 16 [16]

橋	檢	槍
桥 qiáo	检 jiǎn	枪 qiāng
75 16 [16]	75 17 [16]	75 14 [16]

樑	櫻
梁 liáng	樱 yīng
75 15 [74]	75 21 [16]

櫥	機
橱 chú	机 jī
75 19 [17]	75 16 [17]

樞	櫃
枢 shū	柜 guì
75 15 [17]	75 18 [17]

楓	欄
枫 fēng	栏 lán
75 13 [17]	75 21 [16]

稜
棱 léng
115 13 [16]

積
积 jī
115 16 [18]

稈
秆 gǎn
115 12 [18]

種
种 zhǒng zhòng
115 14 [52]

穢
秽 huì
115 18 [18]

穫
获 huò
115 19 [65]

穩
稳 wěn
115 19 [18]

稱
称 chēng chèn
115 14 [50]

釋
释 shì
165 20 [18]

糧
粮 liáng
119 18 [53]

糰
团 tuán
119 20 [37]

牠
它 tā
93 7 [70]

犧
牺 xī
93 21 [52]

壯
壮 zhuàng
33 7 [3]

妝
妆 zhuāng
38 7 [3]

狀
状 zhuàng
94 8 [3]

將
将 jiāng jiàng
41 11 [3]

牆
墙 qiáng
90 17 [10]

規
规 guī
147 11 [48]

丁 工 王 矢 缶

丁

頂
顶 dǐng
181 11 [19]

工

項
项 xiàng
181 12 [48]

王

珊	現	瑪	瓏	環	瓊
珊 shān	现 xiàn	玛 mǎ	珑 lóng	环 huán	琼 qióng
96 9 [19]	96 11 [48]	96 14 [49]	96 20 [19]	96 17 [47]	96 18 [19]

矢

矯
矫 jiǎo jiáo
111 17 [20]

缶

罎	罈
坛 tán	坛 tán
121 22 [10]	121 18 [10]

方 ネ 礻

於
于 yú
70 8 [39]

視
视 shì
147 11 [20]

祕
秘 mì
113 10 [18]

祐
佑 yòu
113 10 [9]

禍
祸 huò
113 14 [20]

禪
禅 chán shàn
113 17 [20]

禮
礼 lǐ
113 18 [20]

禱
祷 dǎo
113 18 [20]

祇
只 zhǐ
145 9 [68]

補
补 bǔ
145 12 [20]

裡
里 li lǐ
145 12 [75]

褲
裤 kù
145 15 [20]

襯
衬 chèn
145 21 [43]

複
复 fù
145 14 [76]

襖
袄 ǎo
145 18 [20]

襪
袜 wà
145 20 [45]

襬
摆 bǎi bēi
145 20 [12]

糹⬚ ⬚ 糹⬚ 糹⬚ 糹⬚ 糹⬚ 糹⬚ 糹⬚

糹⬚

糾	紀	紅	級	納	純
纠 jiū	纪 jì	红 hóng gōng	级 jí	纳 nà	纯 chún
120 8 [15]	120 9 [15]	120 9 [15]	120 10 [49]	120 10 [15]	120 10 [42]

紙	紐	組	細	紳	緬
纸 zhǐ	纽 niǔ	组 zǔ	细 xì	绅 shēn	缅 miǎn
120 10 [15]	120 10 [53]	120 11 [15]	120 11 [15]	120 11 [52]	120 15 [15

練	絲	繩	繡
练 liàn	丝 sī	绳 shéng	绣 xiù
120 15 [15]	120 12 [73]	120 19 [15]	120 19 [15]

糹⬚

維	縱	綁	鄉
维 wéi	纵 zòng	绑 bǎng	乡 xiāng
120 14 [15]	120 17 [15]	120 13 [54]	163 12 [38]

繳	緻	緞	綴
缴 jiǎo	致 zhì	缎 duàn	缀 zhuì
120 19 [51]	133 15 [51]	120 15 [55]	120 14 [15]

糹⬚

纏
缠 chán
120 21 [15]

糹⬚

約	絨	織	纖
约 yuē yāo	绒 róng	织 zhī	纤 xiān
120 9 [50]	120 12 [15]	120 18 [15]	120 23 [15]

糹⬚

繼	縫
继 jì	缝 féng fèng
120 20 [15]	120 17 [15]

糹⬚

綢	綱	網	納
绸 chóu	纲 gāng	网 wǎng	纳 nà
120 14 [15]	120 14 [15]	120 14 [36]	120 10 [15]

紋	絞	紡	統	締	縴
纹 wén	绞 jiǎo	纺 fǎng	统 tǒng	缔 dì	纤 qiàn
120 10 [15]	120 12 [15]	120 10 [44]	120 11 [15]	120 15 [15]	120 17 [15]
綜	縮	編	綿	線	總
综 zōng zèng	缩 suō	编 biān	绵 mián	线 xiàn	总 zǒng
120 14 [15]	120 17 [15]	120 15 [15]	120 14 [15]	120 15 [15]	120 17 [58]
紗	結	緒	繞	績	續
纱 shā	结 jié jiē	绪 xù	绕 rào rǎo	绩 jī	续 xù
120 10 [44]	120 12 [15]	120 14 [15]	120 18 [15]	120 17 [15]	120 21 [15]
縛	縷	緯	繡	繃	
缚 fù	缕 lǚ	纬 wěi	绣 xiù	绷 bēng bèng běng	
120 16 [15]	120 17 [15]	120 15 [15]	120 19 [15]	120 17 [15]	
緣	綠	絲	綫		
缘 yuán	绿 lǜ lù	丝 sī	线 xiàn		
120 15 [15]	120 14 [15]	120 12 [73]	120 14 [15]		
絹	緝	紹	經	緬	
绢 juàn	缉 jī qī	绍 shào	经 jīng jing	缅 miǎn	
120 13 [15]	120 15 [15]	120 11 [56]	120 13 [15]	120 15 [15]	
緩	綉				
缓 huǎn	锈 xiù				
120 15 [15]	120 13 [15]				
終	絡	絶	纔		
终 zhōng	络 luò	绝 jué	才 cái		
120 11 [15]	120 12 [15]	120 12 [15]	120 23 [38]		
紛	給	繪			
纷 fēn	给 gěi jǐ	绘 huì			
120 10 [15]	120 12 [15]	120 19 [15]			
綴					
缀 zhuì					
120 14 [15]					

釒					
針	釘	鈍	鈣	欽	
针 zhēn	钉 dīng dìng	钝 dùn	钙 gài	钦 qīn	
167 10 [21]	167 10 [21]	167 12 [21]	167 12 [21]	76 12 [50]	
鈾	鉗	鈕	銀	敘	敍
铀 yóu	钳 qián	钮 niǔ	银 yín	叙 xù	叙 xù
167 13 [21]	167 13 [21]	167 12 [21]	167 14 [53]	66 11 [31]	66 11 [31]
鍊	鋪	錘	鍾	鏽	
链 liàn	铺 pū pù	锤 chuí	钟 zhōng	锈 xiù	
167 17 [21]	167 15 [21]	167 17 [21]	167 17 [21]	167 21 [21]	

釒		
鍫	鋤	鍛
锹 qiāo	锄 chú	锻 duàn
167 17 [21]	167 15 [21]	167 17 [21]

釒			
鋸	鐮	鍍	鏟
锯 jù	镰 lián	镀 dù	铲 chǎn
167 16 [21]	167 21 [21]	167 17 [21]	167 19 [21]

釒			
釣	鉤	鉋	鐵
钓 diào	钩 gōu	刨 bào	铁 tiě
167 11 [21]	167 13 [21]	167 13 [42]	167 21 [46]

釒	
鍵	鏈
键 jiàn	链 liàn
167 17 [21]	167 19 [21]

釒		
銅	鋼	鍋
铜 tóng	钢 gāng gàng	锅 guō
167 14 [21]	167 16 [21]	167 17 [21]

鋅	鎊	鏡	鐘	鑲	錦
锌 xīn	镑 bàng	镜 jìng	钟 zhōng	镶 xiāng	锦 jǐn
167 15 [21]	167 18 [21]	167 19 [21]	167 20 [21]	167 25 [21]	167 16 [21]
鈔	鎮	錶	鑄	鏽	
钞 chāo	镇 zhèn	表 biǎo	铸 zhù	锈 xiù	
167 12 [21]	167 18 [21]	167 16 [67]	167 22 [21]	167 21 [21]	
錄	錢				
录 lù	钱 qián				
167 16 [77]	167 16 [21]				
銳	鎂	銷	鎖	錯	
锐 ruì	镁 měi	销 xiāo	锁 suǒ	错 cuò	
167 15 [21]	167 17 [21]	167 15 [21]	167 18 [21]	167 16 [21]	
鉛	鋁	鍋	錫	鑼	鏢
铅 qiān	铝 lǚ	锅 guō	锡 xī	锣 luó	镖 biāo
167 13 [21]	167 15 [21]	167 17 [21]	167 16 [21]	167 27 [21]	167 19 [21]
錘	鍾	銹	銘	鋒	
锤 chuí	钟 zhōng	锈 xiù	铭 míng	锋 fēng	
167 17 [21]	167 17 [21]	167 15 [21]	167 14 [21]	167 15 [21]	
鈴	鑰				
铃 líng	钥 yuè yào				
167 13 [21]	167 25 [21]				
鑑	鑽				
鉴 jiàn	钻 zuān zuàn				
167 22 [66]	167 27 [56]				

口一	啞 哑 yǎ yā 30 11 [24]	嗎 吗 ma má mǎ 30 13 [24]	嘯 啸 xiào 30 16 [24]			
口冂	喲 哟 yo yō 30 12 [24]	噸 吨 dūn 30 16 [42]	嚨 咙 lóng 30 19 [24]	嚇 吓 hè xià 30 17 [47]		
口日	嗚 呜 wū 30 13 [24]	鳴 鸣 míng 196 14 [54]	噢 噢 ō 30 16 [23]	噴 喷 pēn pèn 30 15 [23]	嘍 喽 lóu lou 30 14 [23]	嘯 啸 xiào 30 16 [24]
	噹 当 dāng 30 16 [59]	嘩 哗 huá huā 30 15 [23]	嘆 叹 tàn 30 14 [24]	嘛 苏 sū 30 23 [65]	嚥 咽 yàn yān yè 30 19 [24]	
	噁 恶 ě wù 30 15 [72]	唸 念 niàn 30 11 [59]	喚 唤 huàn 30 12 [23]	囉 罗 luō 30 22 [68]	嘮 唠 láo 30 15 [23]	
口品	囑 嘱 zhǔ 30 24 [24]					
口吅	嘰 叽 jī 30 15 [24]	嗎 吗 ma má mǎ 30 13 [24]	嗚 呜 wū 30 13 [24]	鳴 鸣 míng 196 14 [54]		
口巴	呌 叫 jiào 30 7 [24]					
口匚	嘔 呕 ǒu 30 14 [52]					

時 时 shí 72 10 [43]	曉 晓 xiǎo 72 16 [25]	暉 晖 huī 72 13 [25]	曠 旷 kuàng 72 19 [25]	曬 晒 shài 72 23 [25]

睜 睁 zhēng 109 13 [25]	瞭 了 liǎo liào 109 17 [39]	瞞 瞒 mán 109 16 [25]	矇 蒙 méng 109 19 [64]	瞇 眯 mī mǐ 109 15 [25]	矚 瞩 zhǔ 109 25 [25]

財 财 cái 154 10 [28]	敗 败 bài 66 11 [28]	則 则 zé 18 9 [42]

貼 贴 tiē 154 12 [28]	賠 赔 péi 154 15 [28]	賭 赌 dǔ 154 15 [28]	賤 贱 jiàn 154 15 [43]	贖 赎 shú 154 22 [28]

贈 赠 zèng 154 19 [28]	購 购 gòu 154 17 [28]	賺 赚 zhuàn zuàn 154 17 [28]

賜 赐 cì 154 15 [28]	賬 账帐 zhàng 154 15 [14]	貶 贬 biǎn 154 12 [28]	賂 赂 lù 154 13 [28]

販 贩 fàn 154 11 [28]	賄 贿 huì 154 13 [28]	賦 赋 fù 154 15 [43]	賊 贼 zéi 154 13 [43]

畊 耕 gēng 102 9 [18]	疇 畴 chóu 102 19 [25]	暢 畅 chàng 72 14 [49]

耳

恥	聰	聽	職	聯
耻 chǐ	聪 cōng	听 tīng	职 zhí	联 lián
61 10 [25]	128 17 [25]	128 22 [51]	128 18 [25]	128 17 [25]

歹

殘	殲
残 cán	歼 jiān
78 12 [26]	78 21 [26]

石

碩	碼	確	碌
硕 shuò	码 mǎ	确 què	碌 lù liù
112 14 [48]	112 15 [26]	112 15 [26]	112 13 [26]

磚	礎	礦	礙
砖 zhuān	础 chǔ	矿 kuàng	碍 ài
112 16 [46]	112 18 [57]	112 20 [26]	112 19 [26]

足

跡	蹤	踐
迹 jī	踪 zōng	践 jiàn
157 13 [34]	157 18 [26]	157 15 [43]

躊	蹟	踴	躍
踌 chóu	迹 jī	踊 yǒng	跃 yuè
157 21 [26]	157 18 [34]	157 16 [26]	157 21 [26]

酉

醜	醞	釀
丑 chǒu	酝 yùn	酿 niàng niáng
164 17 [39]	164 17 [25]	164 24 [25]

軋 軋 yà zhá gá 159 8 [19]	軒 軒 xuān 159 10 [19]	軌 軌 guǐ 159 9 [19]	軟 软 ruǎn 159 11 [50]	斬 斩 zhǎn 69 11 [51]
軸 轴 zhóu 159 12 [19]	輔 辅 fǔ 159 14 [19]	輛 辆 liàng 159 15 [19]	轍 辙 zhé 159 18 [51]	
較 较 jiào 159 13 [19]	轄 辖 xiá 159 17 [19]	轉 转 zhuǎn zhuàn 159 18 [46]		

輯 辑 jí 159 16 [19]	輻 辐 fú 159 16 [19]	輕 轻 qīng 159 14 [19]	轎 轿 jiào 159 19 [19]	輪 轮 lún 159 15 [19]	輸 输 shū 159 16 [19]

幹 干 gàn 51 13 [39]	韓 韩 hán 178 17 [29]

執 执 zhí 32 11 [13]	報 报 bào 32 12 [13]	親 亲 qīn qìng 147 16 [74]

辦 办 bàn 160 16 [1]	辮 辫 biàn 120 20 [54]	辯 辩 biàn 160 21 [37]

螞 蚂 mǎ mà 142 16 [29]	蝦 虾 xiā 142 15 [29]	蟻 蚁 yǐ 142 19 [29]	蠅 蝇 yíng 142 19 [29]	蟬 蝉 chán 142 18 [29]	蠟 蜡 là 142 21 [29]

月

腫
肿 zhǒng
130 13 [52]

腳
脚 jiǎo
130 13 [54]

鵬
鹏 péng
196 19 [54]

勝
胜 shèng
19 12 [27]

騰
腾 téng tēng
187 20 [27]

臟
脏 zàng
130 22 [27]

膽
胆 dǎn
130 17 [27]

脹
胀 zhàng
130 12 [43]

腸
肠 cháng
130 13 [49]

臉
脸 liǎn
130 17 [27]

膠
胶 jiāo
130 15 [27]

腦
脑 nǎo
130 13 [27]

臘
腊 là xī
130 19 [27]

脈
脉 mài mò
130 10 [27]

膩
腻 nì
130 16 [27]

舟

艙
舱 cāng
137 16 [56]

艦
舰 jiàn
137 20 [28]

身

軀
躯 qū
158 18 [28]

臼

帥
帅 shuài
50 9 [1]

師
师 shī
50 10 [1]

血

衊
蔑 miè
143 21 [64]

颐
颐 yí
181 16 [48]

臥
卧 wò
131 8 [41]

臨
临 lín
131 17 [1]

歐
欧 ōu
76 15 [28]

毆
殴 ōu
79 15 [28]

鷗
鸥 ōu
196 22 [28]

飪
饪 rèn
184 12 [20]

飲
饮 yǐn yìn
184 12 [20]

蝕
蚀 shí
142 14 [52]

餓
饿 è
184 15 [43]

餃
饺 jiǎo
184 14 [20]

館
馆 guǎn
184 16 [20]

餅
饼 bǐng
184 14 [20]

饒
饶 ráo
184 20 [20]

饋
馈 kuì
184 20 [20]

餵
喂 wèi
184 17 [23]

饅
馒 mán
184 19 [20]

餘
馀 余 yú
184 15 [59]

餡
馅 xiàn
184 16 [20]

飾
饰 shì
184 13 [20]

饞
馋 chán
184 25 [20]

飯
饭 fàn
184 12 [20]

飼
饲 sì
184 13 [20]

飽
饱 bǎo
184 13 [20]

饑
饥 jī
184 20 [20]

計 計 jì 149 9 [4]	訂 订 dìng 149 9 [4]	記 记 jì 149 10 [49]	訣 诀 jué 149 11 [46]	訝 讶 yà 149 11 [4]	詛 诅 zǔ 149 12 [53]
許 许 xǔ 149 11 [4]	詐 诈 zhà 149 12 [50]	託 托 tuō 149 10 [13]	証 证 zhèng 149 12 [4]	評 评 píng 149 12 [47]	誣 诬 wū 149 14 [4]

訓 训 xùn 149 10 [4]	訛 讹 é 149 11 [42]	誰 谁 shuí shéi 149 15 [55]	誹 诽 fěi 149 15 [4]	謝 谢 xiè 149 17 [4]

訴 诉 sù 149 12 [4]	詭 诡 guǐ 149 13 [4]

討 讨 tǎo 149 10 [4]	訊 讯 xùn 149 10 [4]	詞 词 cí 149 12 [49]	詢 询 xún 149 13 [4]

試 试 shì 149 13 [4]	誡 诫 jiè 149 14 [43]	誠 诚 chéng 149 13 [4]	識 识 shí zhì 149 19 [4]	譏 讥 jī 149 19 [48]

謎 谜 mí mèi 149 17 [4]	誕 诞 dàn 149 17 [4]	譴 谴 qiǎn 149 21 [4]

調 调 tiáo diào 149 15 [4]	諷 讽 fěng 149 16 [4]

註 注 zhù 149 12 [44]	訪 访 fǎng 149 11 [44]	該 该 gāi 149 13 [4]	諒 谅 liàng 149 15 [54]	謗 谤 bàng 149 17 [4]	讓 让 ràng 149 24 [4]
詠 咏 yǒng 149 12 [23]	詫 诧 chà 149 13 [4]	誼 谊 yì 149 15 [4]	談 谈 tán 149 15 [4]	誇 夸 kuā 149 13 [67]	
詩 诗 shī 149 13 [4]	諸 诸 zhū 149 15 [4]	誌 志 zhì 149 14 [72]	請 请 qǐng 149 15 [4]	讀 读 dú dòu 149 22 [4]	
説 说 shuō shuì 149 14 [4]	詳 详 xiáng 149 13 [4]	譜 谱 pǔ 149 19 [4]	謙 谦 qiān 149 17 [4]	議 议 yì 149 20 [4]	護 护 hù 149 21 [11]
謀 谋 móu 149 16 [4]	諾 诺 nuò 149 16 [4]	謊 谎 huǎng 149 17 [4]	譁 哗 huá 149 19 [23]	謹 谨 jǐn 149 18 [4]	講 讲 jiǎng 149 17 [57]
誤 误 wù 149 14 [4]	課 课 kè 149 15 [4]	謂 谓 wèi 149 16 [4]	譯 译 yì 149 20 [4]	譚 谭 tán 149 19 [4]	
設 设 shè 149 11 [55]	認 认 rèn 149 14 [46]	語 语 yǔ 149 14 [4]	誦 诵 sòng 149 14 [4]	話 话 huà 149 13 [4]	誘 诱 yòu 149 14 [4]
詭 诡 guǐ 149 13 [4]	謠 谣 yáo 149 17 [4]	讒 谗 chán 149 24 [4]			
詮 诠 quán 149 13 [4]	診 诊 zhěn 149 12 [4]	論 论 lùn lún 149 15 [4]	訟 讼 sòng 149 11 [4]	誒 欸 ēi éi ěi èi ǎ 149 14 [50]	
諮 咨 zī 149 16 [78]	證 证 zhèng 149 19 [4]	諧 谐 xié 149 16 [4]	謬 谬 miù 149 18 [4]	讚 赞 zàn 154 26 [77]	

馬

駄	馳	駛
驮 tuó duò	驰 chí	驶 shǐ
187 13 [28]	187 13 [28]	187 15 [57]

駐	駭	駝	騎	騙	駿
驻 zhù	骇 hài	驼 tuó	骑 qí	骗 piàn	骏 jùn
187 15 [28]	187 16 [28]	187 15 [28]	187 18 [28]	187 19 [28]	187 17 [28

駱	驕	騾	騷
骆 luò	骄 jiāo	骡 luó	骚 sāo
187 16 [56]	187 22 [28]	187 21 [28]	187 20 [28]

駁	驗	驟
驳 bó	验 yàn	骤 zhòu
187 14 [28]	187 23 [28]	187 24 [28]

驢	驅
驴 lǘ	驱 qū
187 25 [44]	187 21 [52]

魚

鮮	穌	鯨	鮑	觸
鲜 xiān xiǎn	稣 sū	鲸 jīng	鲍 bào	触 chù
195 17 [29]	115 16 [29]	195 19 [29]	195 16 [50]	148 20 [29]

艱
艰 jiān
138 17 [53]

歎
叹 tàn
76 15 [24]

難
难 nán nàn
172 19 [55]

體
体 tǐ tī
188 23 [9]

髒
脏 zāng
188 23 [27]

髓
髓 suǐ
188 23 [31]

豔
艳 yàn
139 24 [30]

豐
艳 yàn
151 28 [30]

豐盍
艳 yàn
151 27 [30]

申 虫 亩

暢	蝦	畝
畅 chàng	虾 xiā	亩 mǔ
72 14 [49]	142 15 [29]	102 10 [62]

光 皀 雇

輝	歸	顧
辉 huī	归 guī	顾 gù
159 15 [18]	77 18 [1]	181 21 [48]

音 竞 音 亲 彦

韻	競	龍	親	顏
韵 yùn	竞 jìng	龙 lóng	亲 qīn qìng	颜 yán
180 19 [30]	117 20 [62]	212 16 [33]	147 16 [74]	181 18 [48]

屯 柬 皮

頓	賴	頗
顿 dùn	赖 lài	颇 pō
181 13 [48]	154 16 [30]	181 14 [48]

真 夾 麥

顛	頰	麵	麭
颠 diān	颊 jiá	面 miàn	面 miàn
181 19 [48]	181 16 [48]	199 20 [39]	199 15 [39]

壳 棠 青 柰

殼	穀	靜	隸
壳 ké qiào	谷 gǔ	静 jìng	隶 lì
79 12 [71]	150 14 [59]	174 16 [37]	171 17 [77]

隹 乡

鶴	鄉
鹤 hè	乡 xiāng
196 21 [30]	163 12 [38]

步 虍 鹵 齒

頻	虧	鹹	齡
频 pín	亏 kuī	咸 xián	龄 líng
181 16 [48]	141 17 [60]	197 20 [36]	211 20 [30]

昔 革

鵲	靭
鹊 què	韧 rèn
196 19 [54]	177 12 [49]

豆 臼 干

矛 牙 豕

甲 果 票

果 原

戈 奚

角

令 余

分 幺

頑 顽 wán 181 13 [48]	頭 头 tóu tou 181 16 [74]	門 门 mén 169 8 [1]	鬥 斗 dòu 191 10 [1]
預 预 yù 181 13 [48]	務 务 wù 19 11 [76]	鴉 鸦 yā 196 15 [19]	豬 猪 zhū 152 15 [14]
號 号 hào háo 141 13 [68]	鴨 鸭 yā 196 16 [54]	顆 颗 kē 181 17 [48]	飄 飘 piāo 182 20 [57]
縣 县 xiàn 120 16 [77]	縣 县 xiàn 120 16 [77]	願 愿 yuàn 181 19 [32]	
貓 猫 māo máo 153 16 [14]	鵝 鹅 é 196 18 [31]	鷄 鸡 jī 196 21 [54]	
夠 够 gòu 36 11 [57]	觸 触 chù 148 20 [29]		
鴿 鸽 gē 196 17 [54]	領 领 lǐng 181 14 [48]	敘 叙 xù 66 11 [31]	敍 叙 xù 66 11 [31]
頌 颂 sòng 181 13 [48]	頒 颁 bān 181 13 [48]	殺 杀 shā 79 11 [69]	

厂 尸 广

厂

歷	曆	厲	壓	厭	脣
历 lì	历 lì	厉 lì	压 yā yà	厌 yàn	唇 chún
77 16 [32]	72 16 [32]	27 15 [32]	32 17 [32]	27 14 [32]	130 11 [78]

尸

層	屬	屢	屍	屜	屆
层 céng	属 shǔ zhǔ	屡 lǚ	尸 shī	屉 tì	届 jiè
44 15 [32]	44 21 [32]	44 14 [32]	44 9 [39]	44 11 [32]	44 8 [32]

广

庫			
库 kù			
53 10 [33]			

廂	廁	廟	廚
厢 xiāng	厕 cè sì	庙 miào	厨 chú
53 12 [32]	53 12 [32]	53 15 [33]	53 15 [32]

廠	龐	廳
厂 chǎng	庞 páng	厅 tīng
53 15 [39]	53 19 [33]	53 25 [32]

廣	廈	廬
广 guǎng	厦 shà xià	庐 lú
53 15 [38]	53 13 [32]	53 19 [33]

廢	麼	應	鷹	慶	塵
废 fèi	么 me	应 yīng yìng	鹰 yīng	庆 qìng	尘 chén
53 15 [33]	200 14 [77]	61 17 [33]	196 24 [33]	61 15 [33]	32 14 [75]

痹
痹 bì
104 13 [33]

痪
痪 huàn
104 14 [33]

疗
疗 liáo
104 17 [33]

瘉
愈 yù
104 14 [72]

瘡
疮 chuāng
104 15 [33]

癒
愈 yù
104 18 [72]

癢
痒 yǎng
104 20 [33]

癡
痴 chī
104 19 [33]

癮
瘾 yǐn
104 22 [33]

癱
瘫 tān
104 24 [33]

瘧
疟 nüè yào
104 14 [33]

瘋
疯 fēng
104 14 [33]

慮
虑 lǜ
61 15 [33]

膚
肤 fū
130 15 [27]

虜
虏 lǔ
141 13 [33]

處
处 chǔ chù
141 11 [35]

盧
卢 lú
108 16 [66]

廬
庐 lú
53 19 [33]

彥
彦 yàn
59 9 [62]

產
产 chǎn
100 11 [62]

辶

連
连 lián
162 11 [34]

進　游 yóu　遜
进 jìn　游 yóu　逊 xùn
162 12 [34]　162 13 [7]　162 14 [34]

這　適　遠　達　違　遺
这 zhè zhèi　适 shì　远 yuǎn　达 dá　违 wéi　遗 yí wèi
162 11 [34]　162 15 [34]　162 14 [34]　162 13 [34]　162 13 [34]　162 16 [34]

遼　邊　邁　遙
辽 liáo　边 biān bian　迈 mài　遥 yáo
162 16 [34]　162 19 [34]　162 17 [34]　162 14 [34]

還　邏　遷　過
还 hái huán　逻 luó　迁 qiān　过 guò guo guō
162 17 [34]　162 23 [34]　162 15 [34]　162 13 [34]

運　選　蓮
运 yùn　选 xuǎn　莲 lián
162 13 [34]　162 16 [34]　140 15 [65]

遞　遲　週　迴
递 dì　迟 chí　周 zhōu　回 huí
162 14 [34]　162 16 [34]　162 12 [36]　162 10 [37]

走

趙　趕　趨
赵 zhào　赶 gǎn　趋 qū
156 14 [35]　156 14 [35]　156 17 [35]

…

題　翹　颱　麵　麨
题 tí　翘 qiào qiáo　台 tái　面 miàn　面 miàn
181 18 [35]　124 18 [35]　182 14 [78]　199 20 [39]　199 15 [39]

直　置　眞
直 zhí　置 zhì　真 zhēn
24 8 [67]　122 13 [68]　109 10 [67]

貳
貳 èr
154 12 [36]

幾
几 jǐ
52 12 [39]

載
载 zǎi zài
159 13 [36]

飛
飞 fēi
183 9 [39]

馬
马 mǎ
187 10 [73]

鳥
鸟 niǎo
196 11 [58]

烏
乌 wū
86 10 [58]

區　滙
区 qū ōu　　汇 huì
23 11 [37]　22 13 [57]

齒
齿 chǐ
211 15 [66]

岡　風　鳳
冈 gāng　风 fēng　凤 fèng
46 8 [36]　182 9 [36]　196 14 [36]

門　閃　閉　閑　開　閏
门 mén　闪 shǎn　闭 bì　闲 xián　开 kāi kai　闰 rùn
169 8 [1]　169 10 [36]　169 11 [36]　169 12 [36]　169 12 [39]　169 12 [36]

問　間　閒　聞　閘　悶
问 wèn　间 jiān jiàn　闲 xián　闻 wén　闸 zhá　闷 mēn m
30 11 [36]　169 12 [36]　169 12 [36]　128 14 [36]　169 13 [36]　61 12 [36]

閨　閡　閣　閱　闡　闖
闺 guī　阂 hé　阁 gé　阅 yuè　阐 chǎn　闯 chuǎn
169 14 [36]　169 14 [36]　169 14 [78]　169 15 [36]　169 20 [36]　169 18 [36]

闊　閥　關　闆　闢
阔 kuò　阀 fá　关 guān　板 bǎn　辟 pì bì
169 17 [36]　169 14 [36]　169 19 [58]　169 17 [17]　169 21 [54]

鬥　鬧
斗 dòu　闹 nào
191 10 [1]　191 15 [36]

兩　為　歲　蘭　繭
两 liǎng　为 wéi wèi　岁 suì　兰 lán　茧 jiǎn
11 8 [60]　86 9 [38]　77 13 [76]　140 21 [58]　120 19 [65]

園	圍	圓	國	圖	團
园 yuán	围 wéi	圆 yuán	国 guó	图 tú	团 tuán
31 13 [37]	31 12 [37]	31 13 [37]	31 11 [37]	31 14 [37]	31 14 [37]
囂	蠶				
嚣 xiāo	蚕 cán				
30 21 [68]	142 24 [79]				

術	衒	衝	衛
术 shù zhú	街 xián	冲 chòng	卫 wèi
144 11 [41]	167 14 [10]	144 15 [52]	144 15 [39]
辮	辯	辦	
辫 biàn	辩 biàn	办 bàn	
120 20 [54]	160 21 [37]	160 16 [1]	

務	殼	穀	殺	
务 wù	壳 ké qiào	谷 gǔ	杀 shā	
19 11 [76]	79 12 [71]	150 14 [59]	79 11 [69]	
競	韻	靜	隸	歸
竞 jìng	韵 yùn	静 jìng	隶 lì	归 guī
117 20 [62]	180 19 [30]	174 16 [37]	171 17 [77]	77 18 [1]

鬆	鬚	鬍	艷	豔	豑
松 sōng	须 xū	胡 hú	艳 yàn	艳 yàn	艳 yàn
190 18 [16]	190 22 [1]	190 19 [53]	139 24 [30]	151 28 [30]	151 27 [30]

夾	來	氷
夹 jiā jiá gā	来 lái lai	冰 bīng
37 7 [38]	9 8 [38]	85 5 [3]
車	東	肅	甚
车 chē jū	东 dōng	肃 sù	什 shén shèn
159 7 [38]	75 8 [38]	129 13 [69]	99 9 [43]
弔	亞	兩	冊
吊 diào	亚 yà	两 liǎng	册 cè
57 4 [68]	7 8 [39]	11 8 [60]	12 5 [39]

■ 、 ノ 丨 卜 キ 刂

、			
祕 秘 mì 113 10 [18]	跡 迹 jī 157 13 [34]	嚇 吓 hè xià 30 17 [47]	掛 挂 guà 64 11 [55]
恥 耻 chǐ 61 10 [25]	減 减 jiǎn 0 12 [43]	滅 灭 miè 85 13 [60]	鍬 锹 qiāo 167 17 [21]

□少 → A
□代 → A
□戈 → A
□犬 → A
□甫 → A

ノ	
冰 冰 bīng 85 5 [3]	鍬 锹 qiāo 167 17 [21]

丨	
訓 训 xùn 149 10 [4]	糾 纠 jiū 120 8 [15]

卜
掛 挂 guà 64 11 [55]

キ
誹 诽 fěi 149 15 [4]

刂				
刪 删 shān 18 7 [31]	剝 剥 bāo bō 18 10 [42]			
剛 刚 gāng 18 10 [42]	劇 剧 jù 18 15 [42]	劉 刘 liú 18 15 [42]	測 测 cè 85 12 [42]	側 侧 cè 9 11 [9]
劃 划 huà huá 18 14 [42]	劑 剂 jì 18 16 [42]	別 别 bié biè 18 7 [42]	則 则 zé 18 9 [42]	廁 厕 cè si 53 12 [32]
劍 剑 jiàn 18 15 [42]	創 创 chuàng chuāng 18 12 [42]			

軋 轧 yà zhá gá 159 8 [19]	亂 乱 luàn 5 13 [26]

訛 讹 é 149 11 [42]

純 纯 chún 120 10 [42]	鈍 钝 dùn 167 12 [21]

牠 它 tā 93 7 [70]	馳 驰 chí 187 13 [28]

術 术 shù zhú 144 11 [41]	銜 衔 xián 167 14 [10]	衝 冲 chòng 144 15 [52]	衛 卫 wèi 144 15 [39]	虧 亏 kuī 141 17 [60]

十 寸 少 弋 戈

十

針	計
针 zhēn	计 jì
167 10 [21]	149 9 [4]

寸

討	謝	樹	對	廚	財
讨 tǎo	谢 xiè	树 shù	对 duì	厨 chú	财 cái
149 10 [4]	149 17 [4]	75 16 [17]	41 14 [1]	53 15 [32]	154 10 [28]

少

鈔	紗
钞 chāo	纱 shā
167 12 [21]	120 10 [44]

弋

試	賦	膩	貳
试 shì	赋 fù	腻 nì	贰 èr
149 13 [4]	154 15 [43]	130 16 [27]	154 12 [36]

戈

戰	戲	餓
战 zhàn	戏 xì	饿 è
62 16 [30]	62 17 [1]	184 15 [43]

誡	絨	賊
诫 jiè	绒 róng	贼 zéi
149 14 [43]	120 12 [15]	154 13 [43]

誠	滅	減	鹹
诚 chéng	灭 miè	减 jiǎn	咸 xián
149 13 [4]	85 13 [60]	0 12 [43]	197 20 [36]

識	織	鐵	殲
识 shí zhì	织 zhī	铁 tiě	歼 jiān
149 19 [4]	120 18 [15]	167 21 [46]	78 21 [26]

註 注 zhù 149 12 [44]	**駐** 驻 zhù 187 15 [28]		
較 较 jiào 159 13 [19]	**餃** 饺 jiǎo 184 14 [20]	**絞** 绞 jiǎo 120 12 [15]	**紋** 纹 wén 120 10 [15]
訪 访 fǎng 149 11 [44]	**紡** 纺 fǎng 120 10 [44]		
該 该 gāi 149 13 [4]	**駭** 骇 hài 187 16 [28]		
涼 凉 liáng liàng 15 11 [54]	**諒** 谅 liàng 149 15 [54]	**鯨** 鲸 jīng 195 19 [29]	

羊　并

羊	詳 詳 xiáng 149 13 [4]	鮮 鮮 xiān xiǎn 195 17 [29]
并	餅 饼 bǐng 184 14 [20]	併 并 bing 9 8 [74]

臥 卧 wò 131 8 [41]	**夾** 夹 jiā jiá gā 37 7 [38]	**來** 来 lái lai 9 8 [38]		
狹 狭 xiá 94 10 [46]	**俠** 侠 xiá 9 9 [9]	**挾** 挟 xié 64 10 [13]	**峽** 峡 xiá 46 10 [14]	**陝** 陕 shǎn 170 10 [46]
狀 状 zhuàng 94 8 [3]	**獻** 献 xiàn 94 20 [46]	**獄** 狱 yù 94 14 [46]	**獸** 兽 shòu 94 19 [58]	**馱** 驮 tuó duò 187 13 [28]
鋤 锄 chú 167 15 [21]	**動** 动 dòng 19 11 [46]	**勁** 劲 jìn jìng 19 9 [46]	**勵** 励 lì 19 17 [31]	**勸** 劝 quàn 19 20 [1]
執 执 zhí 32 11 [13]	**軌** 轨 guǐ 159 9 [19]			
決 决 jué 15 7 [46]	**訣** 诀 jué 149 11 [46]			

丁 干 几 長 壬 氏

丁	訂 订 dìng 149 9 [4]	釘 钉 dīng dìng 167 10 [21]			
干	軒 轩 xuān 159 10 [19]	汙 污 wū 85 6 [7]			
几	凱 凯 kǎi 16 12 [48]	汎 泛 fàn 85 6 [48]			
長	帳 帐 zhàng 50 11 [14]	張 张 zhāng 57 11 [43]	脹 胀 zhàng 130 12 [43]	賬 账帐 zhàng 154 15 [14]	漲 涨 zhǎng zhàng 85 14 [7]
壬	餁 饪 rèn 184 12 [20]	姙 妊 rèn 38 9 [48]			
氏	祇 只 zhǐ 112 8 [68]	紙 纸 zhǐ 120 10 [15]			

靭 靭 rèn 178 12 [49]	**靭** 靭 rèn 177 12 [49]	
紀 纪 jì 120 9 [15]	**記** 记 jì 149 10 [49]	
詞 词 cí 149 12 [49]	**飼** 饲 sì 184 13 [20]	
釣 钓 diào 167 11 [21]	**約** 约 yuē yāo 120 9 [50]	**哟** 哟 yo yō 30 12 [24]
鉋 刨 bào 167 13 [42]	**飽** 饱 bǎo 184 13 [20]	
鉤 钩 gōu 167 13 [21]	**夠** 够 gòu 36 11 [57]	**詢** 询 xún 149 13 [4]

欠

軟	欽	飲	歐
软 ruǎn	钦 qīn	饮 yǐn yìn	欧 ōu
159 11 [50]	76 12 [50]	184 12 [20]	76 15 [28]

欵	歎	歡	畝
款 kuǎn	叹 tàn	欢 huān	亩 mǔ
76 11 [50]	76 15 [24]	76 22 [50]	102 10 [62]

攵

敗	敘	敵	數	
败 bài	叙 xù	敌 dí	数 shù shǔ shuò	
66 11 [28]	66 11 [31]	66 15 [26]	66 15 [51]	

倣	徵	徹	轍	敘
仿 fǎng	征 zhēng	彻 chè	辙 zhé	叙 xù
9 10 [8]	60 15 [10]	60 14 [10]	159 18 [51]	66 11 [31]

繳	緻	廠
缴 jiǎo	致 zhì	厂 chǎng
120 19 [51]	133 15 [51]	53 15 [39]

反

販	飯
贩 fàn	饭 fàn
154 11 [28]	184 12 [20]

斤

斬	斷	漸	慚	訴
斩 zhǎn	断 duàn	渐 jiàn jiān	惭 cán	诉 sù
69 11 [51]	69 18 [51]	85 14 [51]	61 14 [2]	149 12 [4]

殳

設	殺	穀	殼	沒
设 shè	杀 shā	谷 gǔ	壳 ké qiào	没 méi mò
149 11 [55]	79 11 [69]	150 14 [59]	79 12 [71]	85 7 [6]

緞	鍛	澱	甌	蝦
缎 duàn	锻 duàn	淀 diàn	瓯 ōu	虾 xiā
120 15 [55]	167 17 [21]	85 16 [5]	79 15 [28]	142 15 [29]

鋅	辭	辦	辯	辮	倖
锌 xīn	辞 cí	办 bàn	辩 biàn	辫 biàn	幸 xìng
167 15 [21]	160 19 [54]	160 16 [1]	160 21 [37]	120 20 [54]	9 10 [67]

瑪	馮	媽	嗎	螞	碼
玛 mǎ	冯 féng	妈 mā	吗 ma má mǎ	蚂 mǎ mà	码 mǎ
96 14 [49]	187 12 [3]	38 13 [49]	30 13 [24]	142 16 [29]	112 15 [26]

鴉	鴨	鳴	嗚		
鸦 yā	鸭 yā	鸣 míng	呜 wū		
196 15 [19]	196 16 [54]	196 14 [54]	30 13 [24]		

鵝	鶴	鴿	鵲	鷄	
鹅 é	鹤 hè	鸽 gē	鹊 què	鸡 jī	
196 18 [31]	196 21 [30]	196 17 [54]	196 19 [54]	196 21 [54]	

鴻	鵬	鷗			
鸿 hóng	鹏 péng	鸥 ōu			
196 17 [54]	196 19 [54]	196 22 [28]			

維	誰	進	確		
维 wéi	谁 shuí shéi	进 jìn	确 què		
120 14 [15]	149 15 [55]	162 12 [34]	112 15 [26]		

雖	雜	離	雞	難	
虽 suī	杂 zá	离 lí	鸡 jī	难 nán nàn	
172 17 [79]	172 18 [69]	172 19 [62]	172 18 [54]	172 19 [55]	

灘	攤				
滩 tān	摊 tān				
85 22 [7]	64 22 [55]				

占	佔 占 zhàn zhān 9 7 [66]	貼 贴 tiē 154 12 [28]	黏 粘 zhān nián 202 17 [18]	點 点 diǎn 203 17 [72]	
由	鈾 铀 yóu 167 13 [21]	軸 轴 zhóu 159 12 [19]			
甫	鋪 铺 pū pù 167 15 [21]	輔 辅 fǔ 159 14 [19]	補 补 bǔ 145 12 [20]		
見	視 视 shì 147 11 [20]	規 规 guī 147 11 [48]	現 现 xiàn 96 11 [48]	狽 狈 bèi 94 10 [14]	
	親 亲 qīn qìng 147 16 [74]	襯 衬 chèn 145 21 [43]	觀 观 guān guàn 147 25 [48]		
且	詛 诅 zǔ 149 12 [53]	組 组 zǔ 120 11 [15]			
丑	鈕 钮 niǔ 167 12 [21]	紐 纽 niǔ 120 10 [53]			

鬥	門 门 mén 169 8 [1]	憫 悯 mǐn 61 15 [49]	潤 润 rùn 85 15 [7]	嫻 娴 xián 38 15 [22]	嫺 娴 xián 38 15 [22]	鬥 斗 dòu 191 10 [1]
	們 们 men 9 10 [9]	擱 搁 gē gé 64 17 [49]	攔 拦 lán 64 20 [11]	欄 栏 lán 75 21 [16]	爛 烂 làn 86 21 [3]	問→

頃	頂	項	頓	賴	偵
顷 qǐng	顶 dǐng	项 xiàng	顿 dùn	赖 lài	侦 zhēn
181 11 [48]	181 11 [19]	181 12 [48]	181 13 [48]	154 16 [30]	9 11 [8]

頰	頗	頤
颊 jiá	颇 pō	颐 yí
181 16 [48]	181 14 [48]	181 16 [48]

煩	順	傾	噸	懶
烦 fán	顺 shùn	倾 qīng	吨 dūn	懒 lǎn
86 13 [3]	181 12 [48]	9 13 [48]	30 16 [42]	61 19 [2]

頻	穎	顛	類
频 pín	颖 yǐng	颠 diān	类 lèi
181 16 [48]	115 16 [48]	181 19 [48]	181 19 [59]

額	顏	顫
额 é	颜 yán	颤 zhàn chàn
181 18 [48]	181 18 [48]	181 22 [48]

頑	頭	頸	預
顽 wán	头 tóu tou	颈 jǐng gěng	预 yù
181 13 [48]	181 16 [74]	181 16 [48]	181 13 [48]

顆	顯	題	籲
颗 kē	显 xiǎn	题 tí	吁 yù
181 17 [48]	181 23 [68]	181 18 [35]	118 32 [24]

須	頹	頌	頒	領
须 xū	颓 tuí	颂 sòng	颁 bān	领 lǐng
181 12 [1]	181 16 [48]	181 13 [48]	181 13 [48]	181 14 [48]

碩	頗	顏	願	顧
硕 shuò	颇 pō	颜 yán	愿 yuàn	顾 gù
112 14 [48]	181 14 [48]	181 18 [48]	181 19 [32]	181 21 [48]

頤
颐 yí
181 16 [48]

卩	卻 却 què 26 9 [54]	腳 脚 jiǎo 130 13 [54]	氾 泛 fàn 85 5 [48]	
阝	郵 邮 yóu 163 12 [54]	鄉 乡 xiāng 163 12 [38]	綁 绑 bǎng 120 13 [54]	擲 掷 zhì zhī 64 18 [54]
	郤 隙 xì 170 10 [22]	鄰 邻 lín 163 15 [31]	鄭 郑 zhèng 163 15 [54]	鄧 邓 dèng 163 15 [54]
艮	銀 银 yín 167 14 [53]	艱 艰 jiān 138 17 [53]		
鬼	塊 块 kuài 32 13 [10]	醜 丑 chǒu 164 17 [39]		
風	楓 枫 fēng 75 13 [17]	諷 讽 fěng 149 16 [4]	飄 飘 piāo 182 20 [57]	
冊	柵 栅 zhà shān 75 9 [17]	珊 珊 shān 96 9 [19]		
區	樞 枢 shū 75 15 [17]	摳 抠 kōu 64 14 [13]	嘔 呕 ǒu 30 14 [52]	驅 驱 qū 187 21 [52]

鈴　齡
铃 líng　　龄 líng
167 13 [21]　211 20 [30]

絡　駱　賂　銘
络 luò　　骆 luò　　赂 lù　　铭 míng
120 12 [15]　187 16 [56]　154 13 [28]　167 14 [21]

永文亦它宅	詠	紋	跡	駝	詫
	咏 yǒng	纹 wén	迹 jī	驼 tuó	诧 chà
	149 12 [23]	120 10 [15]	157 13 [34]	187 15 [28]	149 13 [4]
才巾隶盉益	財	帥	隸	豔	豐盍
	财 cái	帅 shuài	隶 lì	艳 yàn	艳 yàn
	154 10 [28]	50 9 [1]	171 17 [77]	151 28 [30]	151 27 [30]
丩甘井弗	糾	拑	鉗	畊	佛
	纠 jiū	钳 qián	钳 qián	耕 gēng	佛 fú
	120 8 [15]	64 8 [21]	167 13 [21]	102 9 [18]	60 8 [9]
大九女糸	駄	軌	妝	絲	
	驮 tuó duò	轨 guǐ	妆 zhuāng	丝 sī	
	187 13 [28]	159 9 [19]	38 7 [3]	120 12 [73]	
攴虎皮内	敍	號	皺	納	
	叙 xù	号 hào háo	皱 zhòu	纳 nà	
	66 11 [31]	141 13 [68]	107 15 [51]	120 10 [15]	
中史虫申	沖	駛	蝕	紳	
	冲 chōng	驶 shǐ	蚀 shí	绅 shēn	
	15 7 [52]	187 15 [57]	142 14 [52]	120 11 [52]	
車東柬	陣	陳	棟	練	鍊
	阵 zhèn	陈 chén	栋 dòng	练 liàn	链 liàn
	170 10 [22]	170 11 [22]	75 12 [45]	120 15 [15]	167 17 [2?]
午乍布軍	許	詐	飾	輝	
	许 xǔ	诈 zhà	饰 shì	辉 huī	
	149 11 [4]	149 12 [50]	184 13 [20]	159 15 [18]	
久色	畞	艷			
	亩 mǔ	艳 yàn			
	102 10 [62]	139 24 [30]			

正 丏 丐

紅 红 hóng gōng 120 9 [15] | 証 证 zhèng 149 12 [4] | 鈣 钙 gài 167 12 [21] | 麪 面 miàn 199 15 [39]

平 牙

汙 污 wū 85 6 [7] | 評 评 píng 149 12 [47] | 訝 讶 yà 149 11 [4]

帀 面

虧 亏 kuī 141 17 [60] | 師 师 shī 50 10 [1] | 緬 缅 miǎn 120 15 [15] | 麵 面 miàn 199 20 [39]

貝 田 里

鋁 铝 lǚ 167 15 [21] | 狽 狈 bèi 94 10 [14] | 細 细 xì 120 11 [15] | 裡 里 li lǐ 145 12 [75]

長 又

氾 泛 fàn 85 5 [48] | 報 报 bào 32 12 [13] | 蝦 虾 xiā 142 15 [29]

及 尋

訊 讯 xùn 149 10 [4] | 級 级 jí 120 10 [49] | 歸 归 guī 77 18 [1]

禾 乏 舌 斤

託 托 tuō 149 10 [13] | 穌 稣 sū 115 16 [29] | 貶 贬 biǎn 154 12 [28] | 話 话 huà 149 13 [4] | 訴 诉 sù 149 12 [4]

戈

係 系 xi 9 9 [60] | 孫 孙 sūn 39 10 [41] | 縣 县 xiàn 120 16 [77] | 縣 县 xiàn 120 16 [77] | 餓 饿 è 184 15 [43]

参 仐 全 余

於 于 yú 70 8 [39] | 診 诊 zhěn 149 12 [4] | 幹 干 gàn 51 13 [39] | 詮 诠 quán 149 13 [4] | 餘 余 yú 184 15 [59]

文

賄 贿 huì 154 13 [28] | 駁 驳 bó 187 14 [28]

′	烏	島	鳥	樂	衆
	乌 wū	岛 dǎo	鸟 niǎo	乐 yuè lè	众 zhòng
	86 10 [58]	46 10 [58]	196 11 [58]	75 15 [60]	143 12 [59]

、	氷	為
	冰 bīng	为 wéi wèi
	85 5 [3]	86 9 [38]

﹀	並	義	養
	并 bing	义 yì	养 yǎng
	1 8 [74]	123 13 [71]	184 15 [58]

八	爺	貧
	爷 yé	贫 pin
	88 13 [59]	154 11 [59]

⺍	糞
	粪 fèn
	119 17 [71]

	賞	嘗	黨	當
	赏 shǎng	尝 cháng	党 dǎng	当 dāng dàng
	154 15 [77]	30 14 [59]	203 20 [59]	102 13 [59]

人	傘	貪	倉	會
	伞 sǎn	贪 tān	仓 cāng	会 huì kuài
	9 12 [59]	154 11 [77]	9 10 [79]	73 13 [77]

晉 晋 jìn 72 10 [79]	爾 尔 ěr 89 14 [72]	兩 两 liǎng 11 8 [60]	盃 杯 bēi 108 9 [17]	
亞 亚 yà 7 8 [39]	惡 恶 è ě wù 61 12 [72]	頁 页 yè 181 9 [60]	貢 贡 gòng 154 10 [77]	憂 忧 yōu 61 15 [2]
爭 争 zhēng 87 8 [61]	愛 爱 ài 61 13 [60]	覓 觅 mì 147 11 [77]		
氣 气 qì 84 10 [61]	氫 氢 qīng 84 11 [61]	無 无 wú 86 12 [33]		
軍 军 jūn 159 9 [61]				
魚 鱼 yú 195 11 [61]	負 负 fù 154 9 [61]	魯 鲁 lǔ 195 15 [61]	龜 龟 guī jūn 213 16 [61]	

■□　　亠　宀　穴

棄	牽	齊	齋	裏	贏
弃 qì	牵 qiān	齐 qí	斋 zhāi	里 lǐ lǐ	赢 yíng
75 11 [62]	93 11 [75]	210 14 [62]	210 17 [62]	145 13 [75]	154 20 [62]

彥	產
彦 yàn	产 chǎn
59 9 [62]	100 11 [62]

宮	寢
宫 gōng	寝 qǐn
40 10 [63]	40 14 [63]

寧	憲	寫	審
宁 níng nìng	宪 xiàn	写 xiě xiè	审 shěn
40 14 [63]	61 16 [63]	40 15 [73]	40 15 [63]

寬	賽	賓	實	寶	寵
宽 kuān	赛 sài	宾 bīn	实 shí	宝 bǎo	宠 chǒng
40 15 [63]	154 17 [77]	154 14 [71]	40 14 [63]	40 20 [63]	40 19 [63]

窯	窩	竄	窮	竊
窑 yáo	窝 wō	窜 cuàn	穷 qióng	窃 qiè
116 15 [63]	116 14 [63]	116 18 [63]	116 15 [63]	116 23 [63]

直 直 zhí 24 8 [67]	專 专 zhuān 41 11 [38]	喪 丧 sāng sàng 30 12 [77]	麥 麦 mài 199 11 [67]		
壺 壶 hú 33 12 [73]	賣 卖 mài 154 15 [74]	臺 台 tái 133 14 [78]	壽 寿 shòu 33 14 [33]	堯 尧 yáo 32 12 [71]	
奪 夺 duó 37 14 [67]	奮 奋 fèn 37 16 [67]				
齒 齿 chǐ 211 15 [66]	歲 岁 suì 77 13 [76]				
豈 岂 qǐ 151 10 [66]	巖 岩 yán 46 23 [66]	嶺 岭 lǐng 46 17 [56]	崗 岗 gǎng 46 11 [66]	嶺 岭 lǐng 46 17 [56]	嶄 崭 zhǎn 46 14 [66]

艹

萊 莱 lái 140 12 [65]	華 华 huá huà 140 12 [70]	蕭 萧 xiāo 140 17 [64]	黃 黄 huáng 201 12 [67]		

艹

茲 兹 zī 140 10 [58]	菸 烟 yān 140 12 [3]	莊 庄 zhuāng 140 11 [33]	蔣 蒋 jiǎng 140 15 [65]	蘋 苹 píng 140 20 [64]	
蕩 荡 dàng 140 16 [65]	蔭 荫 yìn yīn 140 15 [65]	薩 萨 sà 140 18 [65]	蘇 苏 sū 140 15 [65]	蘊 蕴 yùn 140 15 [65]	藹 蔼 ǎi 140 20 [65]

艹

葉 叶 yè 140 13 [24]	蓋 盖 gài 140 14 [58]	蒐 搜 sōu 140 14 [11]	蔥 葱 cōng 140 15 [64]	蕭 萧 xiāo 140 16 [64]	
莖 茎 jīng 140 11 [64]	夢 梦 mèng 36 14 [76]	蘿 萝 luó 140 23 [76]	萬 万 wàn 0 13 [39]	薑 姜 jiāng 140 17 [58]	黃 黄 huáng 201 12 [67]
蒼 苍 cāng 140 14 [79]	舊 旧 jiù 134 18 [53]	藍 蓝 lán la 140 18 [64]	藥 药 yào 140 19 [65]	藝 艺 yì 140 19 [65]	

艹

薦 荐 jiàn 140 17 [65]	蘆 芦 lú lǔ 140 20 [64]	蒼 苍 cāng 140 14 [79]

艹

蔔 卜 bo 140 15 [1]

艹

蓮 莲 lián 140 15 [65]

艹

蘭 兰 lán 140 21 [58]	繭 茧 jiǎn 120 19 [65]

竹 羽 火火

筆　篤
笔 bǐ　笃 dǔ
118 12 [76]　118 16 [66]

範　節　篩　籠　籬　籲
范 fàn　节 jié jiē　筛 shāi　笼 lóng lǒng　篱 lí　吁 yù
118 15 [65]　118 13 [65]　118 16 [66]　118 22 [66]　118 25 [66]　118 32 [24]

箏　簽　質
筝 zhēng　签 qiān　质 zhì
118 14 [66]　118 19 [73]　154 15 [32]

築　籮　籌　籃
筑 zhù zhú　箩 luó　筹 chóu　篮 lán
118 16 [66]　118 25 [76]　118 20 [66]　118 20 [66]

筍　籤　簾　簡
笋 sǔn　签 qiān　帘 lián　简 jiǎn
118 12 [66]　118 23 [73]　118 19 [63]　118 18 [66]

習
习 xí
124 11 [36]

勞　榮　螢　營　鶯
劳 láo　荣 róng　萤 yíng　营 yíng　莺 yīng
19 12 [64]　75 14 [64]　142 16 [64]　86 17 [64]　196 21 [64]

吳 吴 wú 30 7 [74]	**呂** 吕 lǚ 30 7 [68]	**員** 员 yuán 30 10 [77]		
單 单 dān 30 12 [58]	**囂** 嚣 xiāo 30 21 [68]	**嚴** 严 yán 30 20 [60]		
買 买 mǎi 154 12 [69]	**罵** 骂 mà 122 15 [68]	**罰** 罚 fá 122 14 [68]	**罷** 罢 bà 122 15 [68]	**羅** 罗 luó luō 122 19 [68]
置 置 zhì 122 13 [68]	**眾** 众 zhòng 109 11 [59]			
昇 升 shēng 72 8 [60]	**暈** 晕 yūn yùn 72 13 [75]	**疊** 叠 dié 72 19 [61]		
貝 贝 bèi 154 7 [36]	**見** 见 jiàn 147 7 [36]			
異 异 yì 102 11 [69]	**畢** 毕 bì 102 11 [70]	**壘** 垒 lěi 32 18 [61]	**疊** 叠 dié 102 22 [79]	**貫** 贯 guàn 154 11 [77]

賈
贾 gǔ
154　13　[68]

雲
云 yún
173　12　[77]

電
电 diàn
173　13　[38]

靈
灵 líng
173　24　[69]

霧
雾 wù
173　19　[68]

書
书 shū
73　10　[41]

晝
昼 zhòu
72　11　[73]

畫
画 huà
102　12　[37]

盡
尽 jìn
108　14　[36]

肅
肃 sù
129　12　[69]

髮
发 fà
190　15　[41]

鬆
松 sōng
190　18　[16]

鬚
须 xū
190　22　[1]

鬍
胡 hú
190　19　[53]

⼘ ⼟ 龶 ⼔	貞 贞 zhēn 154 9 [77]	堯 尧 yáo 32 12 [71]	責 责 zé 154 11 [67]	眞 真 zhēn 109 10 [67]
⾀ ⾀ 朿	肅 肃 sù 129 12 [69]	盡 尽 jìn 108 14 [36]	棗 枣 zǎo 75 12 [70]	
虫 虫 車	貴 贵 guì 154 12 [77]	蟲 虫 chóng 142 18 [38]	轟 轰 hōng 159 21 [69]	
⼙ 㐫 女 ⾎	韋 韦 wéi 178 9 [38]	彙 汇 huì 58 13 [57]	姦 奸 jiān 38 9 [22]	眾 众 zhòng 143 12 [59]
戈 力 厶	盞 盏 zhǎn 108 13 [80]	脅 胁 xié 130 10 [27]	參 参 cān cēn shēn 28 11 [70]	
其 廿 弗 业	甚 什 shén shèn 99 9 [43]	黃 黄 huáng 201 12 [67]	費 费 fèi 154 12 [77]	叢 丛 cóng 29 18 [73]
非 曲 卅	輩 辈 bèi 159 15 [75]	農 农 nóng 161 13 [77]	帶 带 dài 50 11 [75]	

不 彐 ㄐ

貢	盃	尋	長
贡 gòng	杯 bēi	寻 xún xín	长 cháng zhǎng
154 10 [77]	108 9 [17]	41 12 [70]	168 8 [38]

耳 凸

貫	聶	骨
贯 guàn	聂 niè	骨 gǔ gú gū
154 11 [77]	128 18 [69]	188 1 [69]

匆

喬	怱
乔 qiáo	cōng
30 12 [60]	61 9 [3]

災
灾 zāi
86 7 [63]

臼

兇	兒
凶 xiōng	儿 ér
10 6 [37]	10 8 [42]

學	覺
学 xué	觉 jué jiào
39 16 [59]	147 20 [59]

譽	與	輿	興	釁
誉 yù	与 yǔ yù yú	舆 yú	兴 xīng xìng	衅 xìn
149 21 [78]	134 14 [35]	159 17 [71]	134 16 [59]	164 25 [30]

示示 旡旡 柹柹

發	麗	蠶	鬱
发 fā	丽 lì	蚕 cán	郁 yù
105 12 [41]	198 19 [60]	142 24 [79]	192 30 [54]

八

貝	頁	黃	異	糞
贝 bèi	页 yè	黄 huáng	异 yì	粪 fèn
154 7 [36]	181 9 [60]	201 12 [67]	102 11 [69]	119 17 [71]

與	輿	興	眞
与 yǔ yù yú	舆 yú	兴 xīng xing	真 zhēn
134 14 [35]	159 17 [71]	134 16 [59]	109 10 [67]

儿

兇	兒	見
凶 xiōng	儿 ér	见 jiàn
10 6 [37]	10 8 [42]	147 7 [36]

堯	蒐
尧 yáo	搜 sōu
32 12 [71]	140 14 [11]

彡

彥	參
彦 yàn	参 cān cēn shēn
59 9 [62]	28 11 [70]

一

豈	豎	豐
岂 qǐ	竖 shù	丰 fēng
151 10 [66]	151 15 [73]	151 18 [38]

畫	薑	晝	疊	疉
画 huà	姜 jiāng	昼 zhòu	叠 dié	叠 dié
102 12 [37]	140 17 [58]	72 11 [73]	102 22 [79]	72 19 [61]

並	亞	莖	壺	靈
并 bìng	亚 yà	茎 jīng	壶 hú	灵 líng
1 8 [74]	7 8 [39]	140 11 [64]	33 12 [73]	173 24 [69]

灬　心

魚	無	馬	烏	鳥	為
鱼 yú	无 wú	马 mǎ	乌 wū	鸟 niǎo	为 wéi wèi
195 11 [61]	86 12 [33]	187 10 [73]	86 10 [58]	196 11 [58]	86 9 [38]
熱	黨	窯	嚥		
热 rè	党 dǎng	窑 yáo	咽 yàn yān yè		
86 15 [72]	203 20 [59]	116 15 [63]	30 19 [24]		
寫	薦	鶯	鷹		
写 xiě xiè	荐 jiàn	莺 yīng	鹰 yīng		
40 15 [73]	140 17 [65]	196 21 [64]	196 24 [33]		
罵	篤	駕	驚		
骂 mà	笃 dǔ	驾 jià	惊 jīng		
122 15 [68]	118 16 [66]	187 15 [73]	187 23 [2]		
嗎	嗚	鳴			
吗 ma má mǎ	呜 wū	鸣 míng			
30 13 [24]	30 13 [24]	196 14 [54]			
惡	忽	憲	蔥		
恶 è ě wù	cōng	宪 xiàn	葱 cōng		
61 12 [72]	61 9 [3]	61 16 [63]	140 15 [64]		
憑	慾	態	憊	懲	
凭 píng	欲 yù	态 tài	惫 bèi	惩 chéng	
61 16 [71]	61 15 [50]	61 14 [72]	61 16 [72]	61 19 [72]	
戀	懇	懸			
恋 liàn	恳 kěn	悬 xuán			
61 23 [62]	61 17 [72]	61 20 [72]			
噁	唸	應	癒	慮	
恶 ě wù	念 niàn	应 yīng yìng	愈 yù	虑 lǜ	
30 15 [72]	30 11 [59]	61 17 [33]	104 18 [72]	61 15 [33]	

火	災 灾 zāi 86 7 [63]	燙 烫 tàng 86 16 [74]		
大	吳 吴 wú 30 7 [74]	獎 奖 jiǎng 37 14 [74]	奬 奖 jiǎng 94 15 [74]	
木	棄 弃 qì 75 11 [62]	彙 汇 huì 58 13 [57]	樂 乐 yuè lè 75 15 [60]	槳 桨 jiǎng 75 15 [74]
	業 业 yè 75 13 [40]	葉 叶 yè 140 13 [24]	藥 药 yào 140 19 [65]	築 筑 zhù zhú 118 16 [66]
巾	帶 带 dài 50 11 [75]	幣 币 bì 50 14 [75]	幫 帮 bāng 50 17 [75]	
山	島 岛 dǎo 46 10 [58]			

榮
荣 róng
75 14 [64]

準 准 zhǔn 85 13 [3]	傘 伞 sǎn 9 12 [59]	華 华 huá huà 140 12 [70]	畢 毕 bì 102 11 [70]	單 单 dān 30 12 [58]
尋 寻 xún xín 41 12 [70]	專 专 zhuān 41 11 [38]	奪 夺 duó 37 14 [67]	導 导 dǎo 41 16 [69]	

舉 举 jǔ 134 17 [74]

犂 犁 lí 93 12 [75]	牽 牵 qiān 93 11 [75]

堅 坚 jiān 32 11 [75]	塗 涂 tú 32 13 [6]	墊 垫 diàn 32 14 [75]	墾 垦 kěn 32 16 [75]	墜 坠 zhuì 32 15 [75]	墮 堕 duò 32 15 [75]
壟 垄 lǒng 32 19 [75]	壘 垒 lěi 32 18 [61]	臺 台 tái 133 14 [78]			
壓 压 yā yà 32 17 [32]	塵 尘 chén 32 14 [75]				

糸　水　瓜　衣

糸

紮	紮	緊	繫
扎 zhá zā	扎 zhá zā	紧 jǐn	系 xì
120 11 [13]	120 10 [13]	120 14 [66]	120 19 [60]

水

漿	衆	眾
浆 jiāng jiàng	众 zhòng	众 zhòng
85 15 [77]	143 12 [59]	109 11 [59]

瓜

喪	農	長
丧 sāng sàng	农 nóng	长 cháng zhǎng
30 12 [77]	161 13 [77]	168 8 [38]

衣

裝	製	襲	裏
装 zhuāng	制 zhì	袭 xí	里 lǐ lǐ
145 13 [77]	145 14 [42]	145 22 [77]	145 13 [75]

隻 只 zhǐ zhī 172 10 [68]	**雙** 双 shuāng 172 18 [1]	**髮** 发 fà 190 15 [41]

愛 爱 ài 61 13 [60]	**麥** 麦 mài 199 11 [67]	**憂** 忧 yōu 61 15 [2]	**變** 变 biàn 149 23 [76]	**廈** 厦 shà xià 53 13 [32]	**慶** 庆 qìng 61 15 [33]
髮 发 fà 190 15 [41]	**夢** 梦 mèng 36 14 [76]				

嬰 婴 yīng 38 17 [76]	**屢** 屡 lǚ 44 14 [32]

勞 劳 láo 19 12 [64]	**勢** 势 shì 19 13 [76]

摯 挚 zhì 64 15 [76]	**擊** 击 jí 64 17 [67]

口

呂 吕 lǚ 30 7 [68]	宮 宫 gōng 40 10 [63]	啓 启 qǐ 30 11 [32]	營 营 yíng 86 17 [64]	譽 誉 yù 149 21 [78]
倉 仓 cāng 9 10 [79]	蒼 苍 cāng 140 14 [79]			

曰

書 书 shū 73 10 [41]	習 习 xí 124 11 [36]	暫 暂 zàn 72 15 [79]	響 响 xiǎng 180 21 [23]
晉 晋 jìn 72 10 [79]	會 会 huì kuài 73 13 [77]	嘗 尝 cháng 30 14 [59]	魯 鲁 lǔ 195 15 [61]
曆 历 lì 72 16 [32]	層 层 céng 44 15 [32]	簡 简 jiǎn 118 18 [66]	

田

奮 奋 fèn 37 16 [67]	審 审 shěn 40 15 [63]	當 当 dāng dàng 102 13 [59]

月

腎 肾 shèn 130 12 [79]	脅 胁 xié 130 10 [27]	骨 骨 gǔ gú gū 188 1 [69]	脣 唇 chún 130 11 [78]	膚 肤 fū 130 15 [27]

皿

盃 杯 bēi 108 9 [17]	盡 尽 jìn 108 14 [36]	盞 盏 zhǎn 108 13 [80]			
盪 荡 dàng 108 17 [65]	監 监 jiān jiàn 108 14 [66]	鹽 盐 yán 197 24 [80]	盤 盘 pán 108 15 [80]		
蓋 盖 gài 140 14 [58]	藍 蓝 lán la 140 18 [64]	籃 篮 lán 118 20 [66]	盧 卢 lú 108 16 [66]	廬 庐 lú 53 19 [33]	蘆 芦 lú lǔ 140 20 [64]

螢 萤 yíng 142 16 [64]

蠻 蛮 mán 142 25 [79]

輩 辈 bèi 159 15 [75]

暈 晕 yūn yùn 72 13 [75]

軍 军 jūn 159 9 [61]

單 单 dān 30 12 [58]

頁 页 yè 181 9 [60]

貢 贡 gòng 154 10 [77]

員 员 yuán 30 10 [77]

貞 贞 zhēn 154 9 [77]

負 负 fù 154 9 [61]

貴 贵 guì 154 12 [77]

買 买 mǎi 154 12 [69]

賈 贾 gǔ 154 13 [68]

責 责 zé 154 11 [67]

費 费 fèi 154 12 [77]

貫 贯 guàn 154 11 [77]

貪 贪 tān 154 11 [77]

貧 贫 pín 154 11 [59]

賣 卖 mài 154 15 [74]

貳 贰 èr 154 12 [36]

賞 赏 shǎng 154 15 [77]

賓 宾 bīn 154 14 [71]

實 实 shí 40 14 [63]

賽 赛 sài 154 17 [77]

寶 宝 bǎo 40 20 [63]

貸 贷 dài 154 12 [77]

貨 货 huò 154 11 [77]

資 资 zī 154 13 [77]

貿 贸 mào 154 12 [77]

賀 贺 hè 154 12 [77]

質 质 zhì 154 15 [32]

賢 贤 xián 154 15 [66]

贊 赞 zàn 154 19 [77]

覓 觅 mì 147 11 [77]

覺 觉 jué jiào 147 20 [59]

覽 览 lǎn 147 21 [66]

寬 宽 kuān 40 15 [63]

◨ 耳 酉 馬 鳥

耳

聲 声 shēng
128 17 [67]

聾 聋 lóng
128 22 [80]

聳 耸 sŏng
128 17 [80]

酉

醫 医 yī
164 18 [37]

醬 酱 jiàng
164 18 [80]

馬

罵 骂 mà
122 15 [68]

篤 笃 dǔ
118 16 [66]

駕 驾 jià
187 15 [73]

驚 惊 jīng
187 23 [2]

鳥

鶯 莺 yīng
196 21 [64]

鷹 鹰 yīng
196 24 [33]

習 习 xi 124 11 [36]	嚮 向 xiàng 30 18 [78]	譽 誉 yù 149 21 [78]	麗 丽 lì 198 19 [60]
棗 枣 zǎo 75 12 [70]	獎 奖 jiǎng 94 15 [74]		
歷 历 lì 77 16 [32]	鞏 巩 gǒng 177 15 [48]		
寧 宁 níng nìng 40 14 [63]	莖 茎 jīng 140 11 [64]	聖 圣 shèng 128 13 [61]	斃 毙 bì 66 17 [80]
雲 云 yún 173 12 [77]	藝 艺 yì 140 19 [65]	禦 御 yù 113 16 [54]	
學 学 xué 39 16 [59]	釁 衅 xìn 164 25 [30]	彎 弯 wān 57 22 [62]	
甚 什 shén shèn 99 9 [43]	釐 厘 lí 166 18 [32]	囂 嚣 xiāo 30 21 [68]	蠶 蚕 cán 142 24 [79]
疊 叠 dié 102 22 [79]	疊 叠 dié 72 19 [61]	電 电 diàn 173 13 [38]	單 单 dān 30 12 [58]
夢 梦 mèng 36 14 [76]	昇 升 shēng 72 8 [60]	義 义 yì 123 13 [71]	舊 旧 jiù 134 18 [53]
養 养 yǎng 184 15 [58]	鑒 鉴 jiàn 167 22 [66]	鑿 凿 záo zuò 167 28 [69]	

Left margin radicals: 向 言 鹿 / 犬 / 革 / 工 王 死 / 示 / 分 弓 / 厘 叩 虫 / 甩 甲 / 升 我 臼 / 金

Table 1: Characters which sometimes simplify

The characters in the first row do occur in simplified text, even though they have simplified forms. Hence they are included in the main section of the Fast Finder. The simplified forms as shown by the bottom row are mostly used, but in some contexts, or to avoid ambiguity, the traditional forms can be retained.

覆	乾	夥	藉	麼	像	餘	摺	後	於
						(餘)			
复	干	伙	借	么	象	余	折	后	于

Table 2: Numbers

Numbers are usually written in simple characters, as shown by the middle row. However, to avoid mistakes or guard against alterations, more complex characters (bottom row) are often used in relation to money. Note that the relationship between the characters in the rows is different from that of simplified versus traditional characters.

1	2	3	4	5	6	7	8	9	10	100	1,000	10,000
一	二	三	四	五	六	七	八	九	十	百	千	万
壹	贰	叁	肆	伍	陆	柒	捌	玖	拾	佰	仟	萬

Table 3 : 'Heavenly Stems' and 'Earthly Branches'

This table lists the 10 'Heavenly Stems' and 12 'Earthly Branches': characters which were used in historical methods of writing dates (related to the 'year of the tiger' and so on), and which have traditionally been linked with times of day, directions and various other things. (For example, 丑 is associated with the period 1 a.m. to 3 a.m., the 12th lunar month, and a north-easterly direction.) Apart from being of general interest, these characters (especially the first few Heavenly Stems characters) are used for numbering, in the same way that English uses letters (a), (b), (c) ... or Roman numerals (i), (ii), (iii) ...

Heavenly Stems		Earthly Branches			
1	甲	1	子	鼠	rat
2	乙	2	丑	牛	ox, cow
3	丙	3	寅	虎	tiger
4	丁	4	卯	兔	hare, rabbit
5	戊	5	辰	龍	dragon
6	己	6	巳	蛇	serpent, snake
7	庚	7	午	馬	horse
8	辛	8	未	羊	goat, sheep
9	壬	9	申	猴	monkey
10	癸	10	酉	鸡	cock, hen, rooster
		11	戌	狗	dog
		12	亥	豬	pig, boar

Table 4: Traditional Radical Chart

Table 4 give the traditional 214 radicals, their variant forms, and (where applicable) their modem equivalents (referring to the numbers in Table 5). Unlike the situation for modem radicals, the numbering of these traditional radicals is universally agreed.

Traditional	Mod.	Traditional	Mod.	Traditional	Mod.	Traditional
1 一	2	23 匸 匚	15	45 屮	61	67 文
2 丨	3	24 十	12	46 山	60	68 斗
3 丶	1	25 卜	16	47 巛 川	78	69 斤
4 丿 丿	4	26 卩 㔾	32	48 工	48	70 方
5 乙 乛 乚	5, 6, 7	27 厂 厂	13	49 己 巳	72	71 无 旡
6 亅	-	28 厶	37	50 巾	57	72 日
7 二	11	29 又	35	51 干	-	73 曰
8 亠	9	30 口	58	52 幺	76	74 月
9 人 亠 亻	20,21,23	31 囗	59	53 广	44	75 木
10 儿	29	32 土	49	54 廴	36	76 欠
11 入	23	33 士	49	55 廾	51	77 止
12 八 丷 八	24	34 夂	65	56 弋	56	78 歹
13 冂 冂	19	35 夊	65	57 弓	71	79 殳
14 冖	18	36 夕	64	58 彐 彑 彑	70	80 母 毋 毌
15 冫	8	37 大	52	59 彡	63	81 比
16 几 凡	30	38 女	73	60 彳	62	82 毛
17 凵	38	39 子 孑	74	61 心 小 忄	41, 81	83 氏
18 刀 刂	17, 27	40 宀	45	62 戈	101	84 气
19 力	28	41 寸	54	63 戶	86	85 水 氺 氵 4
20 勹	26	42 小 ⺌ ⺍	79	64 手 扌	55, 111	86 火 灬 8
21 匕	39	43 尢	53	65 支	-	87 爪 爫
22 匚	15	44 尸	67	66 攵	113	88 父

itional	Mod.	Traditional		Mod.	Traditional		Mod.	Traditional		Mod.
爻	-	121	缶	175	153	豸	198	185	首	-
爿	42	122	网 四 罒	145	154	貝	106	186	香	215
片	114	123	羊 ⺶ 羋	157	155	赤	190	187	馬	75
牙	99	124	羽	183	156	走	189	188	骨	214
牛	110	125	老 耂	92	157	足 ⻊	196	189	高	218
犬 犭	69, 96	126	而	169	158	身	200	190	髟	220
玄	-	127	耒	176	159	車	100	191	鬥	46
玉 王	88, 131	128	耳	163	160	辛 辛	186	192	鬯	-
瓜	151	129	聿 聿 畫	124	161	辰	187	193	鬲	219
瓦	98	130	肉 月	118	162	辵 辶	47	194	鬼	216
甘	135	131	臣	164	163	邑 阝	34	195	魚	210
生	-	132	自	180	164	酉	193	196	鳥	152
用	-	133	至	171	165	釆	197	197	鹵	-
田	142	134	臼	179	166	里	195	198	鹿	222
疋 正	156	135	舌	177	167	金	147, 209	199	麥	188
疒	127	136	舛	-	168	長	-	200	麻	221
癶	154	137	舟	182	169	門	46	201	黃 黄	-
白	150	138	艮 艮	184	170	阜 阝	33	202	黍	-
皮	153	139	色	-	171	隶	-	203	黑	223
皿	146	140	艸 艹	50	172	隹	208	204	黹	-
目	141	141	虍	173	173	雨	204	205	黽	207
矛	155	142	虫	174	174	青	202	206	鼎	-
矢	148	143	血	181	175	非	205	207	鼓	224
石	136	144	行	-	176	面	-	208	鼠	225
示 礻	87, 132	145	衣 衤	129, 161	177	革	212	209	鼻	226
禸	-	146	西 覀 襾	166	178	韋	91	210	齊 斉	-
禾	149	147	見	107	179	韭	-	211	齒	206
穴 宀	128	148	角	201	180	音	211	212	龍 竜	137
立	126	149	言	10, 185	181	頁	170	213	龜	-
竹 ⺮	178	150	谷	199	182	風	121	214	龠	-
米	159	151	豆	191	183	飛	-			
糸	77	152	豕	194	184	食 飠	68, 217			

Table 5: Modern Radical Chart

This table lists the 'modem' radicals used in the Fast Finder, with their alternative forms, and (where applicable) the corresponding traditional radicals (see Table 4). This set of modem radicals is used in '*A Chinese English Dictionary*' and many modem dictionaries use this set of radicals or a close approximation – albeit allocating to them numbers which differ slightly from dictionary to dictionary.

Modern	Trad.	Modern	Trad.	Modern	Trad.	Modern
1 、	3	25 乂	-	49 土 士	32, 33	73 女
2 一	1	26 勹	20	50 艹	140	74 子 孑
3 丨	2	27 刀 ⼑	18	51 廾	55	75 马
4 丿	4	28 力	19	52 大	37	76 幺
5 乛	5	29 儿	10	53 尢	43	77 纟 糸
6 丁	5	30 几 凡	16	54 寸	41	78 巛
7 乙 乚 乛	5	31 ⼍	-	55 扌	64	79 小 ⺌
8 冫	15	32 卩	26	56 弋	56	80 川
9 亠	8	33 阝	170	57 巾	50	81 心
10 讠	149	34 阝	163	58 口	30	82 斗
11 二	7	35 又	29	59 囗	31	83 火
12 十	24	36 廴	54	60 山	46	84 文
13 厂	27	37 厶	28	61 屮	45	85 方
14 ナ	-	38 凵	17	62 彳	60	86 户
15 匚	22, 23	39 匕	21	63 彡	59	87 礻
16 卜 ⼂	25	40 氵	85	64 夕	36	88 王
17 刂	18	41 忄	61	65 夂	34, 35	89 生
18 ⼌	14	42 ⺘	90	66 丸	-	90 天 夭
19 冂 几	13	43 亡	-	67 尸	44	91 韦
20 ⺍	9	44 广	53	68 饣	184	92 耂
21 亻	9	45 ⼧	40	69 犭	94	93 廿 ⼮
22 厂	-	46 门	169	70 彐 彐 且	58	94 木
23 人 入	9, 11	47 辶	162	71 弓	57	95 不
24 八 ハ ⼋	12	48 工	48	72 己 巳	49	96 犬

ern	Trad.	Modern		Trad.	Modern		Trad.	Modern		Trad.
歹	78	130	夫	-	163	耳	128	196	足 𧾷	157
瓦	98	131	玉	96	164	臣	131	197	釆	165
牙	92	132	示	113	165	戋	-	198	豸	153
车	159	133	去	-	166	西 覀	146	199	谷	150
戈	62	134	业	-	167	束	-	200	身	158
止	77	135	甘	99	168	亚	-	201	角	148
日	72	136	石	112	169	而	126	202	青	174
曰	73	137	龙	212	170	页	181	203	卓	-
中	-	138	戊	-	171	至	133	204	雨	173
贝	154	139	业	-	172	光	-	205	非	175
见	147	140	业	-	173	虍	141	206	齿	211
父	88	141	目	109	174	虫	142	207	黾	205
气	84	142	田	102	175	缶	121	208	隹	172
牛	93	143	由	-	176	耒	127	209	金	167
手	64	144	申	-	177	舌	135	210	鱼 鱼	195
毛	82	145	皿	122	178	竹 ⺮	118	211	音	180
攵	66	146	皿	108	179	臼	134	212	革	177
片	91	147	牛	167	180	自	132	213	是	-
斤	69	148	矢	111	181	血	143	214	骨	188
爪 爫	87	149	禾	115	182	舟	137	215	香	186
尺	-	150	白	106	183	羽	124	216	鬼	194
月 月	74, 130	151	瓜	97	184	艮 艮	138	217	食	184
殳	79	152	鸟	196	185	言	149	218	高	189
欠	76	153	皮	107	186	辛 辛	160	219	鬲	193
风	182	154	癶	105	187	辰	161	220	影	190
氏	83	155	矛	110	188	麦	199	221	麻	200
比	81	156	疋	103	189	走	156	222	鹿	198
聿 聿 聿	129	157	羊 羊 羊	123	190	赤	155	223	黑	203
水	85	158	类	-	191	豆	151	224	鼓	207
立	117	159	米	119	192	束	-	225	鼠	208
广	104	160	齐	-	193	酉	164	226	鼻	209
穴	116	161	衣	145	194	豕	152	227	-	-
礻	145	162	亦 亦	-	195	里	166			

Pinyin (alphabetical) index

At first sight it might seem that a pinyin index is superfluous for this book: after all, the main purpose of the book is to let you find characters *without* knowing their pronunciations. However, a subsidiary purpose of the book is to allow browsing, and for this it is sometimes useful to be able to check which characters share a particular pronunciation.

In the listing below, characters sharing the same pronunciation and tone are grouped by phonetic element (if any) and then ordered by increasing stroke-count. The numbers refer to pages in the main part of the book. Characters are listed under each of their pronunciations. However if a character appears on more than one page in the main part of the book, then only one of these page numbers is given here (since the character information is identical on each of these pages).

ā	阿 22		爱 60		扒 13		班 19		棒 16		卑	
	啊 24	ān	安 63		捌 13		斑 19	bāo	包 36		碑	
á	啊 24	àn	按 11	bá	拔 13		般 28		炮 3		背	běi
ǎ	啊 24		案 63	bǎ	把 13		搬 13		胞 27		北	běi
à	啊 24		暗 25	bà	把 13	bǎn	板 17		剥 42	bèi	被	bèi
a	啊 24		岸 66		爸 59		版 19	báo	薄 65		辈	
āi	唉 23	áng	昂 68		坝 10	bàn	半 38		雹 68		倍	
	埃 10	āo	凹 39		罢 68		伴 9	bǎo	饱 20		惫	
	挨 12		熬 72		霸 68		拌 13		宝 63		背	
	哀 62	áo	熬 72	ba	吧 24		扮 12		保 8		贝	
	哎 23	ǎo	袄 20	bāi	掰 31		瓣 29		堡 75		狈	
ái	挨 12	ào	奥 58	bái	白 58		办 1	bào	暴 68		臂	
	呆 68		澳 5	bǎi	伯 8	bāng	邦 30		曝 25	bei	奔	bēn
	癌 33		傲 9		柏 16		帮 75		爆 3	bēn	本	bèn
ǎi	欸 50	bā	巴 39		百 39	bǎng	绑 15		刨 42	bèn	笨	bèn
	矮 20		吧 24		佰 8		榜 16		抱 13		奔	
	蔼 65		芭 65		摆 12		膀 27		鲍 29		绷	bēng
ài	唉 23		疤 33	bài	败 28	bàng	傍 8		报 13	bēng	崩	béng
	隘 22		笆 66		拜 31		谤 4		豹 14		甭	běng
	碍 26		八 1	bān	颁 31		磅 26	bēi	杯 17	bèi	绷	
	艾 65		叭 24		扳 13		镑 21		悲 72	béng		

绷 15
蹦 26
逼 34
鼻 58
彼 10
比 10
笔 66
鄙 54
闭 36
必 1
秘 18
辟 31
壁 75
避 34
臂 79
毕 70
毙 80
敝 51
弊 74
蔽 65
痹 33
碧 78
币 40
鞭 29
编 15
边 34
扁 32
贬 28
便 9
遍 34
辨 29
辩 29
辫 29
变 62
边 34
镖 21
标 16
彪 35
biǎo 表 67
biē 憋 72
bié 别 42
biè 别 42
bīn 彬 17
宾 63
滨 5
bīng 兵 61
冰 3
bǐng 丙 39
柄 17
屏 32
饼 20
秉 60
bìng 病 33
并 58
bō 玻 19
播 12
拨 13
剥 42
波 7
菠 65
bó 伯 8
泊 5
柏 16
舶 28
魄 25
博 10
搏 11
膊 27
薄 65
驳 28
勃 46
脖 27
bǒ 簸 66
bò 柏 16
簸 66
薄 65
bo 卜 1
bú 不 39
bǔ 捕 11
卜 1
补 20
bù 不 39
部 54
步 66
簿 66
布 32
怖 2
埠 10
cā 拆 13
擦 11
cāi 猜 14
cái 才 38
材 17
财 28
裁 36
cǎi 采 60
彩 41
睬 25
踩 26
cài 采 60
菜 64
蔡 64
cān 参 61
餐 80
cán 残 26
蚕 69
惭 2
cǎn 惨 2
càn 灿 3
cāng 仓 59
沧 6
苍 64
舱 28
cáng 藏 65
cāo 操 12
cáo 曹 79
槽 16
cǎo 草 64
cè 侧 9
测 7
厕 32
册 39
策 66
cēn 参 61
céng 层 32
曾 58
cèng 蹭 26
chā 差 58
叉 39
插 12
chá 茶 64
叉 39
查 67
察 63
chǎ 叉 39
chà 岔 59
差 58
刹 42
诧 4
chāi 差 58
拆 13
chái 柴 74
chān 搀 12
掺 12
chán 谗 4
馋 20
禅 20
蝉 29
缠 15
chǎn 阐 36
产 62
铲 21
chàn 颤 48
chāng 昌 68
猖 14
cháng 长 38
场 10
肠 27
常 59
裳 59
尝 59
偿 8
chǎng 场 10
敞 51
厂 39
chàng 畅 30
倡 8
唱 23
chāo 超 35
吵 23
抄 11
钞 21
cháo 朝 29
嘲 24
潮 7
巢 69
chǎo 吵 23
炒 3
chē 车 38
chě 扯 13
chè 彻 10
撤 13
chén 陈 22
辰 32
晨 68
尘 59
臣 37
沉 6
chèn 趁 35
称 18
衬 20
chēng 称 18
撑 11
chéng 澄 6
成 36
诚 4
城 10
盛 80
乘 60
呈 68
程 18
承 1
惩 72
chèng 秤 18
chī 痴 33
吃 23
嗤 23
chí 池 7
驰 28
匙 35
持 11
迟 34
chǐ 侈 8
尺 32
耻 25
齿 37
chì 斥 32
赤 67
翅 35
chōng 冲 3
充 62
chóng 虫 38

ALPHABETICAL INDEX

pinyin	char	no.	pinyin	char	no.	pinyin	char	no.	pinyin	char	no.	pinyin	char	no.
	重	60		窗	63	cù	醋	25		大	38		道	34
	崇	66	chuáng	幢	14		促	8		逮	34	dé	得	10
chǒng	宠	63		床	33	cuán	攒	12		戴	36		德	10
chòng	冲	3	chuǎng	闯	36	cuàn	窜	63	dān	担	12	de	地	10
chōu	抽	13	chuàng	创	42	cuī	崔	66		单	58		得	10
chóu	绸	15	chuī	吹	24		催	8		耽	25		的	25
	稠	18		炊	3		摧	11		丹	39	děi	得	10
	畴	25	chuí	垂	60	cuì	脆	27	dǎn	胆	27	dēng	灯	3
	筹	66		捶	12		粹	18	dàn	旦	68		登	66
	踌	26		锤	21		翠	69		但	8		蹬	26
	仇	9	chūn	春	67	cūn	村	17		担	12		等	66
	酬	25	chún	淳	5	cún	存	32		弹	14	dèng	凳	66
	愁	72		醇	25	cùn	寸	36		石	33		瞪	25
chǒu	丑	39		唇	32	cuō	搓	13		淡	5		蹬	26
chòu	臭	58		纯	15		磋	26		氮	61		邓	1
chū	出	38	chǔn	蠢	67	cuò	挫	12		诞	4	dī	堤	10
	初	20	cī	差	58		措	11		蛋	69		提	12
chú	厨	32	cí	瓷	80		错	21	dāng	当	59		低	8
	橱	17		词	4	dā	搭	11	dǎng	挡	11		滴	5
	除	22		雌	10		答	66		党	59	dí	迪	34
	蹰	26		慈	58	dá	打	13		荡	65		笛	66
	锄	21		磁	26		答	66		当	59		狄	14
chǔ	处	35		辞	26		瘩	33		挡	11		的	25
	础	26	cǐ	此	10		达	34		档	16		敌	26
	储	9	cì	次	3	dǎ	打	13	dāo	刀	39		涤	6
	楚	75		伺	9	dà	大	38		叨	24		底	33
chù	处	35		赐	28	da	瘩	33	dǎo	倒	9	dǐ	抵	12
	触	29		刺	42	dāi	待	10		蹈	26		地	10
	畜	62	cōng	从	30		呆	68		岛	58		帝	62
chuān	穿	63		匆	40	dǎi	逮	34		捣	11	dì	缔	15
	川	1		聪	25		歹	39		祷	20		蒂	64
chuán	传	9		囱	58	dài	代	8		导	69		弟	58
	船	28		葱	64		贷	77	dào	盗	80		递	34
chuǎn	喘	23	cóng	从	30		袋	77		到	42		的	25
chuàn	串	38		丛	73		怠	61		倒	9		第	66
chuāng	创	42	còu	凑	3		待	10		稻	18	diān	颠	48
	疮	33	cū	粗	18		带	69		悼	2		掂	13

diǎn 点 典 diàn 店 惦 淀 奠 殿 垫 电 diāo 雕 凋 diào 掉 钓 diē 跌 爹 dié 碟 蝶 迭 dīng 丁 叮 盯 钉 dǐng 顶 鼎 dìng 订 钉 定 diū 丢 dōng 东 冬 董 懂

冻 3
栋 17
动 31
洞 7
都 54
兜 58
斗 1
抖 13
陡 22
豆 60
逗 34
斗 1
读 4
都 54
嘟 24
督 79
独 14
毒 67
读 4
堵 10
赌 28
睹 25
笃 66
肚 27
度 33
渡 7
镀 21
妒 22
杜 17
肚 27
端 20
短 20
断 51
段 31
缎 15
锻 21
堆 10
duì 敦 51
兑 58
队 22
对 1
dūn 吨 24
蹲 26
敦 51
墩 10
dùn 钝 21
顿 30
盾 32
duō 多 61
哆 23
duó 度 33
夺 67
duǒ 朵 69
躲 28
duò 舵 28
跺 26
驮 28
堕 75
惰 2
ē 阿 22
é 俄 9
哦 23
鹅 31
蛾 29
讹 4
额 48
ě 恶 69
è 恶 69
饿 20
厄 32
ê̄ 欸 50
ế 欸 50
ê̌ 欸 50
ề 欸 50
ēn 恩 72
ér 而 39
儿 1
ěr 尔 40
耳 39
èr 二 60
贰 36
fā 发 33
fá 伐 8
阀 36
乏 60
罚 68
fǎ 法 5
fà 发 33
fān 番 60
蕃 64
翻 49
帆 14
fán 烦 3
蕃 64
凡 36
繁 77
fǎn 反 32
返 34
fàn 饭 20
贩 28
泛 6
犯 14
范 65
fāng 方 38
坊 10
妨 22
芳 64
fáng 防 22
坊 10
妨 22
房 32
肪 27
fǎng 仿 8
访 4
纺 15
fàng 放 20
fēi 非 41
啡 24
菲 65
飞 39
féi 肥 27
fěi 匪 37
诽 4
菲 65
斐 69
fèi 沸 7
费 69
废 33
肺 27
fēn 分 59
吩 23
纷 15
芬 64
氛 61
fén 焚 74
坟 10
fěn 粉 18
fèn 分 59
份 8
奋 67
愤 2
粪 59
fēng 丰 38
封 30
风 36
枫 17
疯 33
峰 14
锋 21
蜂 29
féng 冯 3
逢 34
缝 15
fěng 讽 4
fèng 缝 15
凤 36
奉 67
fó 佛 9
fǒu 否 60
fū 夫 38
肤 27
敷 51
fú 夫 38
扶 13
芙 65
弗 40
佛 9
拂 13
符 66
幅 14
福 20
辐 19
俘 8
浮 6
服 27
伏 8
袱 20
fǔ 甫 38
辅 19
府 33
俯 9
斧 59
抚 13
腐 33
fù 赴 35
付 9
附 22
副 42
富 63
傅 8
缚 15
复 61
腹 27
父 59
妇 22
覆 68
负 61
赋 28
fu 咐 24
gā 夹 38
咖 24
gá 轧 19
gāi 该 4
gǎi 改 31
gài 丐 39
钙 21
溉 7
概 17
盖 58
gān 干 39
杆 17
肝 27
竿 66
甘 40
gǎn 杆 17
秆 18
赶 35
感 72
敢 51
gàn 干 39
gāng 扛 13
缸 20

ALPHABETICAL INDEX

	冈 36		跟 26		菇 65	guī	闺 36		涵 6		荷
	刚 42	gēng	更 39		辜 67		硅 26	hán	寒 63	hè	吓
	纲 15		耕 18	gú	骨 69		瑰 19		含 59		荷
	钢 21		庚 33	gǔ	古 67		归 1	hǎn	喊 24		喝
gǎng	岗 66		梗 17		鼓 30		龟 61		罕 61		贺
	港 5		耿 25		骨 69		规 30	hàn	汗 7		和
gàng	杠 17		颈 31		谷 59	guǐ	诡 4		旱 68		鹤
	钢 21	gèng	更 39		贾 68		鬼 58		悍 2		赫
gāo	高 62	gōng	工 39		股 27		轨 19		捍 12	hēi	黑
	糕 18		功 19		固 37		癸 66		焊 3		嘿
	膏 62		红 15		雇 32	guì	桂 16		憾 2	hén	痕
gǎo	搞 11		攻 19		顾 31		跪 26		撼 12	hěn	很
	稿 18		供 8		故 30		柜 17		汉 7		狠
gào	膏 62		恭 67	guā	刮 26		贵 69		翰 29	hèn	恨
	告 67		公 59		瓜 32	gǔn	滚 5	háng	吭 23	hēng	亨
gē	鸽 31		宫 63	guǎ	寡 63	gùn	棍 16		杭 16		哼
	哥 69		弓 39	guà	卦 41	guō	锅 21		航 28	héng	恒
	歌 50		躬 28		挂 11		过 34		行 10		横
	胳 27	gǒng	汞 69	guāi	乖 60		郭 54	hàng	巷 67		衡
	戈 38		拱 11	guǎi	拐 12	guó	国 37		号 68		横
	割 42		巩 19	guài	怪 2	guǒ	果 68	háo	毫 62	hèng	哼
	疙 33	gòng	贡 69	guān	官 63		裹 62		豪 62	hng	哄
	搁 13		共 67		棺 16	guò	过 34	hǎo	好 22	hōng	烘
gé	格 16		供 8		关 58	guo	过 34	hào	好 22		轰
	胳 27	gōu	勾 36		观 1	hā	哈 23		浩 5		红
	搁 13		沟 7		冠 61	hǎ	哈 23		耗 18	hóng	虹
	葛 64		钩 21		馆 20	hà	哈 23		号 68		洪
	革 40		狗 14	guǎn	管 66	hāi	咳 23	hē	呵 24		弘
	隔 22	gòu	勾 36		灌 5	hái	还 34		喝 23		宏
	阁 36		构 17	guàn	罐 20		孩 14	hé	阁 36		鸿
gě	合 59		购 28		贯 69		海 6		核 16	hǒng	哄
	葛 64		够 30		惯 2	hǎi	海 6		合 59	hòng	哄
	个 59	gū	估 8		观 1	hài	亥 62		盒 59	hóu	侯
gè	各 61		咕 23		冠 61		骇 28		河 7		喉
	个 59		骨 69	guāng	光 59		害 63		禾 40		猴
gěi	给 15		孤 14	guǎng	广 38	hán	韩 29		和 18		吼
gēn	根 17		姑 22	guàng	逛 34		汗 7		何 9	hòu	后
										hǒu	
										hòu	

後 10
厚 32
候 9
乎 40
呼 23
糊 18
忽 69
胡 30
湖 7
葫 65
瑚 19
糊 18
蝴 29
核 16
狐 14
壶 67
虎 33
糊 18
戶 58
护 11
沪 5
互 39
化 9
花 65
哗 23
华 70
哗 23
滑 6
猾 14
划 42
化 9
华 70
话 4
划 42
画 37
怀 2
槐 16
淮 7
徊 10
huài 坏 10
huān 欢 1
huán 还 34
环 19
huǎn 缓 15
huàn 唤 23
换 12
焕 3
痪 33
患 69
幻 30
huāng 荒 64
慌 2
huáng 皇 58
凰 36
惶 2
煌 3
蝗 29
黄 67
huǎng 谎 4
恍 2
晃 68
huàng 晃 68
huī 挥 12
晖 25
辉 18
灰 32
恢 2
徽 10
huí 回 37
huǐ 悔 2
毁 31
huì 会 59
绘 15
惠 67
贿 28
秽 18
慧 72
汇 7
hūn 昏 69
婚 22
hún 浑 6
魂 31
混 6
hùn 混 6
huō 豁 30
huó 和 18
活 6
huǒ 火 1
伙 9
夥 31
huò 货 77
豁 30
或 36
惑 72
和 18
祸 20
霍 68
获 65
jī 几 39
讥 4
叽 24
饥 20
机 17
肌 27
圾 10
奇 67
基 69
积 18
期 29
迹 34
缉 15
鸡 1
绩 15
激 7
jí 及 39
级 15
极 17
藉 65
籍 66
吉 67
击 38
急 61
辑 19
集 74
脊 69
即 28
疾 33
嫉 22
jǐ 几 39
己 39
挤 11
济 5
给 15
脊 69
jì 继 15
记 4
纪 15
忌 69
季 60
既 28
寂 63
剂 42
济 5
妓 22
技 11
寄 63
祭 72
计 4
际 22
冀 71
jiā 夹 38
家 63
佳 8
加 30
茄 65
嘉 67
jiá 夹 38
颊 30
jiǎ 甲 39
假 9
jià 嫁 22
稼 18
价 8
驾 73
架 74
假 9
jiān 奸 22
艰 1
歼 26
监 66
兼 58
间 36
坚 75
煎 58
渐 7
肩 32
尖 59
jiǎn 拣 13
俭 8
捡 12
检 16
减 3
碱 26
茧 65
简 66
剪 58
柬 38
jiàn 践 26
剑 42
监 66
间 36
建 35
健 9
键 21
件 9
鉴 66
箭 66
见 36
舰 28
渐 7
贱 28
溅 7
荐 65
jiāng 江 7
浆 77
姜 58
僵 8
将 3
疆 31
jiǎng 奖 74
桨 74
蒋 65
讲 4
jiàng 浆 77
酱 80
匠 37
强 14
将 3
降 22
jiāo 椒 17
交 62
郊 54

ALPHABETICAL INDEX

Pinyin	字	Page
	胶	27
	娇	22
	骄	28
	浇	5
	教	51
	焦	72
	蕉	64
jiáo	矫	20
	嚼	23
jiǎo	狡	14
	绞	15
	饺	20
	矫	20
	角	61
	搅	11
	缴	15
	脚	27
jiào	校	16
	较	19
	轿	19
	教	51
	酵	25
	叫	24
	觉	59
jiē	街	10
	结	15
	阶	22
	揭	12
	节	65
	皆	79
	接	11
jié	洁	5
	结	15
	桔	16
	截	36
	竭	20
	劫	46
	杰	67
	节	65
	捷	11
jiě	姐	22
	解	29
jiè	届	32
	介	59
	价	8
	界	68
	借	8
	解	29
	戒	36
	诫	4
	价	8
jīn	禁	72
	襟	20
	斤	32
	今	59
	巾	38
	津	7
	金	59
	筋	66
	谨	4
	瑾	19
	锦	21
	紧	66
jǐn	仅	9
	尽	32
jìn	晋	60
	劲	46
	禁	72
	近	34
	浸	6
	进	34
	尽	32
jīng	京	62
	惊	2
	鲸	29
	菁	64
	睛	25
	精	18
	经	15
	茎	64
	兢	30
	晶	68
jǐng	颈	31
	井	40
	警	78
	景	68
jìng	竟	62
	境	10
	镜	21
	靖	20
	净	3
	劲	46
	径	10
	经	15
	竞	62
	敬	51
	静	30
jiū	究	63
	纠	15
	揪	13
jiǔ	久	40
	灸	69
	玖	19
	九	38
	酒	7
jiù	救	30
	旧	1
	就	30
	舅	69
	居	32
jū	据	13
	拘	13
	鞠	29
	车	38
	桔	16
	菊	65
	橘	16
jú	局	32
jǔ	沮	7
	柜	17
	矩	20
	举	59
jù	具	71
	俱	8
	惧	2
	剧	42
	据	13
	锯	21
	句	36
	巨	37
	拒	13
	距	26
	聚	37
juān	圈	37
	捐	12
juǎn	卷	67
juàn	卷	67
	倦	8
	圈	37
	绢	15
	眷	67
	决	3
	诀	4
	抉	13
jué	爵	60
	嚼	23
	角	61
	绝	15
	觉	59
	掘	13
	军	61
jūn	君	33
	龟	61
	均	10
	菌	65
	俊	8
	峻	14
	骏	28
	菌	65
kā	咖	24
kǎ	卡	66
kāi	开	39
kǎi	慨	2
	凯	48
kai	开	39
kān	刊	31
	勘	46
	堪	10
	看	33
kǎn	砍	26
	看	33
kàn	看	33
kāng	康	33
	慷	2
	糠	18
káng	扛	13
	亢	62
	抗	11
	炕	3
kǎo	考	32
	烤	3
kào	靠	67
kē	棵	16
	颗	48
	柯	17
	科	18
	磕	
	咳	
ké	壳	
kě	可	
	渴	
	刻	
kè	课	
	克	
	客	
kěn	垦	
	恳	
	肯	
	啃	
kēng	吭	
	坑	
kōng	空	
	恐	
	孔	
kòng	空	
	控	
kōu	抠	
	口	
kòu	扣	
	寇	
kū	枯	
	窟	
	哭	
kǔ	苦	
	酷	
kù	库	
	裤	
kuā	夸	
kuǎ	垮	
kuà	挎	
	跨	
kuài	块	
	会	

Pinyin	Char	Pg
	快	2
la	筷	66
	宽	63
	款	50
g	框	17
g	筐	66
g	狂	14
	旷	25
	矿	26
	框	17
	眶	25
	况	3
	亏	60
	魁	35
	葵	64
	愧	2
	溃	5
	馈	20
	坤	10
	昆	68
	捆	13
	困	37
	扩	13
	括	12
	阔	36
	廓	33
	垃	10
	拉	11
	啦	24
	喇	24
	拉	11
	喇	24
	拉	11
	喇	24
	落	65
	腊	27
	蜡	29

Pinyin	Char	Pg
	辣	29
la	啦	24
	蓝	64
lái	来	38
	莱	65
lài	赖	30
lai	来	38
lán	兰	58
	拦	11
	栏	16
	蓝	64
	篮	66
lǎn	览	66
	揽	12
	懒	2
làn	烂	3
	滥	6
láng	狼	14
	郎	28
	廊	33
	螂	29
lǎng	朗	28
làng	浪	5
lāo	捞	11
láo	劳	64
	唠	23
	牢	63
lǎo	老	32
	姥	22
	潦	5
lào	涝	5
	落	65
lè	勒	29
	乐	40
le	了	39
lēi	勒	29
léi	累	68

Pinyin	Char	Pg
	雷	68
lěi	累	68
	垒	61
	蕾	64
lèi	类	59
	累	68
	泪	7
léng	棱	16
lěng	冷	3
lèng	愣	2
lī	哩	23
lí	厘	32
	狸	14
	梨	74
	犁	75
	离	62
	璃	19
	篱	66
	黎	77
lǐ	里	68
	哩	23
	理	19
	礼	20
	李	67
lì	利	18
	俐	9
	莉	65
	例	9
	立	62
	粒	18
	厉	32
	励	31
	历	32
	沥	7
	力	38
	隶	38
	栗	68

Pinyin	Char	Pg
	丽	60
	荔	64
li	里	68
	哩	23
liǎ	俩	9
lián	怜	2
	连	34
	莲	65
	帘	63
	联	25
	廉	33
	镰	21
liǎn	脸	27
liàn	练	15
	炼	3
	链	21
	恋	62
liáng	量	68
	凉	3
	良	58
	粮	18
	梁	74
	梁	74
liǎng	两	39
	俩	9
liàng	量	68
	辆	19
	凉	3
	谅	4
	晾	25
	亮	62
liáo	辽	34
	疗	33
	聊	25
	僚	8
liǎo	了	39
	潦	5

Pinyin	Char	Pg
liào	了	39
	料	18
liē	咧	24
liě	咧	24
liè	列	26
	烈	72
	裂	77
	猎	14
	劣	59
lín	林	17
	淋	7
	琳	19
	霖	68
	邻	31
	磷	26
	临	1
lǐn	凛	3
	淋	7
lìn	伶	8
líng	玲	19
	铃	21
	零	68
	龄	30
	灵	69
	凌	3
	陵	22
	0	40
lǐng	令	59
	岭	14
	领	31
lìng	令	59
	另	68
liū	溜	6
liú	流	5
	硫	26
	刘	30
	留	80

Pinyin	Char	Pg
	榴	16
liǔ	瘤	33
liù	柳	17
	溜	6
	碌	26
	陆	22
	六	62
lōng	隆	22
lóng	龙	32
	咙	24
	珑	19
	笼	66
	聋	69
	隆	22
	窿	63
lǒng	垄	75
	拢	13
	笼	66
lòng	弄	69
lōu	搂	11
lóu	喽	23
	楼	16
lǒu	搂	11
lòu	露	68
	陋	22
	漏	7
	喽	23
lú	庐	33
	芦	64
	炉	3
	卢	66
lǔ	芦	64
	鲁	61
	虏	33
lù	鹿	33
	赂	28
	录	69

pinyin	字	№	pinyin	字	№	pinyin	字	№	pinyin	字	№	pinyin	字	№	pinyin	字
	绿	15	luǒ	裸	20		盲	62	méng	萌	65		灭	60	mǔ	母
	碌	26	luò	络	15		茫	65		盟	80	mín	民	39		姆
	陆	22		骆	28	māo	猫	14		蒙	64	mǐn	敏	51		拇
	路	26		洛	6	máo	猫	14		朦	27		悯	2		牡
	露	68		落	65		矛	61		檬	16	míng	明	25		亩
lú	驴	28	mā	抹	13		茅	64		氓	30		盟	80	mù	募
lǔ	屡	32		麻	33		毛	40	měng	蒙	64		名	33		墓
	缕	15		妈	22		髦	76		猛	14		铭	21		幕
	吕	68		摩	33	mǎo	卯	31	mèng	梦	76		鸣	23		慕
	侣	8	má	麻	33	mào	冒	68		孟	69		冥	61		暮
	铝	21		吗	24		帽	14	mī	咪	23	mìng	命	59		木
	旅	20	mǎ	马	35		茂	64		眯	25	miù	谬	4		沐
	履	32		吗	24		貌	14	mí	弥	14	mō	摸	11		目
lǜ	率	62		玛	19		贸	77		迷	34	mó	模	16		牧
	绿	15		码	26	me	么	1		谜	4		膜	27		睦
	律	10		蚂	29	méi	梅	16	mǐ	米	38		麽	33		穆
	虑	33	mà	蚂	29		酶	25		眯	25		摩	33	nā	那
	滤	7		骂	68		霉	68	mì	泌	5		磨	33	ná	拿
luǎn	卵	31	ma	嘛	24		媒	22		秘	18		蘑	65	nǎ	哪
luàn	乱	26		吗	24		煤	3		密	63		魔	33	nà	呐
lüè	掠	11	mái	埋	10		没	6		蜜	63	mǒ	抹	13		纳
	略	25	mǎi	买	69		枚	17		觅	77	mò	末	38		那
lūn	抡	12	mài	脉	27		玫	19	mián	绵	15		抹	13	na	哪
lún	伦	8		迈	34		眉	33		棉	16		沫	7	nǎi	乃
	论	4		麦	67	měi	每	61		眠	25		陌	22		奶
	抡	12		卖	67		美	58	miǎn	缅	15		莫	64	nài	奈
	沦	6	mán	埋	10		镁	21		免	61		寞	63		耐
	轮	19		瞒	25	mèi	妹	22		勉	35		漠	5		难
lùn	论	4		馒	20		昧	25		面	39		脉	27	nán	男
luō	罗	68		蛮	62		魅	35	miàn	喵	23		墨	69		南
luó	罗	68	mǎn	满	5		谜	4	miāo	苗	65		默	46		喃
	萝	64	màn	曼	68		媚	22	miáo	描	11		磨	33	nàn	难
	逻	34		慢	2	mēn	闷	36	miǎo	秒	18		没	6		囊
	锣	21		漫	6	mén	门	1		渺	7		万	39	náo	挠
	箩	66	máng	忙	2	mèn	闷	36	miào	庙	33	móu	谋	4	nǎo	恼
	骡	28		芒	64	men	们	9		妙	22	mǒu	某	69		脑
	螺	29		氓	30	mēng	蒙	64	miè	蔑	64	mú	模	16	nào	闹

那 54		凝 3		怕 2		佩 9	piàn	骗 28		仆 9
呢 24	nǐng	拧 11	pāi	拍 11		沛 7		片 38	pú	扑 13
哪 24	nìng	宁 63	pái	徘 10	pēn	喷 23	piāo	漂 6		
内 36		拧 11		排 13	pén	盆 59		飘 57		菩 64
那 54	niū	妞 22		牌 19	pèn	喷 23	piáo	朴 17		葡 65
嫩 22	niú	牛 38	pǎi	排 13	pēng	砰 26	piǎo	漂 6	pǔ	埔 10
能 30	niǔ	扭 13		迫 34		澎 7	piào	票 68		浦 5
嗯 23		纽 15	pài	派 7		烹 62		漂 6		朴 17
嗯 23		钮 21	pān	潘 6	péng	朋 27	piē	撇 13		普 58
嗯 23	nóng	农 38		攀 76		棚 17		瞥 79		谱 4
妮 22		浓 5	pán	胖 27		鹏 27	piě	撇 13	pù	铺 21
尼 32	nòng	弄 69		盘 58		彭 41	pīn	拼 11		瀑 6
呢 24	nú	奴 22	pàn	判 42		澎 7	pín	贫 59		曝 25
泥 7	nǔ	努 76		畔 25		膨 27		频 48	qī	栖 17
倪 8	nù	怒 72		盼 25		蓬 65	pǐn	品 68		欺 29
拟 13	nǚ	女 38		叛 51	pěng	捧 11	pìn	聘 25		妻 67
你 9	nuǎn	暖 25	pāng	膀 27	pèng	碰 26	pīng	乒 61		凄 3
泥 7	nüè	疟 33		乓 61	pī	披 13	píng	平 39		期 29
逆 34		虐 33	páng	彷 10		劈 76		评 4		缉 15
腻 27	nuó	娜 22		旁 62		批 13		坪 10		漆 5
粘 18		挪 13		膀 27		坯 10		苹 64		七 38
年 40	nuò	诺 4		磅 26	pí	皮 33		屏 32		戚 36
捻 12	ō	噢 23		螃 29		疲 33		瓶 30		沏 7
撵 12		喔 24		庞 33		啤 23		凭 71		柒 74
念 59	ó	哦 23	pàng	胖 27		脾 27		萍 65	qí	齐 62
廿 40	ò	哦 23	pāo	泡 7	pǐ	否 60	pō	坡 10		歧 10
娘 22	ōu	区 37		抛 13		劈 76		颇 30		奇 67
酿 25		欧 28	páo	刨 42		匹 37		朴 17		崎 14
酿 25		殴 28		炮 3	pì	辟 31		泊 5		骑 28
鸟 35		鸥 28		袍 20		僻 9		泼 7		琦 19
尿 32	ǒu	偶 8	pǎo	跑 26		譬 78	pó	婆 76		其 69
捏 12		呕 24	pào	泡 7	pó	屁 32	pò	破 26		淇 5
聂 69	pā	趴 26		炮 3	piān	扁 32		朴 17		棋 16
您 72		啪 24		炮 3		偏 8		迫 34		旗 20
宁 63	pá	爬 35	péi	陪 22		篇 66		魄 25		祈 20
拧 11		扒 13		培 10		片 38	pōu	剖 42		七 38
柠 16	pà	帕 14	pèi	赔 28	pián	便 9	pū	铺 21	qǐ	岂 66
					配 25					

ALPHABETICAL INDEX

Pinyin	字	No.
	启	32
	起	35
	乞	61
	企	59
qì	泣	5
	气	61
	汽	6
	弃	62
	迄	34
	砌	26
	契	74
	器	68
qi	起	35
qiā	掐	12
qiǎ	卡	66
qià	恰	2
	洽	6
qiān	千	40
	仟	9
	迁	34
	签	66
	铅	21
	谦	4
	牵	67
qián	钱	21
	前	58
	潜	5
	钳	21
	乾	29
qiǎn	浅	5
	遣	34
	谴	4
qiàn	纤	15
	歉	50
	欠	40
	嵌	66
qiāng	腔	27

Pinyin	字	No.
	抢	12
	枪	16
qiáng	强	14
	墙	10
qiǎng	抢	12
	强	14
qiāo	悄	2
	锹	21
	敲	57
qiáo	乔	60
	侨	8
	桥	16
	瞧	25
	翘	35
qiǎo	悄	2
	巧	19
	雀	59
qiào	俏	8
	翘	35
	壳	67
qiē	切	10
qié	茄	65
qiě	且	39
qiè	怯	2
	切	10
	窃	63
qīn	侵	8
	钦	21
	亲	62
qín	勤	46
	芹	65
	禽	59
	擒	12
	秦	67
	琴	80
qǐn	寝	63
qīng	青	67

Pinyin	字	No.
	清	5
	蜻	29
	氢	61
	轻	19
	卿	31
qíng	倾	9
	情	2
	晴	25
	擎	76
qǐng	请	4
	顷	10
qìng	庆	33
	亲	62
qióng	琼	19
	穷	63
qiū	秋	18
	丘	40
qiú	求	38
	球	19
	囚	37
qū	区	37
	驱	28
	躯	28
	趋	35
	曲	40
	屈	32
	渠	74
qú	取	25
	娶	76
qǔ	曲	40
	趣	35
qù	去	67
qu	去	67
quān	圈	37
quán	全	59
	诠	4
	权	17

Pinyin	字	No.
	泉	58
	拳	67
quǎn	犬	38
quàn	券	67
	劝	1
quē	缺	20
qué	瘸	33
què	鹊	30
	确	26
	榷	16
	雀	59
	却	54
qún	裙	20
	群	31
rán	然	72
	燃	3
rǎn	染	74
rāng	嚷	23
rǎng	嚷	23
	壤	10
ràng	让	4
ráo	饶	20
rǎo	扰	11
	绕	15
rào	绕	15
rě	惹	64
rè	热	72
rén	壬	40
	任	9
	人	38
	仁	8
rěn	忍	69
rèn	任	9
	妊	22
	饪	20
	认	4
	刃	1

Pinyin	字	No.
	韧	30
rēng	扔	13
réng	仍	9
rì	日	39
róng	容	63
	溶	5
	蓉	64
	熔	3
	绒	15
	融	52
	荣	64
róu	柔	61
	揉	12
ròu	肉	36
rú	如	22
	儒	8
rǔ	辱	70
	乳	42
	汝	7
rù	入	38
ruǎn	软	19
ruì	锐	21
	瑞	19
rùn	闰	36
	润	7
ruò	弱	31
	若	65
sā	撒	13
sǎ	洒	7
	撒	13
sà	萨	65
sāi	腮	27
	塞	63
sài	塞	63
	赛	63
sān	三	60
	叁	61

Pinyin	字	No.
sǎn	散	
	伞	
sàn	散	
	丧	
sāng	桑	
	嗓	
sǎng	丧	
sào	骚	
sāo	嫂	
	扫	
	扫	
sào	塞	
sè	色	
	瑟	
	涩	
sēn	森	
sēng	僧	
	纱	
shā	砂	
	杉	
	沙	
	杀	
	刹	
	煞	
shǎ	傻	
shà	厦	
	唵	
	煞	
shāi	筛	
	色	
shǎi	晒	
shài	册	
	X	
shān	栅	
	疏	
	杉	
	衫	

山 38
陕 22
闪 36
禅 20
擅 11
扇 32
善 58
g 商 62
伤 8
g 上 38
晌 25
赏 59
g 尚 36
上 38
g 裳 59
上 38
捎 11
梢 16
稍 18
烧 3
勺 36
少 59
哨 23
捎 11
绍 15
少 59
奢 67
蛇 29
折 13
舌 78
摺 12
舍 59
社 20
射 28
舍 59
设 4
涉 5
摄 12
shéi 谁 4
shēn 申 38
伸 9
呻 24
绅 15
参 61
身 58
深 6
shén 神 20
甚 69
什 9
shěn 审 63
婶 22
沈 7
shèn 甚 69
慎 2
渗 6
肾 66
shēng 生 38
牲 19
声 67
升 40
shéng 绳 15
shěng 省 59
shèng 胜 27
盛 80
圣 61
乘 60
剩 42
shī 施 20
诗 4
失 38
师 1
狮 14
湿 6
尸 39
shí 拾 12
识 4
蚀 20
十 38
什 9
石 33
时 25
实 63
食 59
shǐ 屎 32
史 38
使 9
驶 28
始 22
矢 40
shì 逝 34
誓 78
室 63
是 68
释 18
式 36
试 4
侍 8
士 38
仕 9
适 34
市 62
柿 16
饰 20
示 60
视 20
势 76
似 9
氏 40
世 40
事 38
shi 匙 35
shōu 收 30
shóu 熟 72
shǒu 守 63
手 40
首 58
shòu 受 60
授 12
瘦 33
寿 33
售 78
兽 58
shū 殊 26
叔 30
淑 7
输 19
梳 16
枢 17
抒 12
书 38
疏 31
蔬 65
舒 31
shú 赎 28
熟 72
shǔ 数 51
暑 68
属 32
鼠 69
署 68
薯 64
蜀 68
shù 数 51
束 38
竖 73
恕 72
术 38
述 34
树 17
shuā 刷 42
shuǎ 耍 60
shuà 刷 42
shuāi 摔 11
衰 62
shuǎi 甩 39
shuài 率 62
帅 1
shuān 拴 12
shuāng 霜 68
双 1
shuǎng 爽 38
shuí 谁 4
shuǐ 水 1
shuì 睡 25
说 4
税 18
shùn 顺 1
瞬 25
shuō 说 4
shuò 数 51
硕 26
烁 3
sī 斯 29
撕 13
司 36
私 18
思 68
丝 73
sǐ 死 33
sì 伺 9
饲 20
寺 67
巳 39
似 9
肆 31
四 37
食 59
si 厕 32
sōng 松 16
嵩 66
sǒng 耸 80
sòng 诵 4
讼 4
颂 31
送 34
宋 63
sōu 搜 11
艘 28
sòu 嗽 24
sū 苏 65
稣 29
sú 俗 8
sù 肃 69
速 34
诉 4
塑 75
溯 7
宿 63
素 67
suān 酸 25
suàn 算 66
蒜 65
suī 虽 68
尿 32
suí 遂 34
随 22
suǐ 髓 31
suì 遂 34
隧 22
燧 3
碎 26
穗 18

ALPHABETICAL INDEX

Pinyin	Char	Page
	岁	66
sūn	孙	14
sǔn	损	12
	笋	66
suō	唆	23
	缩	15
	莎	65
suǒ	索	67
	所	31
	锁	21
suo	嗦	23
tā	他	9
	她	22
	它	63
	塌	10
	踏	26
tǎ	塔	10
tà	蹋	26
	拓	13
	踏	26
tāi	胎	27
tái	台	61
	抬	12
tài	太	38
	汰	7
	态	67
	泰	67
tān	摊	13
	滩	7
	瘫	33
	贪	59
tán	坛	10
	弹	14
	谈	4
	痰	33
	谭	4
	潭	6
tǎn	坦	10
	毯	35
tàn	叹	24
	炭	66
	碳	26
	探	12
tāng	汤	7
táng	堂	59
	膛	27
	唐	33
	塘	10
	糖	18
tǎng	倘	8
	躺	28
tàng	烫	74
	趟	35
tāo	滔	6
	掏	13
	涛	7
	叨	24
táo	逃	34
	桃	17
	陶	22
	淘	7
	萄	65
tǎo	讨	4
tào	套	67
tè	特	19
tēng	腾	27
téng	腾	27
	疼	33
	藤	65
tī	梯	16
	踢	26
	体	9
tí	啼	23
	蹄	26
	提	12
	题	35
tǐ	体	9
tì	剃	42
	涕	5
	惕	2
	替	79
	屉	32
tiān	天	39
	添	6
tián	填	10
	田	39
	甜	26
tiāo	挑	13
	调	4
	条	61
tiǎo	挑	13
tiào	跳	26
tiē	帖	14
	贴	28
tiě	铁	21
	帖	14
tiè	帖	14
tīng	厅	32
	听	24
tíng	亭	62
	停	8
	廷	35
	庭	33
	蜓	29
	挺	13
tǐng	艇	28
tōng	通	34
tóng	同	36
	彤	41
tǒng	捅	12
	桶	16
	筒	66
	统	15
tòng	通	34
	痛	33
	同	36
tōu	偷	8
tóu	头	1
	投	12
tòu	透	34
tou	头	1
tū	秃	60
	突	63
	凸	39
tú	屠	32
	涂	6
	途	34
	图	37
	徒	10
tǔ	土	38
	吐	24
tù	吐	24
	兔	61
tuán	团	37
tuī	推	13
tuí	颓	48
tuǐ	腿	27
tuì	退	34
tūn	吞	69
tún	屯	38
	豚	27
tuō	拖	12
	脱	27
	托	13
tuó	陀	22
	驼	28
	驮	28
tuǒ	椭	17
	妥	60
tuò	唾	23
	魄	25
	拓	13
wā	哇	23
	蛙	29
	挖	11
wá	娃	22
wǎ	瓦	39
wà	袜	20
	瓦	39
wa	哇	23
wāi	歪	60
wài	外	30
wān	弯	62
	湾	5
	豌	31
wán	玩	19
	顽	31
	丸	38
	完	63
wǎn	挽	12
	晚	25
	宛	63
	婉	22
	惋	2
	碗	26
	萬	64
	腕	27
	万	39
wāng	汪	7
wáng	王	39
	亡	62
	芒	64
	忘	
	枉	
wǎng	往	
	网	
	旺	
wàng	妄	
	忘	
	往	
	望	
wēi	危	
	委	
	萎	
	微	
	魏	
	威	
wéi	韦	
	围	
	违	
	桅	
	唯	
	惟	
	维	
	为	
wěi	伟	
	纬	
	委	
	萎	
	尾	
	唯	
	伪	
wèi	未	
	味	
	位	
	胃	
	谓	
	遗	
	为	

卫 39	舞 61	洗 5	陷 22	xiáo 淆 6	馨 79
畏 68	武 36	细 15	馅 20	xiǎo 晓 25	xín 寻 69
喂 23	xì 恶 69	系 60	现 19	小 1	xìn 芯 64
wù 魏 31	悟 2	隙 22	宪 63	xiào 啸 23	信 8
慰 72	晤 25	戏 1	献 46	效 51	衅 30
温 6	xiā 勿 40	xiā 虾 29	县 77	校 16	xīng 星 68
瘟 33	物 19	瞎 25	腺 27	肖 59	猩 14
文 62	xiá 戊 36	xiá 侠 9	xiāng 相 17	孝 32	腥 27
纹 15	误 4	峡 14	厢 32	笑 66	兴 59
蚊 29	务 61	狭 14	箱 66	xiē 歇 50	xíng 刑 19
闻 36	雾 68	匣 37	襄 62	些 73	邢 54
吻 24	吸 24	辖 19	镶 21	xié 挟 13	形 19
稳 18	西 39	暇 25	乡 38	邪 19	型 75
问 36	牺 19	霞 68	香 60	鞋 29	行 10
翁 59	xià 嘻 23	xià 下 39	xiáng 详 4	斜 31	xǐng 醒 25
涡 6	昔 67	吓 24	祥 20	协 10	省 59
窝 63	惜 2	夏 60	降 22	胁 27	xìng 姓 22
喔 24	腊 27	厦 32	翔 30	谐 4	性 2
我 31	析 17	xia 下 39	xiǎng 想 72	携 11	杏 67
沃 6	xiān 锡 21	xiān 纤 15	享 62	xiě 写 61	幸 67
握 13	熙 72	鲜 29	响 23	血 58	兴 59
卧 31	夕 40	xiàng 先 67	xiàng 项 19	xiè 写 61	xiōng 凶 37
屋 32	矽 26	仙 9	相 17	泻 6	汹 7
巫 30	晰 25	掀 13	象 61	屑 32	兄 68
诬 4	膝 27	xián 咸 36	像 8	械 17	匈 36
乌 35	悉 60	嫌 22	橡 16	泄 7	胸 27
呜 23	息 58	贤 66	向 36	谢 4	xióng 熊 72
污 6	熄 3	弦 14	巷 67	卸 54	雄 30
吾 69	希 69	衔 10	xiāo 萧 64	解 29	xiū 休 9
梧 16	稀 18	闲 36	潇 5	蟹 79	修 9
无 33	溪 6	娴 22	肖 59	xīn 辛 62	羞 58
xí 毋 39	xiǎn 袭 69	xiǎn 险 22	削 42	锌 21	xiǔ 朽 17
吴 68	习 36	鲜 29	宵 63	新 30	宿 63
五 39	媳 22	显 68	消 5	薪 65	xiù 袖 20
伍 9	xí 席 33	xiàn 限 22	逍 34	心 1	秀 60
xǐ 侮 8	喜 67	线 15	销 21	芯 64	绣 15
午 40	禧 20	羡 58	嚣 68	欣 31	锈 21

宿 63
臭 58
嗅 23
xū 吁 24
须 1
虚 33
墟 10
需 68
戌 36
xú 徐 10
xǔ 许 4
xù 绪 15
酗 25
序 33
絮 77
续 15
叙 31
畜 62
蓄 64
xuān 轩 19
宣 63
喧 23
萱 64
xuán 旋 20
玄 62
悬 72
xuǎn 选 34
xuàn 旋 20
券 67
xuē 靴 29
削 42
薛 65
xué 学 59
穴 63
xuě 雪 68
xuè 血 58
xūn 熏 60

薰 64
xún 旬 36
询 4
寻 69
循 10
巡 34
xùn 讯 4
汛 7
迅 34
训 4
熏 60
逊 34
yā 呀 24
鸦 19
哑 24
押 13
鸭 31
丫 1
压 32
yá 牙 39
芽 65
崖 66
涯 7
yǎ 雅 19
哑 24
yà 讶 4
亚 1
轧 19
压 32
ya 呀 24
yān 咽 24
烟 3
殷 31
燕 69
淹 5
yán 研 26
沿 6

岩 66
炎 69
延 35
言 62
严 60
颜 48
盐 80
眼 25
演 5
衍 10
掩 11
yàn 验 28
焰 3
沿 6
咽 24
雁 32
厌 32
彦 33
燕 69
宴 63
艳 30
yāng 央 38
殃 26
秧 18
yáng 扬 13
杨 17
羊 58
洋 5
阳 22
氧 61
痒 33
养 58
仰 9
样 16
yāo 要 68
腰 27
妖 22

幺 38
约 15
邀 34
yáo 姚 22
谣 4
摇 12
遥 34
尧 69
窑 63
yǎo 咬 23
yào 要 68
钥 21
疟 33
药 65
耀 18
yē 耶 25
椰 17
yé 耶 25
爷 59
yě 也 40
冶 3
野 31
yè 咽 24
叶 24
业 1
夜 62
液 5
页 60
医 37
衣 62
依 8
一 39
伊 9
壹 67
宜 63
蛇 29
怡 2

移 18
遗 34
颐 31
一 39
夷 38
姨 22
yín 疑 30
仪 8
乙 39
yǐ 矣 61
倚 8
椅 16
以 30
蚁 29
已 39
异 69
yì 亿 9
忆 2
艺 65
谊 4
译 4
亦 41
易 68
意 62
yíng 翼 69
役 10
疫 33
益 58
溢 5
yǐng 一 39
义 58
 yìng 议 4
抑 13
逸 34
裔 62
yō 艾 65
yo

yīn 因
姻
音
殷
阴
荫
钒
yín 吟
寅
淫
饮
弓
yǐn 隐
瘾
饮
荫
印
yìn 英
应
yīng 婴
樱
莹
鹰
迎
赢
盈
萤
蝇
营
影
颖
映
硬
应
育
哟
yo

佣 9
拥 13
庸 33
勇 61
涌 6
踊 26
永 1
咏 23
泳 5
用 39
佣 9
优 8
忧 2
幽 37
悠 72
由 38
邮 30
油 7
铀 21
尤 38
犹 14
游 7
有 32
友 32
酉 39
诱 4
右 32
佑 9
有 32
又 39
幼 30
于 39
俞 59
愉 2
逾 34
榆 16
瑜 19
愚 68
与 35
余 59
馀 20
予 61
鱼 61
渔 6
娱 22
於 20
輿 71
yǔ 宇 63
语 4
与 35
屿 14
羽 31
予 61
雨 39
yù 吁 24
喻 23
愈 59
寓 63
遇 34
浴 6
欲 50
裕 20
域 10
与 35
预 31
郁 54
玉 39
誉 59
育 62
御 10
狱 14
豫 31
yuān 渊 7
冤 61
yuán 袁 67
猿 14
元 60
园 37
员 68
圆 37
原 32
源 7
缘 15
援 12
yuǎn 远 34
yuàn 苑 65
怨 72
愿 32
院 22
yuē 曰 39
约 15
yuè 说 4
悦 2
阅 36
跃 26
月 39
钥 21
乐 40
岳 61
越 35
粤 58
yūn 晕 68
yún 云 60
匀 36
yǔn 允 61
yùn 晕 68
运 34
酝 25
蕴 65
孕 69
韵 30
zā 扎 13
zá 杂 69
砸 26
zǎ 咋 24
zāi 灾 63
哉 36
栽 36
zǎi 仔 9
载 36
宰 63
zài 载 36
再 39
在 32
zán 咱 23
zǎn 攒 12
zàn 暂 79
赞 77
zan 咱 23
zāng 脏 27
zàng 脏 27
葬 64
藏 65
zāo 遭 34
糟 18
záo 凿 37
zǎo 澡 6
早 68
枣 70
zào 噪 23
燥 3
躁 26
灶 3
造 34
皂 58
zé 则 28
择 12
泽 6
责 67
zéi 贼 28
zěn 怎 69
zēng 曾 58
增 10
憎 2
zèng 赠 28
综 15
zhā 咋 24
扎 13
查 67
渣 5
zhá 炸 3
闸 36
扎 13
轧 19
zhǎ 眨 25
zhà 乍 40
诈 4
咋 24
炸 3
栅 17
榨 16
zhāi 摘 11
斋 62
zhái 择 12
宅 63
zhǎi 窄 63
zhài 债 8
寨 63
zhān 占 66
沾 5
粘 18
瞻 25
zhǎn 盏 80
斩 19
崭 66
展 32
zhàn 栈 16
占 66
站 20
颤 48
战 30
zhāng 章 62
彰 41
蟑 29
张 14
zhǎng 长 38
涨 7
掌 59
zhàng 帐 14
胀 27
账 28
涨 7
丈 38
仗 9
杖 17
障 22
zhāo 招 12
朝 29
着 58
昭 25
zháo 着 58
zhǎo 沼 6
爪 32
找 11
zhào 兆 42
召 69
罩 68
赵 35
照 72
zhē 折 13
遮 34
摺 12

zhé	折 13		证 4		帜 14		蛛 29		装 77	zòng	纵
	哲 78		政 31		秩 18		猪 14	zhuàng	幢 14	zǒu	走
	摺 12		症 33		志 67		诸 4		撞 11	zòu	奏
	辙 19		挣 12		智 79	zhú	逐 34		壮 3		揍
zhě	者 32		郑 54		掷 13		烛 3		状 3	zū	租
zhè	浙 7	zhī	支 67		稚 18		筑 66	zhuī	追 34	zú	卒
	这 34		枝 16		挚 76		术 38	zhuì	坠 75		族
	蔗 65		肢 27		质 32		竹 30		缀 15		足
zhe	着 58		之 58		制 42	zhǔ	主 58	zhǔn	准 3	zǔ	阻
zhèi	这 34		芝 64		滞 5		拄 11	zhuō	拙 13		组
zhēn	珍 19		指 11	zhōng	中 38		煮 32		卓 66		祖
	真 67		脂 27		忠 69		属 32		捉 12	zuān	钻
	针 21		只 68		钟 21		嘱 24		桌 66	zuàn	钻
	贞 66		织 15		终 15		瞩 25	zhuó	浊 7		赚
	侦 8		汁 7		衷 62	zhù	助 46		酌 25	zuǐ	嘴
	甄 48		知 20	zhǒng	肿 27		住 8		啄 24	zuì	罪
zhěn	诊 4		蜘 29		种 18		注 5		琢 19		醉
	疹 33		掷 13	zhòng	中 38		驻 28		着 58		最
	枕 17	zhí	侄 8		仲 9		柱 16	zī	仔 9		尊
zhèn	镇 21		直 67		种 18		铸 21		咨 78		遵
	振 13		值 8		重 60		筑 66		姿 76	zuō	作
	震 68		植 16		众 59		祝 20		资 77	zuó	昨
	圳 10		殖 26	zhōu	周 36		著 64		兹 58		琢
	阵 22		指 11		州 1	zhuā	抓 13		滋 5	zuǒ	左
zhēng	丁 39		职 25		洲 7	zhuǎ	爪 32	zǐ	子 39		佐
	正 39		执 13		舟 58	zhuāi	拽 13		仔 9	zuò	作
	怔 2	zhǐ	旨 69		粥 14	zhuài	拽 13		籽 18		坐
	症 33		指 11	zhóu	轴 19	zhuān	专 38		紫 77		座
	争 40		只 68	zhǒu	肘 27		砖 26		姊 22		凿
	挣 12		止 38	zhòu	宙 63	zhuǎn	转 19	zì	字 63		做
	睁 25		址 10		骤 28	zhuàn	传 9		自 58		
	筝 66		纸 15		皱 30		转 19	zi	子 39		
	蒸 64	zhì	至 60		昼 73		赚 28	zōng	宗 63		
	征 10		致 51		咒 68		撰 12		综 15		
zhěng	拯 12		置 68	zhū	朱 38	zhuāng	庄 33		棕 16		
	整 75		治 6		株 17		桩 17		踪 26		
zhèng	正 39		识 4		珠 19		妆 3	zǒng	总 58		

No.	Components
1	八 丨 丿 冫 彡 刀 又
2	忄
3	氵 扌 火
4	讠
5	氵 厂 泊 泊 泊 泪 泊
6	泊 泊 …
7	泪 泗 泗 …
8	亻 厂 伯
9	伯 伯 伯 …
10	彳 忄 止 此 土
11	扌 拍 拍 拍 拍 掐
12	拍 拍 …
13	扣 扣 扣 …
14	犭 豸 子 弓 巾 山
15	纟
16	木 相
17	柏 柏 柏 …
18	禾 釆 米 光 耒
19	牛 车 片 丁 工 王 开
20	饣 矢 缶 立 方 衤 衤
21	钅
22	女 阝
23	口 吅
24	叩 叩 叩 …
25	日 白 酉 目 耳 田
26	石 牙 牙 舌 足
27	月
28	舟 身 艮 艮 区 贝 马
29	虫 鱼 角 卓 辛 革 其
30	other
31	…
32	厂 厂 广 耂 尸 户
33	广 虍 疒 other
34	辶
35	走 廴 是 鬼 other
36	
37	田
38	
39	
40	

No.	Components
41	丶 卜 丶 七 八 丨 彡 乍
42	刂 丨 乙 乚 比 七 飞 屯
43	十 寸 扌 斗 半 羊 长 代 戈 戋
44	止 土 士 生 主 立 义 文 亢 方 广 户 少
45	尤 龙 尤 也 木 未 末 朱 东 韦 丰
46	人 人 火 犬 丈 失 夹 力 九 夬 央 专
47	丁 下 不 干 平 于 亏 工 王
48	瓦 页 千 壬 天 乏 几 凡 见 贝
49	丁 习 刀 可 司 乃 及 易 己 弓 马
50	欠 尔 乍 勹 勺 包 子 予
51	攵 又 反 皮 斤
52	口 中 虫 由 申 巨 区 凶 西 彐
53	日 白 丑 艮 良 且 月 肖
54	卩 阝 鸟 鬼 辛 京
55	只 支 殳 灵 青 羊 圭 隹 甫
56	占 各 咼 召 台 合 分 令 仓 仑 它
57	other
58	丶 丷 丷 丷 羊
59	小 业 尚 灬 人 八
60	一 厂 四 禾 不
61	勹 勹 夕 夂 夊 厶 丘
62	亠 亡 去 亦 文 立 音
63	宀 宀
64	艹 芦
65	芦 芦 芦 …
66	竹 卝 收 癶 上 止 山
67	十 土 士 生 圭 丰 木 大 奏 类
68	口 口 四 田 目 西 雷
69	other
70	丶 八 丿 丨 乙 匕 七 冫 十 寸
71	八 乂 人 刂 儿 几
72	小 示 小 巛 心
73	一
74	丁 干 火 大 天 干 廾 木
75	土 牛 车 工 王 正 疋 巾 山
76	又 夂 女 夕 力 刀 マ 子 手 毛
77	水 水 糸 衣 仄 衣 厶 见 贝
78	口
79	目 目 且 虫 月 巴 巳 巴
80	耳 母 田 皿 other

HSK grades in this book are taken from materials published by the HSK authorities. The ultimate rights of interpretations of HSK policies remain with the Office of the PRC HSK State Commission at the following address: HSK Office, 15 Xueyuan Road, Haidan District, Beijing, PRC 100083; Fax 86-10-62311093, 86-10-62311037; Tel 86-10-62317150, 86-10-62317531 x 2685 or 2672.

Published by Tuttle Publishing, an imprint of Periplus Editions (HK) Ltd.

www.tuttlepublishing.com

Copyright © 2004 Laurence Matthews
All rights reserved.

LCC Card No.: 2004107692

ISBN: 978-0-8048-4909-8

Distributed by:

ABOUT TUTTLE
"Books to Span the East and West"

Our core mission at Tuttle Publishing is to create books which bring people together one page at a time. Tuttle was founded in 1832 in the small New England town of Rutland, Vermont (USA). Our fundamental values remain as strong today as they were then—to publish best-in-class books informing the English-speaking world about the countries and peoples of Asia. The world has become a smaller place today and Asia's economic, cultural and political influence has expanded, yet the need for meaningful dialogue and information about this diverse region has never been greater. Since 1948, Tuttle has been a leader in publishing books on the cultures, arts, cuisines, languages and literatures of Asia. Our authors and photographers have won numerous awards and Tuttle has published thousands of books on subjects ranging from martial arts to paper crafts. We welcome you to explore the wealth of information available on Asia at **www.tuttlepublishing.com.**

North America, Latin America & Europe
Tuttle Publishing
364 Innovation Drive
North Clarendon, VT 05759-9436, USA
Tel: 1 (802) 773 8930
Fax: 1 (802) 773 6993
info@tuttlepublishing.com
www.tuttlepublishing.com

Asia-Pacific
Berkeley Books Pte Ltd
61 Tai Seng Avenue, #02-12
Singapore 534167
Tel: (65) 6280 1330
Fax: (65) 6280 6290
inquiries@periplus.com.sg
www.periplus.com

Japan
Tuttle Publishing
Yaekari Building 3rd Floor
5-4-12 Osaki Shinagawa-ku
Tokyo 141-0032 Japan
Tel: (81) 3 5437 0171
Fax: (81) 3 5437 0755
sales@tuttle.co.jp
www.tuttle.co.jp

Indonesia
PT Java Books Indonesia
Jl. Rawa Gelam IV No.9
Kawasan Industri Pulogadung
Jakarta 13930, Indonesia
Tel: (62) 21 4682 1088
Fax: (62) 21 461 0206
crm@periplus.co.id
www.periplus.com

22 21 20 19 18   10 9 8 7 6 5 4 3 2 1   1806RR
Printed in China

TUTTLE PUBLISHING® is a registered trademark of Tuttle Publishing, a division of Periplus Editions (HK) Ltd.